Del Tufo & Co.

Artists & Photographers

BY SPECIAL
APPOINTMENT
TO HIS MAJESTY THE
KING OF ITALY

MADRAS
MOUNT ROAD

BANGALORE
SOUTH PARADE

NEGATIVES RESERVED.

BERN. WAC

HONI SOIT QUI MAL Y PENSE
PALMAM QUI MERUIT FERAT

W. D. Holmes

PESHAWAR
INDIA

Photograph

PORTRAITS FROM LIFE
or PHOTO in WATER
or OIL COLOURS

CALCUTTA ART STUDIO

No. 185
BOW BAZAR STREET

CALCUTTA

Copies of this Photograph can
always be had or enlarged
up to life size.

PAPER
JEWELS

POSTCARDS
FROM
THE RAJ

LAHORE. GOLDEN MOSQUE.

PAPER JEWELS

POSTCARDS FROM THE RAJ

OMAR KHAN

MAPIN
PUBLISHING

The Alkazi Collection
of Photography

First published in India in 2018 by
Mapin Publishing Pvt. Ltd
706 Kaivanna, Panchvati, Ellisbridge
Ahmedabad 380006 INDIA
T: +91 79 40 228 228 • F: +91 79 40 228 201
E: mapin@mapinpub.com • www.mapinpub.com

in association with

The Alkazi Collection of Photography, New Delhi
rahaab@acparchives.com

A travelling exhibition of the same name in conjunction
with the publication of this book will open in August 2018
at Dr. Bhau Daji Lad Mumbai City Museum, Mumbai.

The exhibition will continue in New Delhi at Art Heritage
in October 2018 and a part of the exhibition will be
showcased in Goa at Serendipity Arts Festival in December
2018. It will be shown at additional venues in 2019.

The publishers are grateful to the author Omar Khan for
lending his private collection, the Alkazi Foundation
for the Arts and Dr. Bhau Daji Lad Mumbai City Museum
for supporting the exhibition.

The publishers also extend their appreciation to other
venue partners.

International Distribution
Worldwide (except North America and South Asia)
Prestel Publishing Ltd.
14-17 Wells Street
London W1T 3PD
T: +44 (0)20 7323 5004 • F: +44 (0)20 7323 0271
E: sales@prestel-uk.co.uk

North America
Antique Collectors' Club
T: +1 800 252 5231 • F: +1 413 529 0862
E: sales@antiquecc.com • www.accdistribution.com/us

South Asia
Mapin Publishing Pvt. Ltd

ISBN: 978-81-89995-85-0

Copyediting: Suguna Ramanathan / Mapin Editorial
Design: Amit Kharsani / Mapin Design Studio
Production: Gopal Limbad / Mapin Design Studio

Printed in China

PAGE 1
*Mumtaz-I-Mahal. "The Exalted one of the
Palace." (from an ivory miniature). The Taj. Tomb
of Mumtaz-i-Mahal. Built by the Emperor Shah
Jehan.* Lithograph, India Tea Growers Postcard,
USA, 1909.

PAGE 2
Lahore. The Golden Mosque. Coloured halftone,
Raphael Tuck & Sons Lahore Series I, No. 8965,
London, c. 1905.

For my mother, Thera Khan (1933–2016)

She changed worlds.

CITY LINE To & From INDIA.

Preface

The Spark

There were many reasons for the appearance of the picture postcard in the 1890s. These included the invention of photography—photographs were common by the 1870s, and the mass-produced Kodak camera came out in the 1880s and greatly democratized the form. There were more liberal international postal regulations, and printing technologies like rapid press lithography were being exploited by small workshops and artisans in European and Indian cities. The growth of shipping and railway lines exemplified by cards like *City Line To & From India* (Figure 1) contributed to a fertile tourist market. Postcards as a messaging system were literally built on an iron communications network. At the same time, the spark that proved the concept came from advertising. It was business and marketing that helped underwrite the initially rather high costs for printing postcards.

The very first postcards of the subcontinent are, as far as I can tell, the three *India* (Figures 2, 3, 4) and *Ceylon* (Figure 5) postcards published by the Singer Manufacturing Co. in 1892. Strictly speaking, they were advertising cards, made for the World Columbian Exposition in Chicago in 1893. Nusserwanji Merwanji Patel, the Singer country agent in India, Burmah and Ceylon for 35 years[1] and his employees wearing traditional Parsi green and purple hats are possibly shown in these cards. The World Columbian Exposition marked the first official exposure of America to India in other ways too: Swami Vivekananda explained Hinduism in a series of historic lectures, and the painter Raja Ravi Varma won a Gold Medal (in a few years he would become its first major postcard publisher). Why do I consider them postcards? They are the right size, call themselves postcards, and are sold as such today; what they exemplified was the art of putting an image on the front of a paper card the thickness of a few sheets of paper in order to sell something.

Figure 1. *City Line To & From India.* City Line, c. 1904. Lithograph, Divided back, 14 x 9.15 cm, 5.51 x 3.60 in.

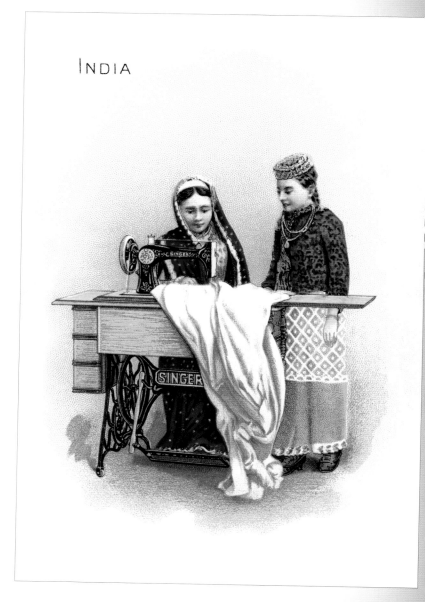

Figure 2. *India*. The Singer Manufacturing Co., 1892. Lithograph, Undivided back, 13.4 x 7.95 cm, 5.28 x 3.13 in.

[*Verso*] "An Extensive Empire of the British Crown, consisting of the Great Southern Penninsula of southern Asia, and a narrow strip along the east side of the Bay of Bengal. It is bounded north by the Himalaya mountains, west by a mountain range, east by parallel offshoots from the opposite extremity of the Himalayas, and on the other side by the Indian Ocean. The surface of the country is extremely diversified. It has the highest mountain peak (Mt. Everest) in the world, the Ganges River - wonderful for its annual inundations of the Gangetic plain. There is great diversity of race and language; in Upper India the inhabitants are of the Indo-European stock, with a language and roots to the Sanscrit. The religions are Mohammedanism and Brahmanism. The Aboriginal races have no literature. The governing races are of the Arabic, Brahmanical and Persian stock. Under British rule India is making rapid strides in modern civilization. Our picture represents the Singer Manufacturing Company's native employees in their usual costume. The Singer Sewing Machine has been a factor in helping people of India toward a better civilization for nearly twenty years, and thousands of them are in use."

Figure 3. *India*. The Singer Manufacturing Co., 1892. Lithograph, Undivided back, 13.4 x 8 cm, 5.28 x 3.15 in.
[*Verso*] Same as Figure 2.

INDIA

Figure 4. *India.* The Singer Manufacturing Co., 1892(?). Lithograph, Undivided back, 13.5 x 9 cm, 5.31 x 3.54 in.

[*Verso*] "INDIA, the land of adventure, of princely wealth and abject poverty, is inhabited by many different tribes, now rapidly becoming civilized under British rule. The women are tall and slender; gentle, timid, loving creatures, painfully desirous of education, which was denied to them until mission schools had been established. Hindoo girls are often betrothed during infancy and are married at the age of twelve. They have dark skins and regular features, a bright, intelligent expression, and fine, straight, black hair. Their usual dress consists of loose, gauze trousers, with a short frock of some bright-colored silk or muslin girded by a wide sash. Ears, neck, hands and feet are loaded with ornaments, sometimes of great value. The chief office of The Singer Manufacturing Co. in India is in Bombay, having more than fifty subordinate offices scattered all over the Empire. The same liberal system of selling is maintained here as elsewhere, and the increasing use of the sewing machine in a country whose inhabitants are so intensely conservative, is one of the strongest indications of the silent change caused in the habits of people through western intercourse. Expert Sewing-Machine Repairs Also sewing-machine oil of absolute purity and the best NEEDLES and PARTS for all machines at Singer Stores. Singer Stores in Every City. See Singer Store in YOUR City."

BELOW

Figure 5. *Ceylon.* The Singer Manufacturing Co., 1892. Lithograph, Undivided back, 13.5 x 9 cm, 5.31 x 3.54 in.

[*Verso*] "There is a picturesque island in the Indian Ocean, separated from Peninsular India by the Gulf of Manaar. It is 271 miles long by 187 wide, is a Crown colony of Great Britain and entirely independent of British India. Its capital city is Colombo. The dominant race is the Singhalese, who are genuine Buddhists and very tenacious of their castes. There are also many natives of Arabic descent, besides the Portuguese, Dutch and English. Our photo, taken on the spot, represents the Singer Manufacturing Company's employees in their national costume. The Company have offices in all the principal cities, and sell a large number of machines."

CEYLON

OVER

ABOVE

Figure 6. *Nestle's Swiss Milk 20ᵗʰ Punjab Infantry.* Byla (Sponsor), Paris, c. 1900. Lithograph.

The 20ᵗʰ Punjab had just fought during the massive North West Frontier uprisings of 1897–98 on the border with Afghanistan and had been present at the conquest of the Khyber Pass in 1878. Another postcard advertising Nestle's Condensed Milk postmarked Dec. 21, 1900 in the Author's Collection features the 3ʳᵈ Madras Light Cavalry. Although Nestle website claims its marketing relationship with India began in 1912, cards like this are evidence to the contrary.[2]

Figure 7. *India Postcard* [*verso*]. Art Institute Orell Fussli, Zurich, Switzerland for West End Watch Co. Bombay and Calcutta. c. 1905. Lithograph, Divided back, 14 x 8.95 cm, 5.51 x 3.52 in.

Figure 8. *SOUTH OF INDIA Dancing Temples.* J. Serravallo, Trieste, c. 1900. Lithograph, Undivided back, 13.8 x 9 cm, 5.43 x 3.5 in.

Nestle's Swiss Milk 20th Punjab Infantry (Figure 6) celebrates the 20th Punjab Infantry, a successful British Indian Army regiment on the North-West Frontier. Note how nicely the soldiers sweep up and in from the background, with the rifleman on his knees aiming just to the left of the viewer.

Another engaging military-themed *India Postcard* (Figure 7) shows a soldier charging in the foreground. It was sponsored by the West End Watch Co. in Bombay and Calcutta, and printed by a lithographer in Switzerland.[3]

An evocative postcard with thick colour regions that give it texture is *SOUTH OF INDIA Dancing Temples* (Figure 8). The sponsoring firm J. Serravallo of Trieste in the Austro-Hungarian Empire (now part of Italy) was a supplier of "Bark and Iron Wine."

Postcards crossed cultures like electric wires around 1900. Sponsored advertising cards like these were typically done in limited print runs, and are often found after many years of searching online, combing through dozens of postcard shows all over the world. I estimate that cards like these were printed in runs of a few hundred to a few thousand. Only a small percentage of that output has survived, sometimes perhaps only one or two cards out of the two thousand that were printed. For me, the survivors have the patina of an original painting.

Figure 9. *Footwear of Nations 10 Designs – No. 4 India.* Woonsocket Rubber Co., Rhode Island (US), 1906. Lithograph, Undivided back, 13.95 x 8.9 cm, 5.49 x 3.50 in.

Figure 10. *Britisch Indien. Indes anglaises. India inglesias. Empire of British India and Ceylon* [*overstamped*]. Unknown Publisher (Printed in Bavaria). Embossed lithograph, Divided back, 14 x 9.1 cm, 5.51 x 3.58 in.

An American card distills the perfect poise between East and West that a sophisticated advertising card can contain. *Footwear of Nations 10 Designs – No. 4 India* (Figure 9) shows rubber shoes facing off with Mughal footwear. In the distance is a palace. The woman's dress flutters. Something unknown passes between them. Rubber soles may be better than handcrafted ones, but wish to be associated with traditional wealth and power. Does she convince?

Another early type of commercial card was an advertisement for place. The first widely popular postcard type from about 1895 were postcards from hotels in the German-speaking Alps featuring the phrase "Gruss Auss [Greetings from . . .]" on the front (see *Ceylon*, Figure 5, for two such cards from Ceylonese hotels). The phrase spread to towns and city postcards. "Greetings from" postcards are said to have been

a big part of what 'launched' the postcard industry.[4] They offered higher and consistent production volumes compared to one-off advertising cards, permitting some of the larger presses in Germany and Austria to be financed. They helped drive down printing costs. "Gruss Aus" cards gave tourists an easy way to tell friends and relatives what they were up to, and lure the next wave of travellers – viral marketing at its best. The earliest Indian "Gruss Aus" card I have been able to date so far is *Greetings from South India* (Figure 11), published by an obscure German firm in 1896.[5] Probably the earliest from an Indian publisher is *Greetings from India*

Figure 11. *Greetings from South India*. Carl Bohm, Germany, c. 1896. Lithograph, Undivided back, 14 x 9.2 cm, 5.51 x 3.62 in.

Figure 12. *Greetings from India*. W. Rossler, Kolkata, c. 1897. Lithograph, Undivided back, 12.2 x 8.75 cm, 4.80 x 3.44 in.

Postmarked May 19, 1900, Sea Post Office, Kolkata. Addressed to "Signorina Olga Prochioles, Via Sorento 21.32. III fl [floor?], Trieste, Austria."

[*Recto*] "Calcutta, 17/5/1900 Saluts [Greetings] Gus Ghern."

(Figure 12) by W. Rossler in Kolkata, about 1897 (see *Introduction*). It seems to have been so rare, I only found it twice in 15 years of searching.

The large white blocks on the front of this and *Greetings from India* by D. Macropolo in Calcutta (Figure 13) invite the sender to say something. It was so easy to send a postcard, there was very little to write compared to a letter. A critic lamented in 1910 that "like a heaven-sent relief, the souvenir postal card has come to the man of few ideas and a torpid vocabulary . . . It represented one general gasp of relief 'See it for yourself; I can't describe it' – and there was no question of its success."[6]

A specific Indian "Gruss Aus" variation that became popular was *Salaams from India* (Figure 14) by H.A. Mirza in Delhi. I prefer the understated, nicely designed map composition *Greetings from Jubbulpore* [*Jabalpur*] (Figure 15) which includes the postcard's likely destination – the British Isles. Postcards forged connections between places, and it may be this more than anything else that drives my attention to them and makes me imagine that in a world where distances were so vast, and people had seen so little of other places, they were extraordinary.

Figure 13. *Greetings from India.* D. Macropolo, Calcutta, c. 1900. Lithograph, Undivided back, 13.95 x 9.2 cm, 5.49 x 3.62 in.

Sallans from India

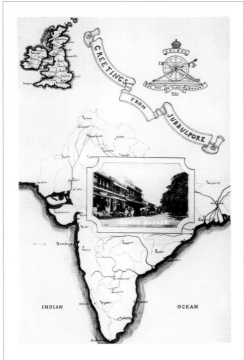

LEFT

Figure 14. *Sallans [Salaams] from India.*
H.A. Mirza & Sons, Delhi, c. 1905. Embossed real
photo postcard, Divided back, 13.8 x 8.85 cm,
5.43 x 3.48 in.

Figure 15. *Greetings from Jubbulpore.* c. 1905.
Real photo postcard, Divided back, 13.9 x 8.8 cm,
5.47 x 3.46 in.

Notes

1. Report of the proceedings at the presentation of an address to R.M. Patell, Esquire, J.P., agent for India, Burmah, and Ceylon, of the Singer Manufacturing Company, on his retirement, p. 11–12, Smithsonian Institution.

2. Nestle, founded in 1867, claims that its relationship with India started in 1912. *Nestle*, accessed November 25, 2016, https://www.nestle.in/aboutus/allaboutnestle.

3. Art Institute, Orell Fussli in Zurich, Switzerland.

4. Frank Staff, *The Picture Postcard & Its Origins*, Frederick A. Praeger, New York/Washington, 1966, p. 57–58.

5. The basis for this claim is a card where the font and set-up are dated to 1896 and attributed to Carl Bohm in "Haiti's First Postcard" by Peter C. Jeannopoulos in *Postcard Collector*, January 1999, Vol. 17, No. 1, p. 91.

6. "Upon the Threatened Extinction of the Art of Letter Writing" in *American Magazine*, Vol. 70, (June 1910): pp. 172–75, accessed November 25, 2016 Postcardy.com/article1910. html.

Women baking bread.

Introduction

It all began with *Women Baking Bread* (Figure 1). I was at my first postcard show in Concord, northern California, when the beauty of this little court-size card struck me. It carried me back to 5 Queens Road in Lahore, where my grandmother and a servant girl crouched on the veranda of a dilapidated mansion, chatting and making chapattis to be carried across the courtyard and cooked in a clay oven with straw awnings and charred wooden beams. It caught the warmth of that place. I marvelled at the *tromp l'oeil* on the postcard of the lantern and cloth, so effortlessly did they float above the women depicted. I bought the postcard. It is one I have rarely run into again, but I have since found many signed by the same artist, Paul Gerhardt, the search for whom is one of the things that propelled this book. His career shows how creatively driven the postcard medium was in its earliest years. *Women Baking Bread* began a twenty-year collecting spree that is far from over.

Once upon a time, postcards were works of art. It was just before 1900, and the "infesting modern microbe, the picture postal"[1] was spreading across the globe. The "picture-mad age" had begun. Billions of postcards exchanged hands between 1898 and 1903. Postcard production in Germany went from under 100 million to almost 1.2 billion, two postcards for everyone on earth.[2] It involved more people more quickly than the rise of any other media form. The world was pulled together by the "poor man's phantasm."[3]

Postcards are barely collected by institutions; they are in the hands of private collectors, families, and increasingly, online exchanges around the world. Postcards are being flushed out of albums and attics, and the interactions that ensue have made finding and analysing them a delightful window into history. They have been skipped by most historians, in part because they have been so inaccessible.

The story of the picture postcard in India is closely intertwined with that of Germany and Austria, where the image postcard was invented and most of them were first printed.

Figure 1. *Women Baking Bread.* The Ravi Varma Press, c. 1898–99. Lithograph, Undivided back, 11.7 x 8.6 cm, 4.61 x 3.39 in.

Indien

I grew up in Vienna, Austria, where I discovered that the earliest artist-signed postcards of India were made. Knowing German has led me to archives and dealers, and even a lithographic print shop in Vienna that still had a stone-plate printing press upon which early postcards were manufactured in the basement.. It has taken me back to what was my home for the first 13 years of my life, before we moved to Islamabad, Pakistan. Recognizing the cross-cultural ping pong between the subcontinent and the West as played out in the story of these cards has been one of the most rewarding threads pursued in this book, an echo chamber of my own Pakistani and European roots.

A postcard is always on its way. My interest in them deepened after my first book, *From Kashmir to Kabul*, was published in 2002. I needed to get away from the monotone of sepia images, to get to colour. Postcards offered that in so many ways, with each process used to introduce colour, from painting to stencils to stone plates, offering its own pleasures. Postcards are the first and only mass-scale colour views made by people a century ago. They are more numerous and less expensive than albumen prints. They cover a lot more ground. A new beautiful century-old postcard can pop up on any day.

Indien (Figure 2) shows a visit by German Crown Prince Ferdinand to India in 1911. It represents an apotheosis of the form, with the palm tree and the elephant brought together with magnificent design effect. Note the carefully arranged back of *Indien* (Figure 3), with the stamp of the German heir just across the profile of his cousin,

ZUR ERINNERUNG AN DIE
REISE DES
DEUTSCHEN KRONPRINZEN
NACH OSTASIEN
1910 / 1911

Postcard

FACING PAGE
Figure 2. *Indien*. J. Correggio [signed], Unknown Publisher, 1910. Coloured halftone, Divided back, 14.2 x 9.35 cm, 5.59 x 3.68 in.

Figure 3. *Indien*. Unknown Publisher, 1910. Coloured halftone, Divided back, 14.25 x 9.35 cm, 5.61 x 3.68 in.
[*Verso*] "In Memory of the Journey of the German Crown Prince To East Asia 1910–11".

LA POSTA NELLE INDIE INGLESI

the British monarch. The two men were on the brink of stumbling into World War I. Sanctions a year later cut deeply into German postcard production, the ensuing war destroyed many manufacturing facilities, and when it was all over in 1918, popular taste had shifted decisively to telephones, movies, records and radio. As I was to discover, the picture postcard has also always been more of a German-speaking thing. Even in the US, where I now live, German-Americans were the largest part of the golden-era postcard market.[4]

Postcards were "to the Edwardians what film and television are to us today" claims one writer,[5] and as I have rolled back postcard history, I see how true this was. In 1900, a single postcard image could move thousands of miles before reaching its destination, more than almost anyone at the time would travel in a lifetime. A photograph was sent to Dresden, postcards were struck from it and shipped back to Jaipur, sold outside the Hawa Mahal, mailed from Mumbai to London, due to arrive in two weeks, a minor miracle for a few *anna*s or pennies.

Picking up thick little pieces of paper that have survived intact for a century is like opening trapdoors into the past. I have been employed as a detective in pursuit of the material in *Paper Jewels.* There have been dangerous moments—illegally using my phone camera in the British or Austrian National Library to record discoveries too exciting to await archival copies. The joy of finding the announcement of the first artist-signed Indian postcards in an obscure journal in Vienna, or meeting the postcard collector Michael Powell in Kent who had a set of sister cards to *Women Baking Bread.* He also had a signed card by M.V. Dhurandhar, who, I would find, was the most inventive of postcard artists and whose work forms a major section of *Paper Jewels.* Speaking of Dhurandhar—my mother-in-law undertook a special mission to spirit his little-known autobiography out of the J.J. School of Art in Mumbai and have it translated from Marathi into English by a woman who knew Dhurandhar's family. As I complete this Introduction, I am readying another trip to Vienna, where I have met an Austrian couple who have written two books on the Ravi Varma Press and have a wealth of data on this, the greatest early Indian postcard publisher and a firm run by expatriate Germans like Paul Gerhardt.

If postcards were indebted to and spawned bridges (and misperceptions) between peoples, their birth was also welcomed with an exuberance similar to the high expectations for every new social media form.

The stamp and cancellation on a postcard, sometimes drawn into the design like on *The Mail in British India* (Figure 4) illustrate the triumph of this new form, imbuing them with the authenticity of time and place. Social media today is similar—an image sent with a message to someone specific at a certain time, yet open to friends and the world at large.

Figure 4. *La Posta Nelle Indie Inglesi* [*The Mail in British India*]. K.F. Editeurs, Paris, c. 1900. Lithograph, Undivided back, 14.05 x 8.95 cm, 5.53 x 3.52 in.

[*Verso*] *"D'estatequando le infezioni della polvere trovano nel sudore e nella pelle un terreno comodissimo al loro sviluppo, l'unico disinfettante, che non essendo velenoso ne puzzolente puo venire usato per tuta la persona, e soltanto il Lysoform.* [In the summer when infections are in the dust and sweat in the skin ground convenient to their development, the only disinfectant, not being poisonous or smelly that best suits the person, is Lysoform]."

A French version *La Poste Aux Indes Anglaises* was signed K.F. Editeurs, the Paris branch of the premiere Zurich-based art printing firm, Kunzli Freres, which published this as part of a world postal services series (see also *Kashmir*, Figure 1).

THE BOMBAY LITHOGRAPHIC CO.

Figure 5. *Taj Mahal Palace Hotel Bombay.* The Bombay Lithographic Co, c. 1903. Lithograph, Divided back, 14.15 x 8.95 cm, 5.57 x 3.52 in.

Postmarked Mumbai, Dec. 24, 1911 and addressed to Daily P.J., Seattle, Washi[ngton], U.S.A.

[*Verso*] "Mr. Bone, Editor P.J. Please state in your paper that John C. Goodrich and family were present at the Coronation in Delhi having seats but a few yards from the throne, oblige, J.C. Goodrich (formerly 16th and P., N.W. Wash D.C. now of Seattle) We sail Jan 7 from Colombo to Egypt."

FACING PAGE
Figure 6. *Taj Mahal Palace Hotel Bombay.* The Bombay Lithographic Co, c. 1903. Lithograph, Divided back, 14.3 x 9.05 cm, 5.63 x 3.56 in.

Bombay 4/23=1910

Dear Mamma,

We had a hot trip across
India but glad we took it even if it
was 100 to 110 in the Shade. I drank
too much Ice Tea or water & was knocked
out for two days — Mildred stood the
trip splendidly.
This is the largest hotel we have
found since leaving Frisco. We start
on a 12 [...] 15 day trip to Naples
[...] on the ocean & will be [...] when
ocean trips are over. Love from
Louis J. S.

THE BOMBAY LITHOGRAPHIC Cº.

Figure 7. *Bombay*. Bertarelli & Co., Milan, Italy, c. 1900. Lithograph, Undivided back, 13.95 x 9 cm, 5.49 x 3.54 in.

"Postcards were image-based conversations between specific networks and communities of people."[5] Postcards were among the first social objects to undo longstanding geographical, social and psychological boundaries. Messages give them a written context that photographic and other image exchanges and collecting often lack. As my collection grew, and I started putting postcards into boxes by publishing house, and the boxes kept multiplying, I found myself collecting the same postcard with different messages. Especially interesting are those sent from the Taj Mahal Palace Hotel in Bombay (Figures 5 and 6), which opened at the height of the postcard craze in the city in 1903. A postcard produced by the hotel is one thing: clean, purchased off the rack at the hotel shop (Figure 5): and a postcard with instructions sent by J.C.G. Goodrich to the Editor of a Seattle, Washington newspaper on Christmas Eve is quite another (Figure 6). Other times the writing overwhelms a beautiful card, as in the case of *Bombay* (Figure 8).

Each city and province in the subcontinent had its own publishers, artists and photographers. The axis through *Paper Jewels* from Kolkata to Mumbai, Karachi to Lahore, Colombo to Kandy is place. It is the filter through which I have curated the best few hundred of the thousands of postcards I have found, selecting those images that have the most personal resonance for me living in California, where postcards are pin-prick reminders of a rich cultural history left behind.

A postcard contains no secrets at all, or it contains them very carefully.

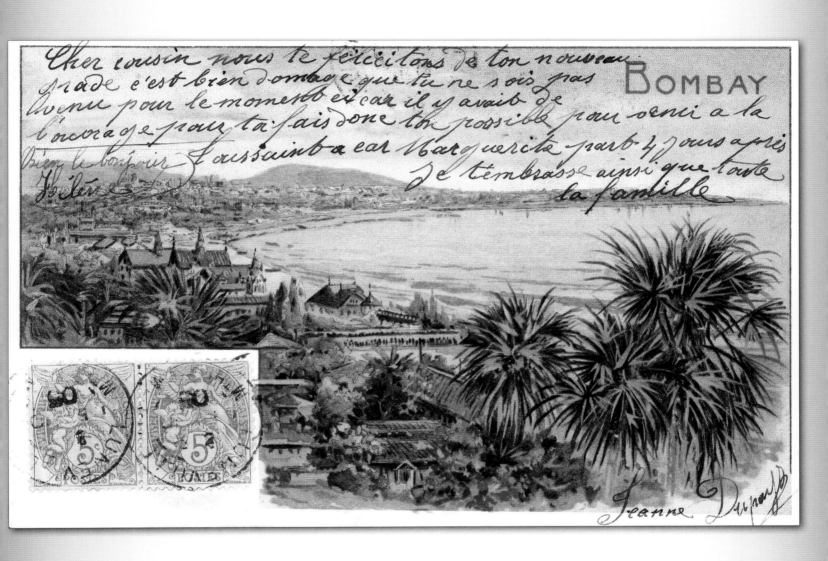

Figure 8. *Bombay.* Bertarelli & Co., Milan, Italy, c. 1900.
Lithograph, Undivided back, 13.95 x 9 cm, 5.49 x 3.54 in.

*"Cher cousin nous te felecitons je ton nouveau frade c'est bien
Bombae que tu ne sois a la l'oorcorage jous ta fais done ton
possible frau sene a la Bien Jeanne Dupuis"* [Dear cousin
I congratulate you your new posting is in good Bombay
may you have the courage to do your best All the best
Jeanne Dupuis].

The Indian Postman

The Indian Postman.
M.V. Dhurandhar [signed], Unknown Publisher,
c. 1903. Chromo-halftone, Undivided back,
12.1 x 8.7 cm, 4.75 x 3.42 in.

ABOVE
*Postmen of the British Empire: Mail Carrier and
Guard, Oudeypore, India.*, Unknown Publisher,
c. 1904. Lithograph, Divided back,
13.7 x 8.8 cm, 5.39 x 3.46 in.

Notes

1. Katharine Perry, "Tirade a La Carte," *Putnam's*, 3:336, reprinted in Postcardy.com, Dec. 1907.

2. One estimate has 200–300 billion postcards produced during the 'Golden Age' of postcards (Bjarne Rogan "An Entangled Object: The Picture Postcard as Souvenir and Collectible, Exchange and Ritual Communication," in *Cultural Analysis* 4 (2005): 1, quoted in Daniel Gifford, *American Holiday Postcards, 1905–1915 Imagery and Context*, Jefferson, North Carolina and London, UK, 2013, p. 203).

3. Malek Alloula, *The Colonial Harem*, University of Minnesota Press, 1986, pp. 4, 9, 36–73.

4. Pictures in the Post – a brief history of the postcard, by Judith and Stephen Holder FRPSL, http://www.rpsl.org.uk/pictures_in_the_post.html.

5. Daniel Gifford, *American Holiday Postcards, 1905–1915: Imagery and Context* (Jefferson, NC: McFarland & Company, 2013), p. 10.

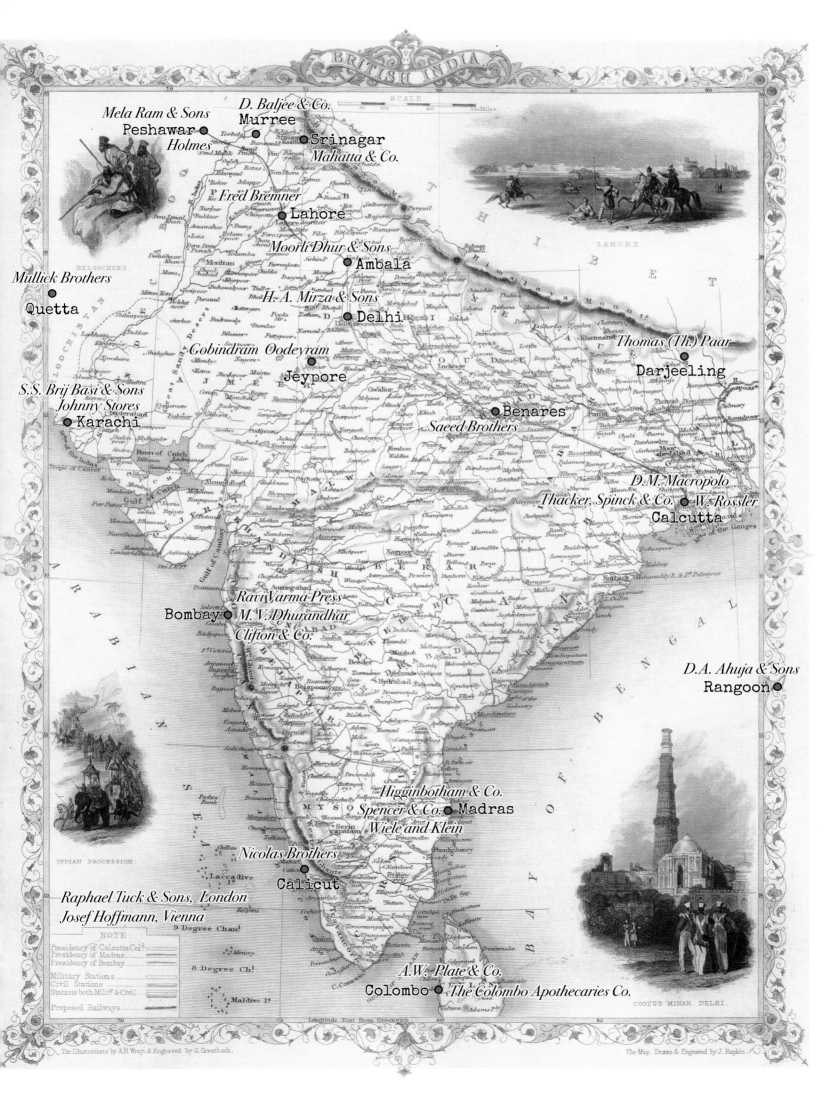

BRITISH INDIA

Mela Ram & Sons
Peshawar
Holmes

D. Baljee & Co.
Murree

Srinagar
Mahatta & Co.

Fred Bremner
Lahore

Moorli Dhur & Sons
Ambala

H. A. Mirza & Sons
Delhi

Mullick Brothers
Quetta

Gobindram Oodeyram
Jeypore

Thomas (Th.) Paar
Darjeeling

S.S. Brij Basi & Sons
Johnny Stores
Karachi

Benares
Saeed Brothers

D. M. Macropolo
Thacker, Spinck & Co. **W. Rossler**
Calcutta

Ravi Varma Press
Bombay M. V. Dhurandhar
Clifton & Co.

D.A. Ahuja & Sons
Rangoon

Higginbotham & Co.
Spencer & Co. **Madras**
Wiele and Klein

Nicolas Brothers
Calicut

Raphael Tuck & Sons, London
Josef Hoffmann, Vienna

A.W. Plate & Co.
Colombo The Colombo Apothecaries Co.

LAHORE.

INDIAN PROCESSION.

COOTUB MINAR, DELHI.

NOTE
Presidency of Calcutta Col.
Presidency of Madras
Presidency of Bombay
Military Stations
Civil Stations
Stations both Milit.ʸ & Civil
Proposed Railways

SCALE

The Illustrations by A.H. Wray. & Engraved by G. Greatbach.

The Map, Drawn & Engraved by J. Rapkin.

Calcutta

[Kolkata]

The story of the first postcards of the city of Kolkata and the hill station of Darjeeling runs through Vienna, the city I grew up in and where I have gone back forty years later with a researcher's eye, ultimately finding, in the basement of a 6th district studio from 1872, the remnants of a "rapid" lithographic press upon which these kinds of postcards were printed. (Figure 1).

An Austrian came up with the idea of the postcard in 1869. Lithographic printing had been invented in Germany 70 years earlier. It involved taking heavy stone plates, usually made of limestone from a single quarry in Germany, upon which an artist or lithographer etched a drawing. These plates were treated with a combination of grease and water to repel and hold colour as paper was pressed against them through multiple runs on a small flatbed press. One stone was used per colour. Paper or card had to be dried just right, especially if colours mixed for the consistency of paper changed when liquids were applied. "Lithographic rapid action presses," "sold for the first time to printers at home [Germany] and abroad," as an advertisement in a craftsman's journal declared (Figure 1), allowed printers to work with card stock in bows that typically were cut into 24 cards. Runs of hundreds and thousands of cards made the set-up and investment worth the gamble that enough could be sold for a profit. Vienna was a hotbed of little presses. Entrepreneurs set up shops in the courtyards of four storey apartment buildings during the twilight of the Hapsburg Empire. It was on one of these presses, probably in the 6th district where most of them were clustered, that the first postcards of Kolkata were printed.

Figure 1. Portion of an advertisement for Schmiers, Werner & Stein, Leipzig in *Freie Kuenste* [Free Arts], Vienna/Leipzig, No. 4, p. 65, 1900. Wood engraving. Courtesy of the *Oesterreichische Nationalbibliothek* [Austrian National Library], Vienna.

Freie Kunste was a trade journal for lithographers, published since the 1880s, in which the latest printing exemplars, technologies and methods were discussed amidst ads for lithographers and new presses (see *Benares*). This *Lichtdruckschnellpresse* [light print rapid press] was identical to the ones used for lithography and came in 6 sizes, and stressed "exact double printing," and its low noise. Note the attached plank from which the lithographer or printer could manage the operation.

GOVERNMENT HOUSE
GANESA.
CALCUTTA
INDIAN BEAUTY
CREMATION
MADE IN AUSTRIA FOR W. ROSSLER

Figure 2. *Calcutta Government House, Ganesha, Indian Beauty, Cremation.* W. Rossler, Kolkata, c. 1897. Lithograph, Court-size, Undivided back, 12.2 x 8.6 cm, 4.80 x 3.39 in. Postmarked Calcutta 24 Nov. 1898 [95?].

The postcard seems to have the year stamp of 1895 on it, but because I have found no cards clearly postmarked from 1896, and the fact that the earliest cards from a number of series start in 1897, I am inclined to think the 5 is an 8, and it was 1898. Note the four tiny titles below each vignette for those eager to know. This postcard was sent via Seapost to Miss Jane P. Barnes, at the Hotel Britannique in Naples, Italy. The space may be small, but the words weighty. A young man offers Miss Barnes a poem in German:

Der Sommerentfliehtmitihm die Blutenpracht
[Summer takes with it the flower's bloom]

Die uns so trost so wonningzugelacht
[Which allowed us such brief laughter]

Ein Kalter Wind durch Wald und Flurengrollt
[A cold wind growls through forest and floors]

Des Lebens Lenz unsvor die Fusserollt
[And rolls life's lint at our feet]

WelkeBlaetter, WelkeBlaetter
[What leaves, what leaves]

HerzlicheGrussevom Restless Spirit
[Best wishes from Restless Spirit]

GOVERNMENT HOUSE, CALCUTTA.

GENERAL · POST · OFFICE

WRITERS BUILDINGS

Calcutta

BENGALI BABOS

MADE IN AUSTRIA FOR W. RÖSSLER CALCUTTA

Ger 1/7 97

Figure 4. *Calcutta General Post Office, Writers Buildings, Bengali Babos.* W. Rossler, Kolkata, c. 1897. Lithograph, Undivided back, 12.2 x 8.7 cm, 4.80 x 3.43 in. Not postmarked.

Rossler was based in Calcutta since at least 1897 and is listed in *Thacker's Indian Directory* from 1900 onwards in the "Photographer and Artists" category. His studio was at 30 Creek Row and then Meadows Street in Kolkata, prime commercial locations. Rossler did not become a major postcard publisher. However the Studio is listed in *Thackers* until 1914, the start of World War I, when many German-speaking residents of the Raj were dispatched to internment camps. Rossler was actually spelt with an umlaut over the "o," often transliterated as Roessler, but he himself dropped that in an English-speaking market.

The card is annotated "GER 1/7 97 [?]." The Writers' Building is today home to the offices of the West Bengal State Government.

FACING PAGE, BELOW

Figure 3. *Government House Calcutta.* Raphael Tuck & Sons, London. Wide Wide World Calcutta Oilette Series #8901, c. 1905. Halftone, Divided back, 13.9 x 8.7 cm, 5.47 x 3.43 in.

[*Verso*, printed caption] "**Government House.** Calcutta has been called a City of Palaces: Government House is the Palace of the Viceroy. It was built by Lord Wellesley in 1799 and is a fine pile, situated in grounds covering six acres and based on the design of Kedleston Hall in Derbyshire, one of the Adam buildings. It has four wings and a fine dome."

Addressed to Mrs. J. McDougall, not stamped. "19-11-18 Bangalore. Mysore. S. India. I have not been in these grounds. But have had a view of the building from the roadway. Fraser."

Government House, to which power shifted from the East India Company after the War of Independence in 1858, is now Raj Bhavan, the residence of the Governor of West Bengal.

Figure 5. *General Post Office, Calcutta.* Raphael Tuck & Sons, London. "Photogravure" Postcard #2185, c. 1903. Halftone sepia, Divided back, 13.9 x 8.9 cm, 5.47 x 3.50 in.

Postmarked Calcutta, March 4, 1938 [?]. Addressed to Bobbie McGeary, 26b. [?] Dudley, Westfield, New Jersey, "Hello to Everybody Hope all is well as we are G M & D. [or M. & D.]"

Sepia cards were printed in a brown colour instead of black inks on halftone, collotype and real photo postcards. They went in and out of fashion from 1900 through the 1940s. Although mailed in 1938 and probably printed that decade, this particular type of card goes back to 1903 (the Tuck's #2185 is one hint).

FACING PAGE

Figure 6. *Holwell Monument, Calcutta.* Raphael Tuck & Sons, London. Wide Wide World Oilette Calcutta Series #8901, c. 1905. Halftone, Undivided back, 13.85 x 8.9 cm, 5.45 x 3.50 in.

[*Verso*] "**Holwell Monument.** John Zephaniah Holwell was the leader of the little band of Europeans left in peril after the Sack of Calcutta by the Nawab of Bengal in June 1756. After a short resistance, Holwell and his gallant party were forced to surrender and were thrust, 146 of them in a guard-room. 18 by 15 feet—the "Black Hole of Calcutta." Only 23 came out alive including Holwell, who wrote an account of their awful sufferings."

GENERAL POST OFFICE, CALCUTTA.

HOLWELL MONUMENT, CALCUTTA.

They were published by Werner Rossler, probably an Austrian photographer based in Kolkata,[1] trying his hand at a new business. *Calcutta* (Figure 2) is a typical "Gruss Aus"-style lithographic postcard and may have been cancelled as early as November 2nd 1895.[2] Across the top half is a detailed view of Kolkata from a photograph by Rossler with Government House in the foreground. The elephant god Ganesha is tucked atop a Greek column, unfamiliar enough to European lithographers to probably be from a photograph too. Together with the regal "Indian Beauty" and "Cremation" scene, they balance the horizontal thrust of modern Kolkata. Below her unfolds a cremation. I marvel at the rich detail of these cards, the precarious balance between East and West.

A postcard of *Government House* by another publisher (Figure 3) gives a better sense of how this single building reflected the self-perceived immensity of British power over India. Completed in 1803, it was designed after a building in England whose heir, Lord Curzon, lived here as Viceroy between 1899 and 1905, the very years when postcards established themselves in Kolkata. From Curzon's point-of-view, this city of just over a million, was the second city of the British Empire, "a European city set down upon Asiatic soil."[3] The city's new buildings celebrated the clearing of space for European order and beauty, transplants, like postcards, from Vienna and London.

A second Rossler lithograph, *Calcutta* (Figure 4), clearly postmarked April 7th, 1897, is among the earliest Indian illustrated postcards sent from Kolkata. It shows the neo-classical General Post Office. The number of postcards sent through the mail in India doubled between 1890 and 1901 to over 200 million. The Calcutta GPO saw more traffic than any other in India.[4] An early sepia card, *General Post Office, Calcutta* (Figure 5), captures the polished blur to life that quickened visual communication offered. Opened in 1865, the GPO is said to have been built on the "Black Hole" commemorating a much-elaborated event where Europeans were held hostage and some of whom died during

an uprising by Indians. Viceroy Lord Curzon (see *Delhi*, Figure 15) inaugurated *Holwell Monument Calcutta* (Figure 6) in front of the GPO in 1901.

To the left of the pillar, and across the top of Rossler's card, (Figure 4), is the Writers' Building. This was where India was governed from the late 1700s until 1857. 'Writers' were recruits who came from England to make their fortunes with the British East India Company; some of them became fabulously wealthy "nabobs". Around the Writers' Building grew Dalhousie Square, the business centre of the city since the 19th century.

Kolkata's antipode was *Bengal Village Scene* (Figure 7), the vast and dense rural areas whose produce, like jute, nourished the capital's wealth. *Bengal Village Scene* has a level of detail hard to capture on a lithograph. The popularity of postcards led to the desire to find ever-cheaper ways to produce them, and by the early 1900s lithographs were finding themselves supplanted by collotypes. Here the photographic image was printed directly on a glass plate, against which paper was pressed and light exposed; the Germans called them "Lichtdruck" or "light prints." The glass plates could wear out after a few thousand cards, but they were cheaper to make and easier to store than lithographic stones. Collotypes are the second major type of early cards. They enabled the texture and

Our Clerical Staff

BABU

CITY CLERK

Figure 7. *Calcutta. Bengal Village Scene.* W. Rossler, Kolkata, c. 1900. Collotype, Court-size, Undivided back, 12.1 x 8.8 cm, 4.76 x 3.46 in.

Postmarked 1904. Addressed to Mr. Bert Roe, 68 Brincliffe Edge Road, Sheffield England "15-11-[19]04 Still awfully busy, Can't get time for that letter to Mother Hope all are well. Weather ideal here. Your uncle is off up to the scene of the elephant kill again tonight. Aunt Ella."

Figure 8. *EAST AND WEST SERIES. Our Clerical Staff BABU CITY CLERK.* Thacker, Spink & Co. Calcutta, c. 1905. Halftone, Undivided back, 13.75 x 8.75 cm, 5.41 x 3.44 in.

Thacker, Spink & Co., 3 Esplanade East, Calcutta billed themselves "The Premier Booksellers, Publishers, Stationers and Printers in India," with "An Immense Stock of Books for Tourists" and "New and Second-hand Books on Sport and Shikar [Hunting] in India."[13] Thackers was a major postcard publisher, with branches in Bombay and Simla as well. Their court-sized cards of Calcutta go back to around 1898.

Figure 9. *Bengalee Babu.* M.V. Dhurandhar, [signed], Unknown Publisher, Bombay, c. 1904. Halftone, Divided back, 13.95 x 9 cm, 5.49 x 3.54 in.

Bengalee Babu

shades of grey in the thatched roof and trees of *Bengal Village Scene.* An early postcard series usually comprised six cards, and Rossler published a set of six court-sized Kolkata lithographs and apparently soon thereafter the collotype postcards.

A Bengali *babu* in *Calcutta* (Figure 4) stands beneath government offices. The *babu,* or educated Bengali bureaucrat, could be said to have held the Raj in the twirl of an umbrella. *Babu*s were a new species that blossomed during colonial rule, hybrids of Western needs and Indian traditions. *Our Clerical Staff Babu City Clerk* (Figure 8) compares the London variant. A more sympathetic portrait of the *Bengalee Babu* (Figure 9) came from the Indian postcard artist M.V. Dhurandhar (see *Bombay*). This soft-faced character standing between East and West is unsure of his place in the world, true to the word *babu*'s "ambiguous connotations, even today. It can mean a dandy and a poseur, or an intellectual and man of culture" writes Krishna Dutta.[5] In short, he is an unsettled hybrid, a character who appeals to me and reflects the borderline dance of the postcard.

Other "first residents" of Kolkata to grace postcards are found in yet a third type of postcard type that followed the collotype, the halftone. It turned out to be most efficient to render a photograph as a series of dots on a metal plate through which ink was sprayed on paper. The human eye puts the dots together. Small Vienna shops were no competition for larger presses and new postcard fashions that would make a firm like London-based Tuck's "arguably, the most important publishing house in the history of picture postcards" soon after the new century began.

Tuck's packet envelope for the firm's first *Native Life, India* (Figure 10) series claims that Oilettes were from "original oil paintings."[7] Actually, some of the images are from photographs by Johnston & Hoffmann, an old Kolkata photo-studio that competed with Rossler. *Calcutta Devil Dancers* (Figure 11) was one of the most popular

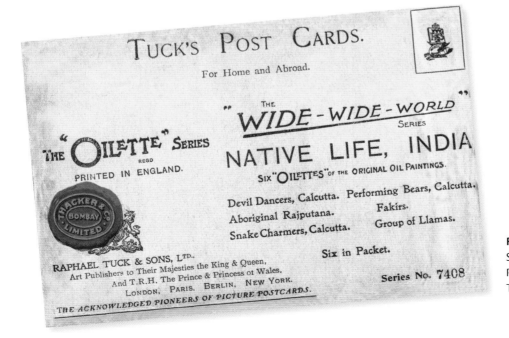

Figure 10. Envelope for Tuck's Post Cards Series #7408 *Native Life, India,* c. 1905. Paper, 15.1 x 9.9 cm, 5.94 x 3.90 in. Sold by Thacker & Co. Ltd. Bombay.

Figure 11. *Calcutta Devil Dancers*. Raphael Tuck & Sons, London. *Wide Wide World Oilette Native Life, India*, Series I, #7408, c. 1905. Halftone, Divided back, 13.85 x 8.8 cm, 5.45 x 3.46 in.

[*Verso*] "**Devil Dancers, Calcutta.** The Devil Dancer with his painted body, hideous mask, and fantastic head-dress is supposed to strike terror unto the beholder; as a rule he but succeeds in amusing him. The attitude struck and the whole performance is more grotesque than alarming."

Figure 12. *Calcutta. Snake Charmers*. Raphael Tuck & Sons, London. Wide Wide World Oilette #7408, Series I, c. 1905. Divided back, 13.8 x 8.7 cm, 5.43 x 3.43 in.

[*Verso*] "**Snake Charmers, Calcutta.** The Snake Charmer, as a rule, is an itinerant being, who is glad to charm his snakes in your compound, or before your house or bungalow, for a small reward. The snakes uncoil and erect themselves to the sound of weird music, and seem thoroughly fascinated. They are usually quite harmless, their poison fangs having been extracted."

Figure 13. *Samp Wallah (Snake Charmers), Calcutta*. Probably Johnston & Hoffmann [?] #40, Kolkata, c. 1904. Real photo, Divided back, 13.7 x 8.7 cm, 5.39 x 3.43 in.

Figure 14. *Calcutta Kalighat, Kali, Burning Ghat, Nautch Girl.* W. Rossler, Kolkata, c. 1897. Lithograph, Court-size, Undivided back, 12.1 x 8.8 cm, 4.76 x 3.46 in.

Nautch dancers inspired stories like Hassan Shah's *The Nautch Girl*, "the first known modern Indian novel" in the 1790s,[14] as well as the first Urdu novel, the story of the Lucknow courtesan Umrao Jaan Ada in 1899.[15]

Postmarked Calcutta December 3, 1898. The card is addressed to Karl Hatta in Bohemia, Austria [now Czechia], and was sent by Rossler himself, and suggests that like many Raj photographers, he ran side businesses as well.

[*Recto*] "1st December 1898. A Merry Xmas and a happy New Year to you W. Rossler Representierung [Representing] J.G.d.A."

Figure 15. *Calcutta. Nautch Girl.* W. Rossler, Kolkata, c. 1903. Collotype, Undivided back, 14.1 x 9 cm, 5.55 x 3.54 in. Postmarked Calcutta 18 Nov. 1903.

The *nautch* was also changing at this time. S.S. Bose, a collector of early *nautch* photographs, opined in the Kolkata *Englishman* in 1903 that these Christian and Indian "moralists," have nothing to say about the new "opera girl" actresses taking over the theatrical stage in Kolkata: "The modern Bengali Opera-girl is a cross-breed between the nautch-girl and the European ballet dancer."[16] A hundred years ago, the *nautch* girl was already morphing into later Bollywood incarnations, a prime example of which is the iconic film *Umrao Jaan* (1981).

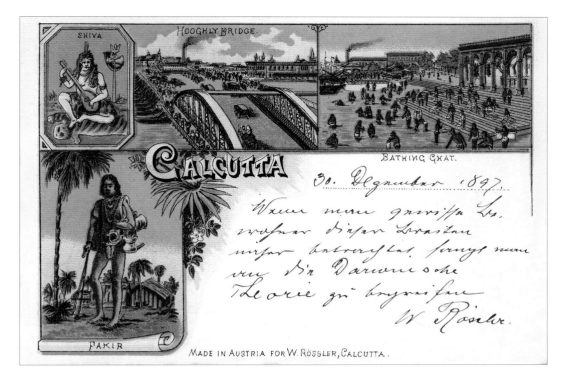

Figure 16. *Calcutta Shiva, Hooghly Bridge, Bathing Ghat, Fakir.* W. Rossler, c. 1897. Lithograph, Court-size, Undivided back, 12.25 x 8.45 cm, 4.82 x 3.33 in.

Addressed to S. Gouthier Esq Turkenstrasse 95, Munich, Germany and postmarked 1 [?] January 1898 Calcutta and 15 Jan 1898 Munich.

[*Recto*] "Wenn man gewisse Bewohner dieser Breiten naeher betrachtet faengt man an die Darwinische (Darwin'sche) Theorie zu begreifen. W. Roessler." [When one looks more closely at certain inhabitants of these lands, one starts to comprehend Darwin's theory].

Kolkata cards. "Devil" dancers were hired to re-enact the moves of demonic spirits and drive diseases from the sick. *Calcutta Snake Charmers* (Figure 12) was another popular card. "They are usually quite harmless, their poison fangs having been extracted," assures the caption. For a British audience, the postcard made the East a manageable spectacle rendered harmless in a view with a hint of danger. One can see what an Oilette added to a photograph by comparing *Snake Charmers* (Figure 12) to the black and white postcard *Snake Charmers, Calcutta* (Figure 13). The Oilette's blend of photography and colour delivers a special zone between reality and fantasy.

A third postcard in Rossler's lithographic *Calcutta* (Figure 14) series, cancelled on December 1st 1898, features Kali, the goddess of destruction and creation, and the city's patron spirit. The Kalighat Temple is the most important in the city, where the poor come to spend their last hours on earth, lovers come to secretly marry, businessmen to place offerings for success, everyone to ask the goddess for something.

Calcutta also features another woman, the *nautch* (*naach*) or dancing girl, a character who helped sell postcards from the very beginning. The attendance of Europeans at *nautch* performances in Kolkata during the 1890s was common[11] even as the practice was under attack by Christian groups who tried to stamp out an "evil practice,"[12] and also by Indian women protesting degradation and its effects on home life. Rossler captures the *nautch* girl's strut ("attitude") in the black and white *Nautch Girl* (Figure 15), postmarked in Kolkata on the 18th of November 1903. It is of the larger, standard European-size approved in Britain in 1899 which became the global standard within a few years.[13] Note the fine detail in the woman's sari, and the out-of-focus walls in the back. The collotype could bring all the intentionality of a photograph to bear.

A fourth card in Rossler's lithographic series *Calcutta* (Figure 16) features a *fakir*, the male counterpoint to the *nautch* dancer. Above the *fakir* is his spiritual guide along lifelong wanderings, Lord Shiva. On the other side of the bridge is a bathing *ghat*. Any musings about what this beautifully laid-out card might have meant to its creator were refracted in an unexpected way when, twenty years into collecting, I found a *Calcutta* postcard sent by Rossler himself in 1897. He wrote "When one looks more closely at certain inhabitants of these lands, one starts to comprehend Darwin's theory." It is a racist comment, at least towards certain Indians and makes me aware of the prejudices that lurk in the beauty of a card like this.

At the top centre of Rossler's card is Kolkata's emblematic bridge, also shown in *The Pontoon Bridge on the Hooghly Calcutta* (Figure 17). The bridge bound the railway station and other sites on the farther bank to the main city in the foreground. In *The River showing Jetties and Howrah Bridge. Calcutta* (Figure 18) ships from all over

Figure 17. *The Pontoon Bridge on the Hooghly.* Johnston & Hoffmann [?] #20, Calcutta, c. 1905. Halftone, Divided back, 13.9 x 8.8 cm, 5.47 x 3.46 in.

[*Verso in pencil*] "Myself. June 22.07 Main St. 5 + 10 c Store"
The same factory exhausts fumes in both postcards.

FACING PAGE, ABOVE
Figure 18. *The River showing Jetties and Howrah Bridge. Calcutta.* Johnston & Hoffmann #7027, Calcutta, c. 1905. Collotype, Undivided back, 13.7 x 8.8 cm, 5.39 x 3.46 in.

Johnston and Hoffmann was "after Bourne & Shepherd, the preeminent commercial photographic studio in northern India," according to Sophie Gordon.[14] The firm was also an early postcard publisher, publishing a court-sized *Greetings from Calcutta* card in 1898.

FACING PAGE, BELOW
Figure 19. *Howrah Bridge.* Bombay Photo Stores Ltd. #21, Bombay, c. 1945. Real photo, Divided back, 14.1 x 8.9 cm, 5.55 x 3.50 in.

The River showing Jetties and Howrah Bridge. *Calcutta.*

No. 21   **Howrah Bridge**

RABINDRANATH
TAGORE

R.B. ANANT
SHIVAJI OBS
BOMBAY

Figure 20. *Rabindranath Tagore.* R.B. Anant Shivaji Das [?] Bombay, c. 1928. Bromide real photo, Clear back [no electrotype], 13.7 x 8.6 cm, 5.39 x 3.39 in.

The victory of Japan over Russia in 1905, the first by an Asian power over Europeans in centuries, fired the imagination of men like Tagore. They began a revival in Asian thought and opposition to Western hegemony that took many forms. In later years, Tagore would distance himself from the more radical opposition to British rule represented by younger Bengali leaders like Subhas Chandra Bose (see *Independence*).

FACING PAGE, ABOVE

Figure 21. *Chowringhee, Calcutta.* Raphael Tuck & Sons, London. Wide Wide World Oilette Calcutta #4005, c. 1903. Embossed halftone, Divided back, 13.9 x 8.8 cm, 5.47 x 3.46 in.

[*Verso*] "**Chowringhee, Calcutta.** Chowringhee Road runs past the sumptuous edifice of the Bengal Club and the finest residential quarter of Calcutta to St. Paul's Cathedral. Half-way is the superb pile of buildings of the Army and Navy Stores, and King Edward's Court: elegant flats with every modern convenience."

This later called oil facsim is from one of Tuck's early India six-card city series. The effect of the brushstrokes is heightened by a light emboss of the whole card. "They are really marvelous veritable miniature oil paintings, & easily are worthy of a frame. Needless to say, when used for Postcard correspondence they will be treasured by the fortunate recipients as WORKS OF ART."[18]

FACING PAGE, BELOW

Figure 22. *Native Street Scene, Harrison Road, Calcutta.* c. 1925. Sepia real photo, Divided back, 13.75 x 8.8 cm, 5.41 x 3.46 in.

the world are docked on the Hooghly, next to 18th and 19th century mansions occupied by successful trading houses. The Howrah Bridge remained a pontoon bridge until February 1943, when the needs of World War II led to its replacement with the steel structure shown in the real photo postcard *Howrah Bridge* (Figure 19).

Real photo postcards like *Howrah Bridge* are the fourth major type of postcard, one that has endured until today. Photographic emulsion is laid down directly on paper, as in the colour glossies we see in tourist kiosks around the world (the halftone also endured in newspapers, books and magazines as the predominant 20th-century print type). Real photo postcards became more common after 1910.

Approximately two million people a day use the Howrah bridge, renamed Rabindra Setu in 1965 after Rabindranath Tagore (Figure 20), Bengal's poet laureate and

CHOWRINGHEE, CALCUTTA.

NATIVE STREET SCENE, HARRISON ROAD, CALCUTTA.

philosopher with an over-arching presence all over Bengal. He was the first Asian to win a Nobel Prize for Literature in 1913; he founded a school, Santiniketan, that trained many of India's leaders and artists. He wrote the national anthems of both India and the eastern half of Bengal that later became Bangladesh. Raised in a Kolkata mansion, his grandfather was a patron of the opium trade with China and his father an Independence champion. He grew up in a home full of Bengali artists, thinkers and *babu*s of every kind, trying to find the right balance between victorious European practices and traditional Indian values.

The European Kolkata of *Chowringhee Lane* (Figure 21) reached an apotheosis in a Tuck's "oil facsims" format which emphasized the materiality of the painting to "show the raised brush marks, the canvas grain, with the actual oil effects of the original painting."[15] The Great Eastern Hotel, the second building down, speaks to the dreams that many brought to Kolkata.

The hazy Impressionism of an "oil facsim" contrasts with a real photo postcard like *Native Street Scene, Harrison Road, Calcutta* (Figure 22). A small temple stands in the middle of the monsoon-soaked city. On my only visit to Kolkata I was struck by the wideness of the Hooghly, and by how decaying everything looked on the outside when you walked through Kolkata's streets, yet how beautiful and refined everything was once you stepped inside.

Pan & Aerated Water Shop, Calcutta (Figure 23) reflects how easily Kolkata mixed past and present. *Paan* is an ancient cornucopia of spices and nuts wrapped in a betel leaf. Next to it are cooling soda bottles. Victorian lamps are bolted to thin bamboo poles. The mirror in the middle reflects an onlooker standing just outside the frame. The boy on the right is fanning his shirt. A lot of effort went into this moment.

The Victoria Memorial (Figure 24), Curzon's gift to the city in honour of Queen Victoria after she died in January 1901, may seem like a European building, but it is actually "a mixture of English baroque and Indo-Sarcenic with some Islamic and Hindu features."[12] The central dome is of white marble from the same quarries as the Taj Mahal. Today Kolkata's traffic flows circumambulate the Memorial, both an icon of the city and repository of Raj history in books and on paper.

My favourite representation of the deeply mixed culture that evolved in Kolkata is *Sheeshu in India* (Figure 25). An embossed real photo postcard shows a girl in a photographer's studio, arm on a wicker chair, ribbon in her hair, wearing leather shoes and dress of local and colonial style. One imagines her at home in Tagore's salon or a *babu*'s mansion.

ABOVE

Figure 24. *Victoria Memorial.* [Attributed] Thacker, Spink & Co. Calcutta/Simla or Thacker & Co. London/Bombay, c. 1925–1930. Sepia photogravure, Divided back, 13.9 x 8.9 cm, 5.47 x 3.50 in. Inked on back "F.M.A."

LEFT

Figure 25. *Sheeshu in India* (pencilled title on back). c. 1920. Real photo, Divided back, 13.85 x 8.85 cm, 5.45 x 3.48 in.

Another postcard of the same girl from the same sitting has this pencilled on the back: "widow. A Little girl I saw who came from India. Age 6 years."

FACING PAGE

Figure 23. *Paan & Aerated Water Shop, Calcutta.* W. Newman & Co. Calcutta. Dalhousie Series, c. 1905. Collotype, Undivided back, 13.65 x 8.7 cm, 5.37 x 3.43 in.

DARJEELING

A seventh Rossler lithographic card, *Greetings from Darjeeling* (Figure 26), celebrates the Himalayan hill station in the north of Bengal where, among tea plantations and Himalayan views, Kolkata's elite spent their summers. I understand the pull of the hill station. When we moved for good from Vienna to Islamabad (I was 13), I stepped for the first time onto the hot tarmac of Chaklala airport in June, and then, a few weeks later, drove up to the hill station of Murree (see *Karachi*). It was intoxicating and bewildering to breathe cool mountain air surrounded by peaks thousands of meters higher than the Alps. You needed a postcard to believe it. *Greetings from Darjeeling* features the train loop that brought the traveller here so much more quickly after 1881. The Tibetan equivalent of the *fakir*, the *Bhotier [Bhutia] with Praying Wheel*, is ready to be your guide.

Greetings from Darjeeling   Himalaya

Th. Paar, Photogr., Darjeeling.

FACING PAGE

Figure 26. *Greetings from Darjeeling.* c. 1897. Lithograph, Divided back, 12.15 x 8.75 cm, 4.78 x 3.44 in.

Postmarked in Darjeeling January 16, 1898, to Mrs. Sr. Danco in Bonn, Germany.

Figure 27. *Greetings from Darjeeling.* c. 1898. Coloured collotype, Court-size, Undivided back, 12.35 x 8.8 cm, 4.86 x 3.46 in.

Postmarked Calcutta 27 February 1902.

[*Verso*] "26/II 1902. [Unknown Esperanto writing]". Addressed to "Faru [Mrs.] Ada v. Sartorns [sp.?], IX. Waisenhasugasse 12, Vienna, Austria."

A major early photographer at the hill station, Thomas Paar, came out with a court-sized *Greetings from Darjeeling* (Figure 27) around the same time as Rossler. Later real photo postcards from the 1930s or so veered towards the psychedelic, like *Sunrise from Tiger Hill* (Figure 28) from S. Singh's studio. "Sunrise on the sea of clouds as we watch it touch Mt. Everest from Tiger Hill near Darjeeling," wrote one anonymous owner. S. Singh, which the striking *Nepali Girls* (Figure 29) makes clear, was a superb publisher of signed photographic postcards.

Rossler's and Paar's Darjeeling cards are extremely rare—it can take ten years to find a single one. While I have all six Kolkata cards and one from Darjeeling, a "Greetings from India" card was also published by Rossler in exactly the same format as the *Calcutta* series and Darjeeling card. I bought it once at an auction, and had it sent by registered mail, but it was lost, the only one of thousands of postcards to go missing. I waited five years before it showed up again, while reading proofs for this book, and inserted it into the *Preface* (Figure 12).

FACING PAGE

Figure 28. *Sunrise from Tiger Hill.* c. 1897. Colored real photo, Divided back, 13.55 x 8.65 cm, 5.33 x 3.41 in.

[*Verso in pencil*] "Sunrise on the sea of clouds as we watch it touch Mt. Everest from Tiger Hill near Darjeeling."

Figure 29. *Nepali Girls.* c. 1897. Real photo postcard, Divided back, 13.8 x 8.7 cm, 5.43 x 3.43 in.

Early Major Types of Postcards

	Lithographs	Invented in 1798, lithography literally means "writing on stone," or the laying down of an original drawing in oil, fat or wax on a smooth stone plate. The drawing is protected or exposed selectively with other chemicals before being pressed against paper to create a print. Today offset lithography is common, where a photographic plate is rendered on aluminium, polyester or other artificial surfaces instead of stone.
	Collotypes	Invented in 1856, a collotype plate was made, usually in glass, from a photographic negative. Chemicals are used to harden the impression, which breaks down into fine patterns. These are then treated with more chemicals and pressed against paper. Collotypes lost the market to halftones, though they were used in books where high-quality photo reproductions were desired through the 1930s, and are still occasionally used by artists.
	Halftones	An image screen is made from a photograph or other drawing, with the size of the dots used to represent the amount of ink that will go into the reproduction. The halftone renders everything one shade of grey, from dark to light, based on the distribution of ink and dots, which ranged from 75 to 175 dots per inch. Higher dpi offer greater depth and detail. Its use became widespread in popular journals like *The Illustrated London News* and *Harper's Weekly* in the 1880s and 1890s.
	Real photo	In 1902 Kodak let photographers turn any image into a postcard, and in 1907 apparently coined the term "real photo postcard." A continuous tone photographic image is printed on postcard stock, often contact-printed from a negative, usually in black and white or sepia, though these could be tinted with colour later. The product has the highest fidelity to the original photograph.

Notes

1. Rossler was likely to have been Austrian not only because his cards were printed there, but because many were addressed to Austria, including one to Agnes Roessler in Bohemia, now Czech Republic, then part of the Hapsburg Empire. An Austrian, Rudolf Roessler is listed as a lithographer in the Albertina, Vienna, in 1907. Arthur Roessler (1877–1955) was a towering figure in the Wiener Secession, although no direct connection between these families has been found yet.

2. If it were from 1895, it would put the card in the same date range as the earliest postmarks from towns in Germany and Austria.

3. Krishna Dutta, quoting from Lord Curzon's speech to the 50th Anniversary Banquet of the Bengal Chamber of Commerce in 1903. In *Calcutta: A Cultural and Literary History* (Oxford, Signal Books, 2003), p. 129.

4. William Wilson Hunter, *Imperial Gazetteer of India*, Volume 3, (London: Trubner & Co., 1885), p. 427.

5. Krishna Dutta, *Calcutta: A Cultural and Literary History* (Oxford: Signal Books, 2003), p. 36.

6. J.H.D. Smith, *The Picture Postcards of Raphael Tuck & Sons*, (London: IPM), p. 3.

7. Anthony Byatt, *Picture Postcards and Their Publishers* (Malvern: Golden Age Postcard Books, 1978), p. 293.

8. *The Englishman*, Kolkata, Nov. 7, 1903.

9. Ibid.

10. A special British and Indian 2.25 by 3.25 inch to 3.5 by 4.5 inch size format. It was replaced by the standard 5.5 inches by 3.5 inch (14 by 8.9 cm) postcard after November 1st, 1899. In 1902, the "divided back" postcard first appeared, which permitted messages next to addresses on the back of postcards.

11. Original Tuck's packet for *Wide Wide World* Madras Series II #7065A, Ph 740 (1-29) The British Library, London.

12. Dutta, op. cit., p. 121.

13. Advertisement inside book cover, *A Handbook for Travellers in India Burma and Ceylon*, London/Calcutta, John Murray/Thacker, Spink, & Co., 1938.

14. Qurratulain Hyder, "Foreword," in *The Nautch Girl: A Novel*, Sterling Publishing, Delhi, 1992.

15. An ad in *The Times of India*, November 15, 1904 by one firm in Bombay listed as its No 1 offering *The Indian Nautch* (8 Different Positions of *Nautch* Girls).

16. Ibid.

17. Robert Flynn Johnson, ed., *Reverie and Reality*, (Fine Arts Museum of San Francisco, 2003), p. 177.

18. Original Tuck's packet for *Wide Wide World* Madras Series II #7065A, Ph 740 (1-29), The British Library, London.

Benares

[Varanasi]

In July 1898, *The Illustrated Post-Card*, the official journal of the "International Association of Postcard Collectors" in Vienna, announced a set of "Artist Postcards of India and China." They are probably the first artist-signed postcards of India,[1] and most likely the first to be sold both to early postcard collectors in Europe and to tourists in Kolkata. They were made from paintings by the popular Viennese painter and opera stage designer Josef Hoffmann. I found an advertisement for these cards (Figure 1) in a Hapsburg Palace, now the Austrian National Library, one afternoon ten years ago; it was nearly as quiet as a morgue. I enjoyed snapping away at ads in this journal, against the posted rules, while thirty people in the main reading room pretended to look elsewhere. A few years later, on another visit, I discovered in the trade journal *Freie Kunste* [Free Arts] a news article with an illustration (Figure 2) that claimed that the Indian postcard series' "exceptional print quality would earn the admiration of every professional."[2] In the summer of 1898, the Hoffmann India cards were on the cutting-edge.

Three of the nine India cards were of Varanasi, the Hindu and Buddhist city on the *ghat*s of the Ganges river. It was then called Benares and before that, for much longer, Kashi or the "City of Light." Here people come to die and have their ashes scattered at the "religious capital of India from beyond historical times,"[3] the center of Brahmanism and the place where Gautama Buddha had some of his fiercest debates with Hinduism's high priests.

Figure 1. *Advertisement.* Classified section, *Die Illustrirte Postkarte. The Illustrated Post-Card. La Carte Postale Illustree.* (Trilingual) Official Organ of the "International Association of Collectors of Illustrated Postcards," Vienna, No. 7, July 1, 1898, p. 15. *Austrian National Library*.

Josef Heim described himself as a "Technical and Art Advertising Publisher" (*Freie Kunste*, No. 6). *The Illustrated Post-Card* was founded in 1896 and ceased publication three years later. Note that India cards were momentarily popular: another ad in the same issue offers postcards of Calcutta and the Himalayas by "Hugo Volke, 12 Government Place East, Calcutta," which could be requested with "Urdu, Bengali, Sanskrit or Hindi" writing. "A member, who for example lived in Calcutta, and wanted a card view of Vienna, would send a card from Calcutta, and receive 8 kroner (which was worth three cards back) and so still have a credit for other cards."[24] *The Illustrated Post-Card* also guaranteed that its members sent postcards with correct exit and entrance postmarks.[25]

Figure 2. *Advertisement.* Classified section, *Freie Kunste*
[*Free Arts*], No. 12, 15. June 1898, p. 183. *Austrian National Library.*

Freie Kunste, a trade journal for lithography, stone and book
printing founded in 1879 was "Edited and Administered" by Josef
Heim,[26] the publisher of the Hoffmann cards. It was filled with
methods of printing, articles on the economics of the business,
new trends, job listings and ads for printers and presses and
testified to the many developments practitioners needed to follow.

DER GROSSE VERBRENNUNGSPLATZ IN BENARES

Figure 3. *Der Grosse Verbrennungsplatz* [The Great Burning Place] *in Benares.* Josef Hoffmann [signed], Joseph Heim *Artist Cards from a World Tour, #5,* Vienna, Austria, 1898. Lithograph, Undivided back, 14 x 9 cm, 5.51 x 3.54 in.

Oscar Meta, the printer at Josef Heim's, wrote just before these cards were published in the trade journal *Freie Kunste* [*Free Arts*]: "In Chromo [lithography] a postcard should be able to be artistically rendered in eight to nine colours. These are: 1 yellow, 1 flesh tone, 2 blue, 2 red, 1 grey and 1 brown. The depiction in Aquarell requires: sugar yellow, blue #1, pink, drawing (brown or neutral), grey, blue #2."[27]

Figure 4. *Burning Ghat Benares* [Verso in pencil]. Saeed Brothers [?] Benares, c. 1915. Real photo postcard, Divided back, 13.8 x 8.6 cm, 5.43 x 3.39 in.

Saeed Brothers was the dominant local postcard publisher in the city after 1900.

FACING PAGE, ABOVE

FACING PAGE, BELOW

Figure 5. *Benares am Ganges* [Benares on the Ganges]. F. Perlberg [signed], C & A. Co. Series 755, India No. 2, c. 1905. Halftone, Divided back, 13.8 x 8.9 cm, 5.43 x 3.50 in.

Postmarked Calcutta 24 Nov. 1905 [?] and addressed to Mrs. James Cooke, No 93 Bentnick Street, Birkenhead, Cheshire, England:

"My darling Nell. I hope you are getting well. I hope you will get my letter all right. Will you write soon. Your loving Lisa XX"

Another version, possibly sent in an envelope and not postmarked: "(1) My Dear Holly In answer to X your P.C. I hope you are going R.I. [?] I am glad to say that I am going on well, waiting for dear Olle England next March I am a little fed up with this country and I want to see all the dear fcos sci [sp?] - I love so well-"

I have never been able to establish who the artist F. Perlman or publisher C. & A. were. The cards were printed in Germany, but the publisher seems to have been based in Budapest, then part of the Austro-Hungarian Empire.

Figure 6. *Verwaltungs-Palast in Benares* [*The Administration Palace in Benares*], Artist Cards from a World Tour 1898. "Supplied by Thacker & Co., Ltd., Bombay," after 1898. Lithograph, Undivided back, 14 x 9 cm, 5.51 x 3.54 in.

Postmarked Seapost, Bombay, Sept. 16, 1899 and addressed to Gentilissima Signorina [Gentle Miss] Lucia Merlato, S. Giorgius St 1 I mo/fr, Trieste, Austria.

[*Recto, Italian*] "Distinti Salutirlla Prinsrettobile Farmiglia" [Distinguished Greetings to the Prinsoltobile [sp?] Family]

Other Hoffmann postcards were "Edited" by Thacker & Co., showing how the terminology for these things was still in flux. Another version of the same card promoted OSAN in German:

"OSAN machtgesunde und schone Zahne! Versuchensie dieses vorrtreffliche Zahn-Antoseptikum, Sie warden hockstzufriedensein! OSAN istzuhaben in allen Geschaeften der Branche Czerny's OSAN-FABRIK Wien XVII [OSAN makes teeth healthy and beautiful. Try this exceptional antiseptic. You will be most satisfied! OSAN can be found in all stores of the Branch Czerny's Osan Factory, Vienna 16].

Figure 7. *Benares – Aurangzeb's Minarets etc.* D.A. Ahuja, Rangoon, No. 489, c. 1905. Coloured halftone, Divided back, 13.75 x 9 cm, 5.41 x 3.54 in.

Postmarked India, 1922 and sent to F.S. Stackpole, 33 Common St., Saco (Maine), United States of America.

"Dear Friend, I am glad to receive your card and I am ready to exchange a few cards with you. Please send me cards as under 'Agnes' of the code. I shall also be glad to exchange stamps with you if you are agreeable please send a selection and when I shall do the same for you. Thanking you in anticipation. With kind regards, Yours sincerely, N. Mukarji BCC 2965/51 [Postcard club number?]."

D.A. Ahuja, a Rangoon, Burma-based Punjabi photographic studio was established in 1885 and lasted through at least 1959. It dominated that colony's early postcard publishing business with a set of very distinctive cards by a German printer (see also *Delhi*).

Supplied by Thacker & Co., Ld., Bombay. — Made in Austria.

THE ADMINISTRATION PALACE IN BENARES.

·Benares - Aurangzeh's Minarets etc.

THE PLACE OF CONTRITION IN BENARES.

Nº 8

ABOVE

Figure 8. *The Place of Contrition in Benares.*
Josef Hoffmann [signed], Joseph Heim,
Edited by Thacker & Co. Ltd. Bombay,
c.1898. Lithograph, Undivided back,
14 x 9 cm, 5.51 x 3.54 in.

Postmarked 24 Jan 1901, Bombay. Sent to
Dr. Edgar Goodspeed, University of Chicago,
Chicago, Illinois, United States of America.

[*Verso*] "28th January 1901 Dear Goodspeed,
Here is one to add to the collection of your
nephew which you were making when we
were last together. Wish it best wishes for
his father and for your father and yourself.
Sincerely yours, Als. Stratton [sp?]."

Thacker's could have picked up the
Hoffmann cards for distribution under
its own name as early as 1899, when they
were advertising "Our Own Specialty India
Scenes and Views" chromolithograph cards
in Kolkata newspapers.[29]

FACING PAGE, BELOW

Figure 9. *The Fakirs of Benares, on the Bank of the Gange[s], India. Les Fakirs a Benares, Au bord du Gange. Inde.* Antoine Druet [signed] #106, I. Lipina, Imp[erial]. Ed[itions], Paris. Coloured halftone, Divided back, 14 x 9 cm. 5.51 x 3.54 in.

Antoine Druet (1857–1921) was a painter and portrait artist, a pupil of Gerome at the Ecole des Beaux Arts in Paris, and apparently later Paris gallery owner and photographer of Cezanne paintings.[30]

Figure 10. *Untitled.* c. 1915. Hand-coloured real photo postcard, Clear back, 13.9 x 8.85 cm, 5.47 x 3.48 in.

At Hoffmann's *Der Grosse Verbrennungsplatz* [*The Great Burning Place*] in Benares (Figure 3) bodies are cremated before their ashes are immersed in the Ganges. Bodies of those *sadhu*s or holy men too worthy to be cremated are floated down the river, shown up close in *Burning Ghat* (Figure 4). Part of the competition among early lithographic postcard publishers had to do with conveying the beauty of sunsets, for which this was the world's most appropriate location.

Another sunset postcard is *Benares am Ganges* (Figure 5), probably made about ten years after Hoffmann's Aquarelles. It shows at least three new temples, two of them large. British rule had allowed Hindus to rebuild a city partially destroyed by Muslim rulers; for example, a great Shiva temple was replaced by the Mughal Emperor Aurangzeb's mosque. Its minarets, reinforced by British archaeologists when they started crumbling, loom over the city in Hoffmann's *The Administration Palace in Benares* (Figure 6). *Benares – Aurangzeb's Minarets etc.* (Figure 7) by D.A. Ahuja shows the *ghat*s from the other bank of the Ganges, using a set of blue and orange hues to simulate sunset (see also *Delhi*).

The Place of Contrition in Benares (Figure 8) is perhaps the most beautiful of the Hoffmann postcards, a masterful use of orange, brown and red. We know that printing them was difficult, as described in an article by Oscar Meta, the manager of publisher Josef Heim's printing press.[4] A few months before the Varanasi cards appeared, he wrote about the manufacture of this new kind of object, the postcard, in *Freie Kunste*.[5] He describes the use of Bolgonese chalk – applied to the paper to help the colours dry well. He describes the parts of a drawing that needed to be more deeply etched in stone to absorb the dyes.[6] A postcard bow of 24 cards had to be dried for just enough hours, sometimes overnight, before applying the next colour. "Because the printing of postcards," he wrote, "is one of the most beautiful branches of lithography, so is everyone who makes his living at it implored to carry out his work with the greatest care."[7]

Benares was a city of learning, of philosophers and *fakirs*, illustrated in *The Fakirs of Benares, on the Bank of the Gange*[*s*]*, India* (Figure 9). Many of Hinduism's sages and grammarians came from Benares, nearly a third of whose 120,000 inhabitants were Brahmins. They discussed philosophy for hours on the steps of the *ghat*s as the cycle of life wore on around them. My favourite *fakir* postcard from Varanasi is [*Untitled*] (Figure 10), a hand-tinted real photo postcard from a later period, with a *fakir's* stare that questions you right back.

Ramdei (Songstress of Benares)

No. 19 — A Benares street.

Figure 12. *A Benares street.* Saeed Brothers, Benares No. 19, c. 1910. Collotype, Divided back, 13.6 x 8.45 cm, 5.35 x 3.33 in.

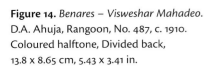

Figure 13. *The Golden Temple, Benares.*
Raphael Tuck & Sons, London, c. 1905.
Coloured halftone, Divided back,
13.9 x 8.8 cm, 5.47 x 3.46 in.

[*Verso*] "**The Golden Temple**. Held
by many to be the oldest and holiest
temple amid the 1,000 temples of
Benares, the holiest city in India. Covered
with gold plates, set on copper, it really
dates from the 18th century and was
built to replace the one razed to the
ground by Aurangzebe."

Figure 14. *Benares – Visweshar Mahadeo.*
D.A. Ahuja, Rangoon, No. 487, c. 1910.
Coloured halftone, Divided back,
13.8 x 8.65 cm, 5.43 x 3.41 in.

TEMPLE AT RAMNAGAR, BENARES.

Where there are *fakirs*, there must be *nautch* women, in this case *Ramdei (Songstress of Benares)* (Figure 11). The link between dancers, musicians and great temples in the city was deep. Singers accompanied boats in the evening down the Ganges. The city of pilgrimage was known for its courtesans, the rates for which were fixed by municipal authorities. Its musical styles boasted some of the finest instrument-playing lineages in India. The inner city in *No. 19 –A Benares Street* (Figure 12) was also a center for the manufacture for silk and brass religious wares sold throughout the Raj.

Figure 15. *Temple at Ramnagar, Benares.* Raphael Tuck & Sons, London, c. 1905. Coloured halftone, Divided back, 5.31 x 3.31 in.

[*Verso*] "Temple of Ramnagar. Commenced to be built by the famous Chait Singh who, in 1781, forced Hastings to retreat from Benares to the fort of Ramnagar. The treatment of Chait Singh by Hastings was one of the charges made against Hastings during his famous trial."

Figure 16. *Temple of Buddhist Shrine – Bodh Gaya.* Published by Medical Mission Auxiliary Baptist Missionary Society. The Photochrom Co. Ltd., London, c. 1905. Lithograph, Divided back, 13.6 x 8.55 cm, 5.35 x 3.37 in.

The Photochrom Co. in London, otherwise a big lithographic and quality publisher of European and American views, printed few India cards.

The Hidden Budhist City.

The oldest and most revered temple in the city is the Kashi Vishwanath Temple dedicated to Lord Shiva. It was rebuilt in the 18th century, with gold gifted by Maharajah Ranjit Singh of Lahore to gild the domes, as in Tuck's early Varanasi card, *The Golden Temple, Benares* (Figure 13). The difference in colour selections between publishers could be large, for artistic, financial or technical reasons. *Benares. Vishar Mahadeo* (Figure 14) by D.A. Ahuja uses bluish-silver instead of gold for the temple's domes. Until real colour photography came to postcards in the 1960s, colour selection could be a matter of taste.

The *ghat*s were the starting point of a six-day religious pilgrimage for a million people annually around 1900. The walk started at the Manikarnika Ghat (Figure 5), then proceeded south to Asi Ghat (Figure 6), and then looped for 36 miles from temple to temple until returning to Barna Ghat in the north (Figure 7). "Anyone of whatever creed, and however great his misdeeds, dying within the compass of the Panch Kosi road, is transported straight to heaven."[8] The pilgrimage led across the river from Asi Ghat to the *Temple at Ramnagar, Benares* (Figure 15), another very popular postcard from the first Tuck Benares series.

Sarnath, Benares.

A Buddhist city also began peeking through postcards at this time. A few miles from the *ghat*s, in Bodh Gaya, Gautama Buddha received his first enlightenment. *Gaya – Buddha Temple* (Figure 16) has become the most sacred temple for Buddhists around the world. Five weeks after the revelations at Gaya, the Buddha began preaching a few miles away at the deer park in Sarnath. The British helped excavate *The Hidden Buddhist City.* (Figure 17) around the Damekh Stupa in *Sarnath, Benares* (Figure 18). They were motivated by scholarly interest in this almost forgotten Indian religion under Emperor Asoka, who ruled all of India in the 3rd century BCE. They were

P. & O. R.M.S. KAISAR-I-HIND, 11,500 TONS GROSS.
India Mail and Passenger Service.

also pleased to undermine Hindu claims to the entire city. Postcards were a part of resurrecting this past and in a small way contributed to these locations achieving such prominence among Buddhists today.

Postcards of religious spectacle drew tourists from all over the world to Varanasi. *City Line To & From India. S.S. City of "Benares"* (Figure 19) depicts the transition in the late 19th century from sailing boats to huge steamships bringing visitors and freight to the subcontinent. It would have been on such a steamship that an American couple came to Varanasi and had a sepia real photo postcard commissioned of themselves at the Scindia Ghat (Figure 20) around 1920. Aurangzeb's minarets are barely a whisper in the background. The well-dressed man and woman are standing on the unfinished columns of a new temple to Shiva, construction for which had begun in the previous century but whose mighty columns were too heavy for the river bank. Beyond them, on another of the proposed columns, a man in a *dhoti* is watching.

Josef Hoffmann[9] was in his sixties when he toured India in 1893-94 and made the paintings behind Figures 3, 6, and 8. According to the official biographical dictionary of Austrian painters, the man was "possessed of an extraordinary work-ethic, and created on these trips thousands of Aquarelle views."[10] Hoffmann exhibited them and

Figure 19. *P. & O. R.M.S. KAISAR-I-HIND 11,500 TONS GROSS. India Mail and Passenger Service.* Unknown Publisher, UK, Coloured halftone, Divided back, 13.8 x 8.7 cm, 5.43 x 3.43 in.

FACING PAGE
Figure 20. [*Unknown Couple at Scindia Ghat*]. c. 1925. Real photo, Divided back, 13.65 x 8.5 cm, 5.37 x 3.35 in.

gave lectures when he returned to Vienna. An industrious self-promoter, he even had the temporary Gallery Hoffmann, "one of the most popular sites" in the city in front of the Baroque Karl's Church,[11] where people could see his "Glimpses of the World."[12] Here the Varanasi postcards would have been sold to their first customers.

I tracked down three addresses for Josef Heim, the printer and publisher of the cards in Vienna, in the 4th and 6th districts (Figure 21). What is surprising is the global reach of a publisher[13] then – the electrotype in *The Place of Contrition in Benares* (Figure 7) says "Edited by Thacker & Co., Bombay," which means Heim must have licensed them to this Raj retailer. (Electrotype - the print put down on the front and back of cards in separate press runs from image and colour - is one of my favorite words in deltiology, or the study of postcards.)

When the Hoffmann Varanasi cards appeared in the summer of 1898, they were one florin, 80 kroners, much more than Calcutta cards at 15 kroner (two and half British pennies) each.[14] Their high price must have reflected their scarcity to the 50,000 to 60,000 "purchase drunk" buyers of the magazine.[15] *The Illustrated Post-Card* at the time carried essays on the national-economic value of the postcard, on postcards and love, on *How to Use Postcards for Room Decoration?* and *Should Postcards be*

Figure 21. Josef Heim inhabited a number of buildings in the city between 1897 and 1898, two of which, 69. Gumpendorferstrassse (left) and 1, Schonbrunnerstrasse (middle and right) are still standing. The press would have been on the ground floor or basement, and these buildings typically have courtyards where small manufacturing operations could be facilitated.

Made from Drawings or Photographs?[16] Despite the many men's names associated with the art and production of cards, many of the actual collectors at this early stage were women. A poem in one issue had it that,

> *The right thermometer to*
> *Measure the beauty of women*
> *Is the number of postcards they have.*
> *So say I what I believe, Amen.*

Most of the cards in this book were sent or probably collected by women,[18] as are most of the cards in my collection. Dealers in Vienna - and the names on the empty albums harvested of postcards[19]- suggest that women comprised the primary Western market for postcards. Saloni Mathur relates this to the "feminization of mass culture,"[17] and quotes a male writer at the time who believed that the "feminine love of ornament" explained the rise of the postcard.[20] Leonard Pitt, the postcard historian, notes that women were in charge of the parlor in Western countries, where postcard albums were kept and displayed to visitors.[21]

Neither Hoffmann nor Josef Heim (nor in fact Rossler in Kolkata) stayed in the postcard business for more than a round or two. *The Illustrated Post-Card* survived only a few years, even though the height of postcard fever was still to come (and hadn't really arrived in Britain in 1898[22]). As collotypes started taking over from lithographs around 1900 (glass plates could easily replace stones on the same press), it would be German companies with their huge volumes, proximity to ports and large domestic markets, that took over from small shops like Josef Heim which had put their artistic energies into whetting the appetite for postcards. In fact, much of the same ferment around postcards in Vienna took place in German cities like Leipzig and Dresden as well.[23] But it is curious that the Austrians, with none of the same links to India as the British, should have been the first to bat. Or were they?

Notes

1. As early as 1898, Thackers were advertising "Our Own Specialty India Scenes and Views" chromolithograph cards in Kolkata's *The Englishman*, and as we shall see in the next chapter, Paul Gerhardt in Bombay or others might have been earlier. *Die Illustrite Postkarte. The Illustrated Post-Card. La Carte Postale Illustree.*, Vienna, No. 7, 1 July 1898, p. 4.

2. *Freie Kunste*, No. 12, p. 183.

3. *A Handbook for Travellers in India, Burma and Ceylon*, 14th Edition, (London: John Murray, 1933), p. 87.

4. *Freie Kunste*, No. 12, p. 183.

5. *Die Herstellung der Ansichtspostkarten* [The Manufacture of Postcards], in *Freie Kunste*, No. 21. January 1898 (Part I), No. 31 February 1898 (II), Vienna and Leipzig, pp. 1–2.

6. *Die Herstellung der Ansichtspostkarten* [The Manufacture of Postcards], in *Freie Kunste*, No. 31 February 1898, Vienna and Leipzig, p. 1.

7. Ibid., 1 January 1898, p. 34.

8. *Handbook*, op. cit., p. 87.

9. Josef Hoffmann (1831–1904) was a prodigy who published a series of lithographs at the age of 15. At 19, he undertook a trip to Persia, returned to Vienna to continue his art studies, exhibited at the Viennese equivalent of the Paris Salon in 1864, and became a prominent designer of Mozart and Wagnerian stages for the national opera (a particularly quarrelsome artist, he had a big falling out with the composer Richard Wagner).

10. Hans Vollmer, *Allgemeines Lexikon der Bildenden Kunstler*, 1924, p. 266.

11. *Orient & Okzident Oestterichische Maler des 19. Jahrhunderts auf Reisen*, (Vienna: Hirmer/Belvedere, 2012), p. 202.

12. Ibid., p. 203. This temporary structure was right on Karlsplatz, in front of an imperial Baroque Hapsburg cathedral. Inside people could look at the world through his paintings, and follow him on a journey "over India and Ceylon to Singapore, Java and China, then further to Japan and over the Pacific…" in his words.

13. Josef Heim, principally a religious publisher, put out an album of premiere lithographic printing examples each year from about 1879 onwards.

14. Brazilian cards were 35 kroner, those from Argentina only 10, *Die Illustrierte*, July 1898. Cards could be inscribed in Urdu, Bengali, Sanskrit or Hindi. Each was 40 pfennigs (equivalent to 24 kroners, 4 British pennies or 12 American cents). This was less than postcards from Cairo and San Francisco at 20 kroner (3 pennies, 40 cents US) each; Chinese cards were 30 to 45 kroners, more than twice the price. Six months later prices for cards from Calcutta were still at 15 kroners, but for the first time in *The Illustrated Post-Card*. Bombay cards were listed separately at 50 kroners, "Allahabad on the Ganges" at 85, and "Lahore on the Indus" at 90 kroners. Delhi postcards were the most expensive at 2 florin, 80 kroners' more than the set of all twelve Hoffmann cards cost in Vienna! In *The Illustrated Post-Card*, No. 12, December 1899, p. 14.

15. *The Illustrated Post-Card*, No. 3, p. 12.

16. *The Illustrated Post-Card*, No. 9, 1 July 1898, pp. 1, 3, 4. No. 12, December 1899, p. 6.

17. *The Illustrated Post-Card*, No 12, December 1899, p. 13. Original-Postkarten-Versen, by Julius Bretisch.

18. Out of about 650 cards initially selected for this book, twice as many of the postmarked cards are addressed to women (14%) as men (6%). In about 10% of the cases one cannot be sure. About 70% are unaddressed. Vienna dealers when asked about this phenomenon agree that most albums in their trade were assembled by women. The percentage of female to male recipients in another survey of about 2,000 postcards was 70% to 30%. In Daniel Gifford, *American Holiday Postcards, 1905–1915* (Jefferson: McFarland & Co, 2013), p. 26.

20. "A Chat with the Foundress of a Ladies' Postcard Club," *The Picture Postcard: A Magazine of Travel, Philately, Art* I, No. 5 (1900), pp. 71–72, quoted in Saloni Mathur, *India by Design Colonial History and Cultural Display* (Berkeley, CA: University of California Press, 2007), p. 130.

21. Leonard Pitt, personal communication, Berkeley, CA, 2014.

22. *The Illustrated Post-Card*, No. 9, p. 10.

23. *The Illustrated Post-Card* Postkarte, No. 7, Nr. 9, July, 1898.

24. *The Illustrated Post-Card*, No. 7, 1 July 1898, p. 9. Burma postcards were only 70 kroners, and ones from Ceylon at least 1,30 florins. Chinese cards were all 1 florin and American cards from 8 to 20 kroner. Things changed quickly.

25. *Die Illustrierte The Illustrated Post-Card*, No. 1, January 1, 1899.

26. *Freie Kunste*, No. 6, 15. March 1900

27. *Freie Kunste*, No. 1, January 1898, p. 1.

29. *The Englishman*, Kolkata, Nov. 8, 1898.

30. Carla Taban, ed., *Meta and Interimages in Contemporary Visual Art and Culture*, (Belgium: Leuven University Press, 2013), p. 52. Also see, http://www.blouinartinfo.com/artists/53305-antoine-druet, accessed on May 31, 2015.

GENERAL POST OFFICE
BOMBAY.

Bombay
[Mumbai]

The first India postcards may have been published in Vienna and Kolkata, but by 1900 Mumbai had become the centre of innovation in the subcontinent. Among the first postcards printed in Mumbai were a Ravi Varma Press series from 1899 that included the lithograph *General Post Office Bombay* (Figure 1). Mumbai had the largest post office in India. Each year tens of millions of postcards passed through a city of less than a million.

For me, the texture of the postcard and its origins is richest in Mumbai. When I came here as a young man for the first time to meet my wife's family, I revelled in the density of cultures. Bombay, as it was then known, was the global city of the subcontinent. Karachi seemed like a pond in comparison. Mumbai offered just the cosmopolitan milieu the postcard needed to thrive.

Mumbai grew from the 1860s through the 1890s because of the international cotton trade, which started with *Cotton Cleaning* (Figure 2) and led to textile manufacturing mills dotting the city. The wealth generated by the cotton trade financed buildings of a unique "Gothic Indo-Sarcenic" style. These included the *Municipal Hall* (Figure 3), and, right next to it, Victoria Terminus, a railway station imposing enough for a Latin name. In 1899 it was still so fresh in the landscape that the lithographer Paul Gerhardt at the Ravi Varma Press called it *Bori Bunder Station* (Figure 4). One sender noted "Magnificent station but far too big for requirements." Postcards generally favoured the side view to convey the grandiose effect of *Victoria Terminus G.I.P. Ry.* [*Railway*] *Bombay* (Figure 5).

Figure 1. *General Post Office Bombay*. Paul Gerhardt [signed], Ravi Varma Press, Karli and Bombay, c. 1899. Lithograph, Undivided back, 12.2 x 8.75 cm, 4.80 x 3.44 in.

Postmarked 22 March 1905 in Bombay, and April 18 1905 in Salt Lake City, Utah. Addressed to "Miss Etta Vermillion, West 2nd Salt Lake City, Utah via San Francisco"

[*Verso*] "Bombay 22 March Good luck Uncle Will."

Cotton Cleaners

Municipal.
Buildings
Bombay.

RAVI VARMA PRESS, KARLI & BOMBAY, REGISTERED

P.G.
Bombay
99.

FACING PAGE, ABOVE
Figure 2. *Cotton Cleaners.* Clifton & Co.,
c. 1905. Coloured collotype, Divided
back, 13.85 x 8.8 cm, 5.45 x 3.46 in.

FACING PAGE, BELOW
Figure 3. *Municipal Buildings Bombay.*
Paul Gerhardt [signed], Ravi Varma
Press, Bombay, 1899. Lithograph,
Undivided back, 12.3 x 8.8 cm,
4.84 x 3.46 in.

Figure 4. *Bori Bunder Station Bombay.*
Paul Gerhardt [signed], Ravi Varma
Press, Bombay, 1899. Lithograph,
Undivided back, 12.4 x 8.9 cm,
4.88 x 3.50 in.

Postmarked 22 March 1905 in Bombay,
and April 18 1905 in Salt Lake City, Utah.
Addressed to "H. H. Rogers Esq. Konupa
Makme-Kopunuka, Odessa South Russia-
in-Europe"

[*Recto*] "Magnificent station but far too
big for requirements."

Gerhardt is among the first artists who signed his name on a postcard series printed in India. His *Bombay View* (Figure 6) shows the "Queen's necklace" from Victoria Gardens in Malabar Hills. The red colour draws the eye to the two men in the foreground. Gerhardt's aesthetic choices add intrigue. What are the boy and man talking about? The postcard has a hopeful flavour, distinct from another early view from the same picture stop, the classicist *Bombay* (see *Introduction*, Figures 7, 8).

ABOVE
Figure 5. *Victoria Terminus G.I.P. Ry. [Railway] Bombay.* G.B.V. Ghoni, Bombay, 1899. Coloured halftone, Undivided back, 13.75 x 8.65 cm, 5.41 x 3.41 in.

BELOW
Figure 6. *Bombay View.* Paul Gerhardt [signed], Ravi Varma Press, Bombay, 1899. Lithograph, Undivided back, 12.2 x 8.7 cm, 4.80 x 3.43 in.

Postmarked 4 December 1905 Sea Post Office Bombay [?], and April 18 1905 in Salt Lake City, Utah. Addressed to "Master Dore Tydeman, Gordon Villa, Great Western Road Dorchester England" [no message].

University Gardens and Clock Tower (Figure 7), known as Rajabai Tower after the mother of one of the first great cotton brokers, and *Bombay. The Museum* (Figure 8) show the range of architectural styles within the "Indo-Saracenic," from a Gothic tower from Venice to an imperial museum structured around a Persian dome.

A very popular postcard site was *Bombay. Pydownie Street* (Figure 9). Tuck's view celebrates the arrival of the tram, while another fills the picture with the Shia Muslim procession *Mohuram Festival, Bombay* (Figure 10).

Figure 7. *University Gardens and Clock Tower.* G.B.V. Ghoni, Bombay, 1899. Coloured halftone, Undivided back, 13.75 x 8.65 cm, 5.41 x 3.41 in.

Figure 8. *Bombay. The Museum. Wide Wide World Oilette Bombay Series #8969.* Raphael Tuck & Co. Embossed coloured halftone, Divided back, 13.75 x 8.65 cm, 4.41 x 3.41 in.

[*Verso*] "**The Museum**. As befitting an important town like Bombay, the Museum is indeed a very fine one and contains many valuable collections."

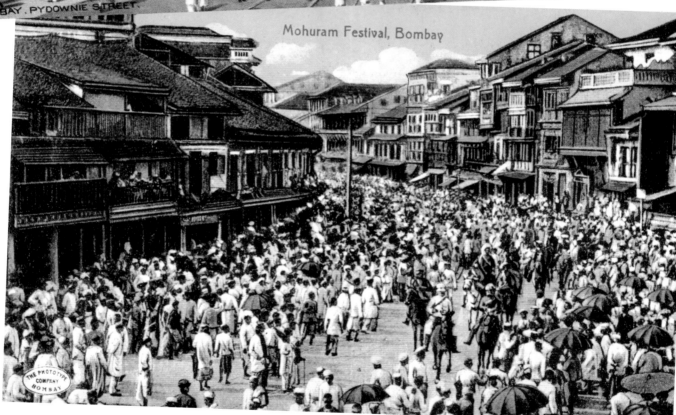

Figure 9. *Bombay. Pydownie Street. Wide Wide World Oilette Bombay, India Series #7022.* Raphael Tuck & Co. London, c. 1905. Coloured halftone, Divided back, 13.9 x 8.75 cm, 5.47 x 3.44 in.

[*Verso*] "**Pydownie Street, Bombay (City)**. Pydownie Street, one of the principal highways of Bombay, is typical of the many animated thoroughfares of this busy city. Forty percent of the trade of India is now done through Bombay, while its chief industries are dyeing, tanning, and working in metal. It possesses no less than seventy large steam mills, and a population of between eight and nine hundred thousand."

Figure 10. *Muharam Festival, Bombay.* The Phototype Company, Bombay, c. 1905. Coloured halftone, Divided back, 13.9 x 8.85 cm, 5.47 x 3.48 in.

[*Verso, pencil*] "**One of the Street Scenes met with at Bombay.**" This street was later and still is named Mohammed Ali Road after the freedom fighter (see *Independence*, Figure 12).

Figure 11. *Greetings from Bombay.*
D. M. Macropolo, Kolkata, c. 1900.
Lithograph, Undivided back,
14.1 x 9.25 cm, 5.55 x 3.64 in.

D.M. Macropolo was a tobacco retailer
in the city from 1863 until he died in
1901. He did not do more than one
printing of this series, opting soon for
cheaper photographic cards.

Figure 12. *Hindu Monkey Temple,
Bombay.* Clifton & Co., c. 1903.
Coloured collotype, Undivided back,
13.75 x 8.75 cm, 5.41 x 3.44 in.

Clifton and Co. began as Schultz &
Clifton as early as 1895, when the
firm was first listed in *Thackers Indian
Directory*. The next year it became just
Clifton & Co. We know Clifton was
a photographer. Schultz and Clifton
produced a set of photographs of
Mumbai, many of which were later used
for postcards.[10]

D.M. Macropolo's lithographic card, *Greetings from Bombay* (Figure 11), uses ornamentation skilfully to drive the forward movement of the elephant.[1] The temple in the top right is the *Hindu Monkey Temple* (Figure 12), in an early colour collotype postcard by Clifton & Co. Clifton became the major Bombay and all-India publisher of postcards between 1900 and 1905. The firm used different design strategies to display large format albumen photographic images. At first there were court-sized cards like *Elphinstone Circle* (Figure 13), this done up with a soft watercolour stencil.

After Clifton made the successful transition to the larger European sized postcard in 1902, the firm went through many variations of the "Lichtdruck," or "light print" chromo-collotype, manufactured by a single firm in Dresden in Germany,[2] to keep up with the competition. These include *Hindu Woman* (Figure 14) and *A Mohamedan dancing Girl in Attitude* (Figure 15), where colours seem to have been lathered on to the card.[3] *Road Sweeper* (Figure 16) idealizes the noble native doing his duty. The most popular of Clifton's type cards was *Water Carrier* (Figure 17), with realistic water spouting from the goatskin.

Another "Lichtdruck," *A Parsee Lady* (Figure 18), has a sky created from an irregular pattern of blues and whites. Mottled orange beads give the woman's cheeks their colour. Parsis were the most Westernized and wealthiest of Mumbai's elite. Given

Hindu Woman.

FACING PAGE

Figure 13. *Elphinstone Circle, Bombay.* Clifton & Co., c. 1903. Handcoloured collotype, Undivided back, 12.1 x 8.8 cm, 4.76 x 3.46 in.

Note how the title and publisher are etched into the negative of this original albumen photograph. It saved an electrotype run in the early days.

Figure 14. *Hindu woman.* Clifton & Co., c. 1903. Chromo-collotype, Undivided back, 13.7 x 8.75 cm, 5.39 x 3.44 in.

A Mohamedan dancing Girl in Attitude

Figure 15. *A Mohamedan dancing Girl in Attitude.* Clifton & Co., c. 1903. Chromo-collotype, Undivided back, 13.9 x 8.9 cm, 5.47 x 3.50 ins.

"Attitude" is the equivalent of striking a pose. A Kolkata critic wrote of the type in 1903:

"The Mohamedan dancing-girl plies her trade from the age of twelve to sixty, for youth and beauty are by no means the 'sine qua non' of the dancing-girl. She must be a thorough mistress of her art, and old fiddles often play the best tune."[11]

Road Sweeper

Clifton & Co., Bombay

Figure 16. *Road Sweeper.* Clifton & Co.,
c. 1903. Chromo-collotype,
Undivided back, 13.75 x 8.9 cm,
5.41 x 3.50 in.

ABOVE

Figure 17. *Water Carrier.* Clifton & Co.,
c. 1903. Chromo-collotype, Undivided back,
13.7 x 8.95 cm, 5.39 x 3.52 in.

Figure 18. *A Parsee Lady.* Clifton & Co.,
c. 1903. Chromo-collotype, Undivided back,
13.8 x 8.8 cm, 5.43 x 3.462 in.

their literacy and the number of Parsi-themed postcards that have survived, Parsis seem to have consumed more postcards per capita than any other community. Parsi women were a popular subject—progressive women with traditional virtues, counterpoints to the *nautch* girl. The *Parsee Lady* is holding what could be a postcard. *Up-to-date Parsee* (Figure 19) presses the same key for men, and reveals a new object mediating social relationships, the newspaper.

Parsee Tower of Silence, Bombay (Figure 20), another of the city's landmarks, spoke to the mysterious in the Zoroastrian religion. Only Parsees are allowed to enter this

Figure 19. *Up-to-date-Parsee.* Unknown Publisher, c. 1903. Lithograph, Divided back, 13.6 x 8.4 cm, 5.35 x 3.31 in.

This card was from a very nicely done series, possibly by Taraporevala, although at least one copy is blind stamped Haji Yusuf Haji Mohammed, Pictures, Postcards & Cutlery Merchant, Grant Road Cross-Lane, Bombay.[7]

Figure 20. *Parsee Tower of Silence.* Clifton & Co., c. 1903. Chromo-collotype, Undivided back, 13.8 x 8.9 cm, 5.43 x 3.50 in.

Who knows what motivated the Austrian writer Stefan Zweig to send this postcard to Miss Hirschfeld in Vienna from Bombay on December 30, 1908? The 27-year old Zweig, a budding novelist whose popularity after World War I was unparalleled among German writers, mailed it to Miss Hirschfeld just after having heard that she was to be engaged:

[*Recto*] "Most honored Miss. I greet you many times still as a Miss – with your understanding I hope." [*Verso*] "I wish you luck for Hannover over everything else. For myself, I can wish for nothing more than India – it is incredibly wonderful and terrific."[12]

Handwritten on the front of another card, unsent: "This is the celebrated Tower of Silence where the Parsees put their dead + the vultures eat all the flesh off them You can see them waiting around the walls for their dinner I saw about 200 of these birds feeding on a dead body in the Hooghley just recently." Many versions of this postcard were published by different publishers and mailed as late as 1952 from Mumbai.

Figure 21. *Malabar Hill, Bombay.* Clifton & Co., c. 1903. Chromo-collotype, Undivided back, 13.55 x 9 cm, 5.33 x 3.54 in.

Figure 22. *Malabar Point. Bombay. Wide Wide World Oilette Bombay Series #8926.* Raphael Tuck & Co., London, c. 1905. Coloured halftone, Divided back, 13.75 x 8.75 cm, 5.41 x 3.44 in.

[*Verso*] "**Malabar Point Bombay**. Malabar Point, showing the Sea and Promenade, where all classes—Europeans and natives—congregate to enjoy the fresh and breezy air in the cool of evening."

Figure 23. *P. & O. S.S. "Kaisar-i-Hind."* [*Emperor of India*]. Unknown Publisher, c. 1920. Coloured halftone, 13.9 x 8.8 cm, 5.47 x 3.46 in.

Postmarked July 8, 1924, Norway and addressed to L.B. Rice 106 Summer Street Newton Center Mss. USA.

"Dear Laurie: Spent last night at North Cape, most northerly point in Europe. It is light as day all night Spending summer in Europe then going around the world. Good luck in tennis. Gordon" temple on top of Malabar Hill, where the bones of the dead are left after final rites for vultures to consume. The Tower of Silence of *Malabar Hill, Bombay* (Figure 21) uses what was a brief flirtation in postcard history, the keyhole view. Tuck's *Malabar Point, Bombay* (Figure 22) exposed a new place in the urban sphere where, as the caption had it, "all classes – Europeans and natives – congregate to enjoy the fresh and breezy air in the cool of the evening."

Figure 24. *The Victoria Docks, Bombay.*
Unknown Publisher, c. 1908. Coloured
halftone, Divided back, 13.8 x 8.75 cm,
5.43 x 3.44 in.

Figure 25. *Lascar* [*Sailor*]. M.V.
Dhurandhar [signed], Mumbai, c. 1903.
Coloured halftone, Undivided back,
11.15 x 8.65 cm, 4.39 x 3.41 in.

Addressed to Miss. G. Stanley, 70 Edward
Street, Burton on Trent, England.

[*Verso*] "AEP." [*Blindstamp*] Nowgong
[Central India]

FACING PAGE, ABOVE
Figure 26. *Native Street.* Paul Gerhardt
[signed], Ravi Varma Press, Bombay,
1899. Lithograph, Undivided back,
12.35 x 8.75 cm, 4.86 x 3.44 in.

FACING PAGE, BELOW
Figure 27. *Abdul Rehiman Street,
Bombay.* Raphael Tuck & Sons #8926,
London, c. 1905. Coloured Halftone,
Divided back, 13.1 x 8.85 cm,
5.16 x 3.48 in.

[*Verso*] "**Abdul Rehiman Street**. This is
one of the busiest spots in the city of
Bombay and also one of the principal
native streets."
Note the building under construction
on the right.

NATIVE STREET.

P. G

ABDUL REHIMAN STREET, BOMBAY.

P. & O. S.S. "Kaisar-i-Hind." [Emperor of India] (Figure 23) gives some sense of the size of the freighters at *The Victoria Docks, Bombay* (Figure 24). Shipping industry needs pushed the *Lascar* (Figure 25) into greater prominence. Lascars were sailors who spoke their own multinational tongue, 'Lascari', while keeping the ships moving from port to port.

Illustrated postcards actually came to Mumbai at an inauspicious moment. The increased ship traffic from Hong Kong and South Africa brought the bubonic plague back to Mumbai in 1896. Its epicentre was the "Native Quarter," already on par with New York in density of population at 760 people an acre,[4] represented in Gerhardt's delicate *Native Street* (Figure 26) and Tuck's beautiful *Abdul Rehiman Street* (Figure 27). "It [the plague] started in the Mandvi quarter and then spread throughout the city," wrote the *Bombay Gazette* in 1900.[5] In response to this crisis, Clifton published cards like *Segregation Camp, Bombay* (Figure 28) and *Innoculation Against Plague* (Figure 29) that showed the authorities taking action. Note the well-dressed people on the right who set-off the little boy with the bloated stomach.

A Ward in Plague Hospital, Bombay showing Patients (Figure 30) and *Plague Patients. Bombay* (Figure 31) depicts a clean interior with an English doctor and nurse standing by. The two cards also represent a postcard phenomenon that deltiologist Leonard Pitt calls "the sequential." *Plague Patients* was shot a few feet closer and to the right of *A Ward*, but clearly on the same day. Some, but not all, patients are the same. The man with the bandaged head in the foreground has moved a little. The European nurse and doctor are gone. How many minutes have gone by?

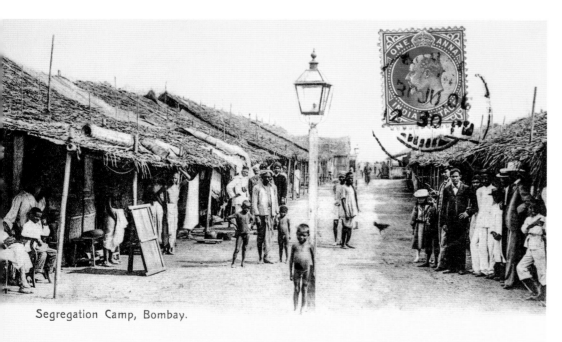

Segregation Camp, Bombay.

Figure 28. *Segregation Camp, Bombay.* Clifton & Co., c. 1903. Collotype, Undivided back, 13 x 8.7 cm, 5.12 x 3.43 in.

Postmarked June 30, 1906, Mumbai. Addressed to "Miss Amy L. Carter Graylingwell Hospital, Chichester, Sussex, England" with ink blind stamp on back "Chas. [Charles] A. E. Huard, Marble Hall, Byculla, Bombay."

[*Recto*] "This is the place Segregation Camp, what do you think of it. C.A.E. Huard, 30.6.06"

As one resident confessed, "Bombay was a trading city; knowledge of the plague would hurt trade... The representation that all was well was critical."[13]

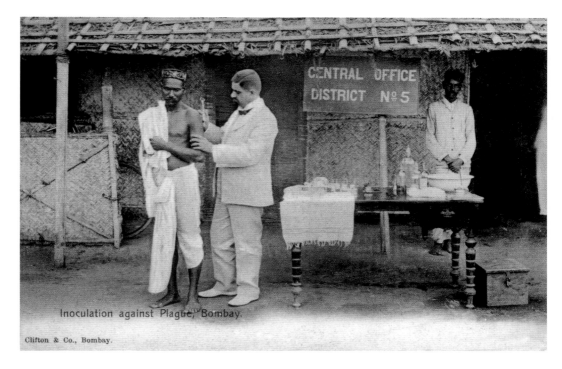

Inoculation against Plague," Bombay.

Clifton & Co., Bombay.

ABOVE

Figure 29. *Innoculation Against Plague.* Clifton & Co., c. 1903. Collotype, Undivided back, 13.6 x 9.1 cm, 5.35 x 3.58 in.

Postmarked May 7, 1904, Sea Post Office, Mumbai. Addressed to "Miss. R. Kennedy, Viewmont Drive, Gilshochill, Mary Hill, Glasgow, Scotland."

"Dear Ruby, when I see you I shall be able to explain this p.c. [postcard] to you. With my love, John [sp?]"

Waldemar Haffkine, a Russian Jewish doctor in Mumbai developed one of the first vaccinations after he arrived in 1896 from the Pasteur Institute in Paris where he helped with the discovery of early cholera vaccinations. By 1897 he was running trials for a serum that inoculated millions in India. Made from resistant animals, it worked about half the time[14] and made him a controversial hero.[15]

CENTRE

Figure 30. *A Ward in Plague Hospital, Bombay showing Patients.* Clifton & Co., c. 1903. Coloured collotype, Divided back, 13.85 x 8.8 cm, 5.45 x 3.46 in.

BELOW

Figure 31. *Plague Patients, Bombay.* Clifton & Co., c. 1903. Collotype, Divided back, 13.9 x 9 cm, 5.47 x 3.54 in.

Not postmarked or addressed.

[*Verso*] "This is how the`se devils are taken care of when they have plague, and as soon as they are well they abuse the doctors and say they tried to kill them. The pity is, that they don't let them die. C.A."

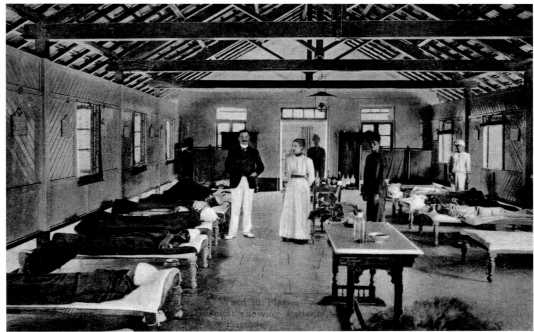

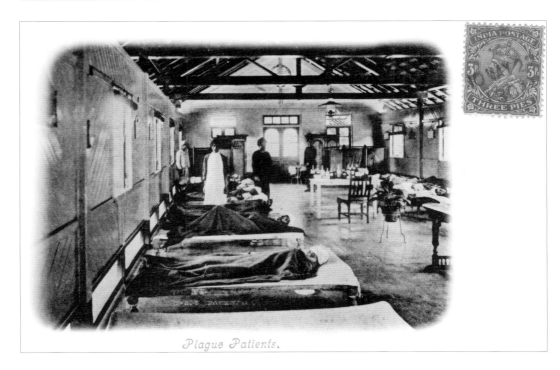

Plague Patients.

Group of famine stricken victims

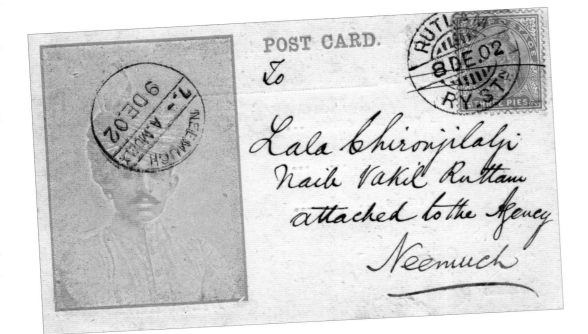

Figure 32. *Famine Group Victims.* The Phototype Company, Bombay, c. 1905. Coloured collotype, Divided back, 13.7 x 8.9 cm, 5.38 x 3.50 in.

While famines were not unknown to India, the use of railways to transport food out of the agricultural areas had unintended consequences. When droughts came, there was little colonial will to use the railways to bring food back to the starving. They in turn had no choice but to walk to the cities in search of food, using up energy.

Figure 33. *Famine Victims* [pencilled title on back]. c. 1910. Real photo postcard, Divided back, 14 x 8.85 cm, 5.51 x 3.48 in.

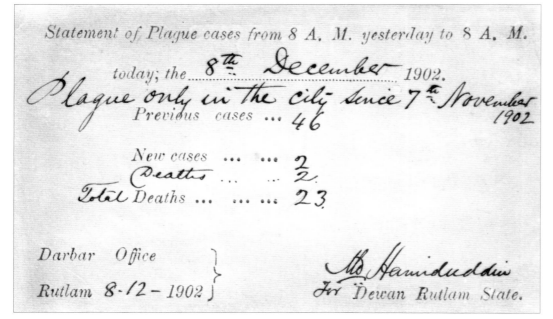

Figure 34. *Statement of Plague cases from yesterday to 8 A. M. today; the 8thDecember 1902.* 1902. Halftone postcard, Undivided back, 14 x 8.85 cm, 5.51 x 3.48 in.

Royal Indian Tour – T.R.H. the Prince & Princess of Wales. Arrival at Apollo Bunder. Bombay 9th Nov: 1905

Figure 35. *Royal Indian Tour – T.R.H. the Prince and Princess of Wales. Arrival at Apollo Bunder, Bombay 9th Nov: 1905.* The Phototype Company, Bombay, c. 1905. Collotype, Divided back, 13.85 x 9.35 cm, 5.45 x 3.68 in.

The event was boycotted by the freedom-minded.

It was not only plague deaths that were reported on a daily basis in newspapers together with postcard advertisements. There were also the *Famine Stricken Victims* (Figure 32), millions of whom died in Maharashtra, Punjab, Central and South India. Later real photo postcards like *Famine Victims* (Figure 33) are truly uncomfortable to look at. It is also hard to believe, but perfectly logical, that postcards like *Statement of Plague cases from 8 A. M. yesterday to 8 am today; the 8ᵗʰ December 1902* (Figure 34) were sent up the reporting chain, in this case of a princely state in Central India.

A more fortunate visitor to the city when the plague temporarily subsided was the Prince of Wales and his wife, heirs to the British throne. They are shown in the early Indian photo-journalistic postcard *Royal Indian Tour – H.R.H. the Prince and Princess of Wales Arrival at Apollo Bunder, Bombay 9ᵗʰ Nov: 1905* (Figure 35). While in India, the Prince of Wales sent his eleven-year old son Bertie (the future George VI, father of Queen Elizabeth II) a steady stream of postcards, assembled in an album by his mother Queen Mary, herself an avid postcard collector.[6] The first three, and most of the India cards in her album are by Clifton & Co.[7] *Native Street Scene, Bombay* (Figure 36) has a handwritten message (both front and back) from the Prince of Wales to his son which offers a glimpse of the world from inside the royal carriage (see caption).

Figure 36. *Native Street Scene, Bombay.* Clifton & Co., c. 1903. Collotype, Undivided back, 13.8 x 8.8 cm, 5.43 x 3.46 in. Royal Collection Trust/© Her Majesty Queen Elizabeth II 2014

[*Recto*] "Nov 12ᵗʰ/05 Bombay

My dear Bertie
Look at all these people" [*Verso*] "in the picture and imagine thousands of them lining the streets cheering and clapping their hands and that will give you an idea of what we see as we drive through the streets of Bombay. It is all most interesting but very hot, much hotter than you have ever felt it in England. We start for Indore on the 14ᵗʰ where I hope it will be cooler. O'Kane got a charming hay trab [sp?] horse which I hope to soon ride. With great love from Yr. devoted Papa, G.I."

After 1910 or so, Clifton published postcards as "Clifton, Photographer, Bombay." In the 1950s the firm was listed as "Map and Book Publishers, Kion, Bombay."[16]

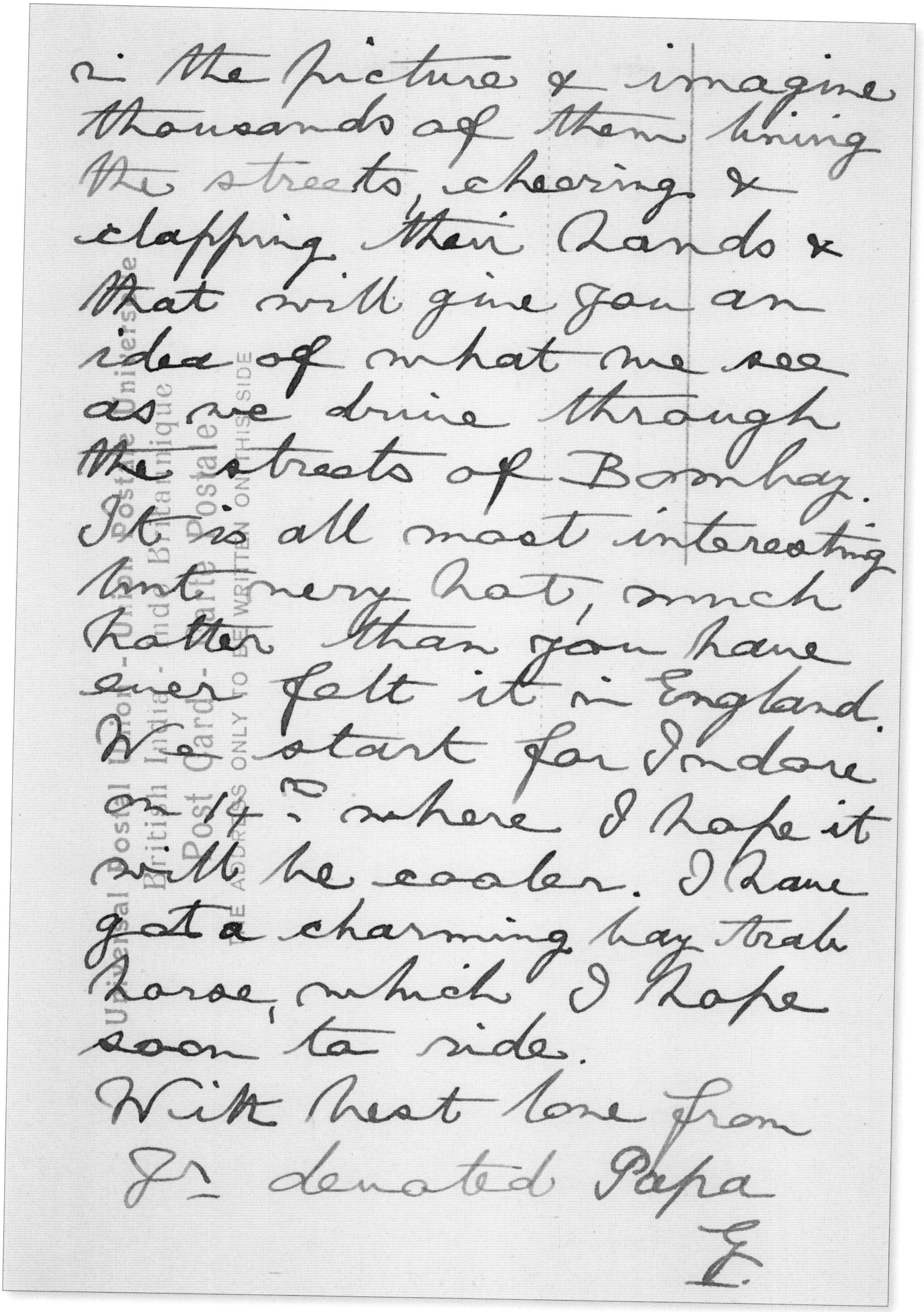

in the picture & imagine
thousands of them lining
the streets, cheering &
clapping their hands &
that will give you an
idea of what we see
as we drive through
the streets of Bombay.
It is all most interesting.
but very hot, much
hotter than you have
ever felt it in England.
We start for Indore
on 14. where I hope it
will be cooler. I have
got a charming bay Arab
horse, which I hope
soon to ride.
With best love from
Jr devoted Papa
E.

The royals included a single hand-painted postcard in their album, *Bullock Cart* (Figure 37). In a tradition where local artists used wood, skin, fabrics to paint images, hand-painted postcards were a new product.[8] As the plague report postcard (see Figure 33) also shows, there was a stream of inexpensive illustrated postcards available in the bazaars, sometimes pre-printed, sometimes hand-painted, but sadly for the many stories they could tell, few have survived.

Figure 37. *Bullock Carriage.* Bombay, 1905. Handpainted, Undivided back, 13.55 x 9 cm, 5.33 x 3.54 in.

A version of this card is postmarked Prince of Wales Camp, Bombay, Dec. 14, 1905 and addressed to Prince Albert of York[sp?], York Cottage, Sandringham, England. "Wishing you many happy returns of the day."[17] [CHG. [sp?].

A *zenana* carriage offered veiled transport for women through the city. These single cards are similar to Chinese handmade postcards and are often court-sized with undivided backs, and were not often mailed abroad.

Figure 38. *Bombay Beauties.* The Phototype Co., Mumbai, c. 1905. Coloured halftone, Divided back, 13.9 x 8.9 cm, 5.47 x 3.50 in.

The image was titled *Hindoo Natch Girls* in F.M. Coleman's *Typical Pictures of Indian Natives, Being Reproductions from Specially Prepared Hand-Coloured Photographs with Descriptive Letterpress*, published in Bombay and London in 1897. A black and white postcard of the same image by The Phototype Co. was called *Bombay Beauties*. Malka Jan, born Victoria Hemmings, married a Muslim nobleman and established herself as a dancer in Calcutta at the court of the exiled former ruler of Lucknow, Wajid Ali Shah. Trained by the best dance and music composers in the city, Gohar Jan gave her first performance in 1896. In 1902 her debut ended with her signature line "My name is Gohar Jan."

Figure 39. *Miss Gohur, Prima Donna of India.* Unknown Publisher, c. 1910. Coloured collotype, Divided back, 13.75 x 8.8 cm, 5.41 x 3.46 in.

Gohar Jan [1873–1930], despite reaching the pinnacle of success as a singer, ended her life as an unhappy court musician in the zenana of the Maharajah of Mysore after a series of bitter disappointments.

Late Lok. Tilak.　　　कै. लोकमान्य टिळक.

(107　जुगतराम एन्ड कुं॰ नरनारायण मंदिर सामे मुंबई, नं. २.

Indian Art Press, Kalbadevi Road Bombay, No. 2.

Figure 40. *Bal Gangadar Tilak.* The
Phototype Company, Bombay, c. 1905.
Coloured halftone, Divided back,
13.85 x 8.8 cm, 5.45 x 3.46 in.

Among my most interesting discoveries among Mumbai postcards is that the popular *Bombay Beauties* (Figure 38) actually shows a young Gohar Jan (right) and her mother Malka Jan.[9] *Miss Gohur, Prima Donna of India* (Figure 39) was born in North India as Angelina Yeoward in Azamgarh in 1873, and became the most famous *nautch* girl of the postcard era, with a voice so popular that it became the first to be recorded on gramophone in India on November 2, 1902—at the height of the famine.

A key political figure to emerge in the city during this period was *Bal Gangadar Tilak* (Figure 40). Tilak (1865-1920) offered a Hindu revivalist message built around Shivaji, the Mahratta (Maratha) Hindu ruler who defeated the Mughal armies in the 17th century. Imprisoned as a violent agitator by the British, Tilak used the plague quarantines and repression of poor populations as a rallying cry for the independence struggle and the city did in fact become its centre (see *Independence*).

Figure 41. *Taj Mahal Hotel Bombay. Wide Wide World Oilette Bombay Series I #8925.* Raphael Tuck & Co., London, c. 1905. Coloured halftone, Divided back, 13.75 x 8.75 cm, 5.41 x 3.44 in.

[*Verso*] "**Taj Mahal Hotel, Bombay**. Bombay, one of the most important cities in India, has an area of not less than 22 square miles. Its harbour, studded with islands and crowded with shipping, is one of the finest in the world, the space available for shipping being 14 miles in length and 5 miles in width. The view from the Taj Mahal Hotel is magnificent."

Sir J. N. Tata.

The Apollo Bunder, Bombay.

GATEWAY AT BOMBAY TO COMMEMORATE THE LANDING OF THEIR IMPERIAL MAJESTIES KING GEORGE V & QUEEN

ABOVE

Figure 42. *The Apollo Bunder, Bombay.* G.B.V. Ghoni [?], Mumbai, c. 1905. Coloured halftone, Divided back, 13.75 x 8.75 cm, 5.41 x 3.44 in.

Figure 43. *Gateway at Bombay to Commemorate the Landing of Their Imperial Majesties King George V & Queen Mary on 2nd December 1911. Copyright Bombay Court, British Empire Exhibition, Wembley,* 1924. Raphael Tuck & Co., London. Sepia Halftone, Divided back, 14.2 x 9.15 cm, 5.59 x 3.60 in.

The iconic *Taj Mahal Hotel, Bombay* (Figure 41) was opened in 1903. It was built by a Parsi who, it is said, was furious that he could not be admitted to European-only clubs. It is my favourite hotel. Whether on my first visit for tea with my in-laws, in a corner overlooking the Arabian Sea, or the time I actually stayed here many years later, I was struck by how much history had flowed through this little embankment, up the steps splashed by seawater in *The Apollo Bunder, Bombay* (Figure 42). The same location in reverse angle is shown in *Gateway at Bombay.* (Figure 43). The Gateway was opened in 1911 to honour King George V and Queen Mary who celebrated their accession with another tour of India. It has since become everyone's gateway to India.

Notes

1. Author's Collection, postmarked Sea Post Office, April 4, 1904. The Michael Stokes Collection has a "Salaam from India" from the same set, mailed from Bombay on July 8, 1901.

2. The firm was Knackstedt und Naether in Dresden, as identified by Howard Woody in *Delivering Views Distant Cultures in Early Postcards* (Washington D.C.: Smithsonian Institution, 1998), p. 40.

3. Howard Woody, a pioneer researcher of early German printing postcard technologies writes of another *Mohamedan Woman* postcard, of how the collotype's "light hues accent the woman's layered costumer and create an attractive luminous image that contrasts with the muted background" in "International Postcards Their History, Production and Distribution (Circa 1895 to 1915)" in *Delivering Views Distant Cultures in Early Postcards*, p. 40.

4. E. Washburn Hopkins, *India Old and New* (New York: Charles Scribner's Sons, 1902), p. 266.

5. *The Bombay Gazette*, Feb. 13, 1900.

6. For example, see the album RCIN 2587841, Windsor Castle, Royal Collection Trust/© Her Majesty Queen Elizabeth II 2014.

7. Clifton & Co. has the majority of cards by a single publisher in the royal album (17 of 79). This seems to reflect Clifton's share, at its height, of the Indian postcard market.

8. The other place where this kind of individually produced postcard is seen is in China and among Chinese expatriate communities, where presumably labour was inexpensive enough to profitably justify the effort.

9. This photograph was taken on behalf of a book by the Mumbai editor of *The Times of India*, F.M. Coleman, where they are described as *Hindoo Nautch Girls.*

10. These include a dozen image set with Apollo Bunder, the Yacht Club and Municipal Hall, and other then new areas in South Bombay. British Library, Ph 156/1-2.

11. *The Englishman*, Kolkata, Nov. 7, 1903, "The *Nautch* Girl. Some Fresh Facts," p. 5.

12. Stefan Zweig, *Ansichtskarten Aus Indien, Herausgegeben von Erich Fitzbauer*, p. 4-5, at the New York Public Library, New York. Translated from German by the author.

13. *India Old and New*, p. 279

14. Another Russian doctor with experience in China, Alexander Yertsin, gave the bubonic plague its official name *yersinia pestis*, by isolating the strain first. In 1907, a number of Punjabi villagers died when the vaccine was administered, Haffkine was blamed and had to flee the country. It took many years of petitions by European scientists before his name was cleared. He returned to India and worked for some more years in Kolkata before retiring to Europe and becoming a dedicated Zionist.

15. *Thacker's India Directory*, 1918, p. 673.

16. British Library F178/84 (1) has a signed photograph of the *Civilian Commission* dated to March, 1931. *The Times of India* directory and yearbook, 1955, as seen in Google Books.

THE RAVI VARMA PRESS

Were the first artist-signed postcards of India really produced in Vienna? If anyone beat them to it, it would have been Paul Gerhardt at the Ravi Varma Press in Mumbai.

Raja Ravi Varma (1848–1906) was a painter from minor royalty in what is today Kerala state in southwest India. From a very early age, he took to painting, and was encouraged by many in an artistic family. After apparently being rejected as a court painter at the age of thirteen because his skin was too dark,[18] he kept learning from visiting Indian and English painters. In his mid-twenties he won a prize at an exhibition in Chennai. From then on, patronage by successive British Governor-Generals and Indian feudal rulers was assured. Ravi Varma's fusion of Western perspective, the new medium of oil painting, Hindu mythology and photography continue to have mass appeal to Indian audiences today.

Ravi Varma and his younger brother Raja Varma worked in a cosmopolitan image tradition. They collected the latest European illustrations,[19] bought at places like the influential Mumbai bookstore D.B. Taraporevala & Sons. In 1892 they took the bold step of investing the enormous sum of Rs. 80,000 in a printing press (at the time, Ravi Varma was earning Rs. 1500 from a reluctant-to-pay Maharajah for a portrait that took weeks to execute).[20] Dadabhai Naoroji (1825–1917), an early Parsi Independence leader from Mumbai (see Figure 5, *Independence*), is said to have arranged for Germans to come over and bring the steam-driven lithographic press with them.[21]

The German (or Austrian) lithographer Paul Gerhardt worked at the Press under master printer and business manager Fritz Schleicher (1862–1935). Gerhardt was in charge of transferring the pictures to stone,[22] which "demanded highly trained and accomplished artists."[23] The working language at the Press was German.[24] Gerhardt sometimes helped Raja Varma and his brother with their work too[25]—the younger Varma, for example, wrote in his diary on Tuesday, January 31st, 1899:

Figure 44. Advertisement, *The Times of India*. Sept. 28, 1899.

RAVI VARMA PRESS, KARLI & BOMBAY. REGISTERED.

RAVI VARMA PRESS, KARLI & BOMBAY. REGISTERED.

ABOVE

Figure 45. *Jumma Masjid Bombay.* Paul Gerhardt [signed], Ravi Varma Press, Bombay, 1899. Lithograph, Undivided back, 12.25 x 8.7 cm, 4.82 x 3.43 in.

Not postmarked. Addressed to "Miss H. Sear – 24 East Bank [?]. Stanford Hill. N. [New Jersey, USA]"

[*Recto*] "With Greet. [?] Lallys line. [sp?]"

BELOW

Figure 46. *Water bearer.* Paul Gerhardt [signed], Ravi Varma Press, Bombay, 1899. Lithograph, Undivided back, 12.1 x 8.85 cm, 4.76 x 3.48 in.

[*Verso*] "With Hearty Greetings From, To," Gerhardt would have known Raja Varma's prize-winning Water Bearer, also finished in 1899.[46]

"We induced Ms Gerhardt to stay with us for one more day as his assistance was valuable. He is a good artist though he has no time to practice painting. We had nothing to give him for dinner except rice and curry. [Next day] The morning was very windy though not so cold. Ms Gerhardt left for Bombay by the 1 o'clock train. He is such a good man that we like him very much. We were sorry when he left us."[26]

In January 1899 Schleicher presented an order for 100,000 holiday postcards on behalf of local photographic retailer Babajee Sakharam to the Varma brothers.[27] A newspaper advertisement for the postcards (Figure 44) first appears in the September 28, 1899 issue of *The Times of India*. A series of a dozen cards each are offered from watercolours by Gerhardt; a later ad mentions, "for the first time in India," a total of 42 postcards.[28]

Jumma Masjid Bombay (Figure 45) is deftly rendered, like the backdrop in a theatrical production, a skill which Gerhardt was apparently expert in.[29] *Water bearer* (Figure 46) has the message ("With Hearty Greetings") printed on the back. The face of the *bhistee* is indistinct enough to suggest it did not come from a photograph. Instead Gerhardt focuses attention on the man's strapping body. One of my favourite cards was simply entitled *Happy* (Figure 47). The sender could fill in the blank, a nod to the fact that elite customers—Christian, Parsee, Hindu, Muslim—all had their own words to add after "Happy". The title also works perfectly, with no annotation, to describe a woman thrilled to be holding a sickle.

Figure 47. *Happy.* Paul Gerhardt [signed], Ravi Varma Press, Bombay, 1899. Lithograph, Undivided back, 12.25 x 8.8 cm, 4.82 x 3.46 in.

Postmarked March 4, 1905. Addressed to "Col. And Mrs. [Charles] A. Gibson, 2713 Sacramento Street, San Francisco, California, U.S.A."

[*Recto*] "Bombay, India, Feb. 5, 1905. 13,000 miles from 2714 Sac[ramento] St. Had a fine voyage from Egypt.- weather cool. – Usually 100° here and no breeze from the Sea.- Pop. 900,000- Interesting city – Very Oriental About 80 Different Styles of Fancy Turbans worn. Hotels all crowded. Will be 5 weeks in India or more then to Ceylon.- We are now ½ way around the world. Wish you were with us. How's little Charlie and the dog Jack. Best wishes from Mr. and Mrs. Frank W. Marstens."

Copyright.

Camp·life
(Magistrate holding his court.)

Figure 48. *Camp Life (Magistrate holding his court).* The Ravi Varma Press, c. 1898–99. Lithograph, Undivided back, 11.7 x 8.6 cm, 4.61 x 3.39 in.

The title and printing of this and *Women Baking Bread* (Figure 1, Introduction) are similar to Gerhardt's signed postcards and so is the use of red in the turbans, the palm trees and the quickly sketched backdrops.

BELOW

Figure 49. *Shakuntala Patra-lekhana.* The Ravi-Varma-Press Karla Series No. 834, c. 1898-99. Coloured halftone, Divided back, 13.65 x 8.75 cm, 5.37 x 3.44 in.

[*Verso*] "Shakuntala writing love-letter :– Shakuntala while she was dwelling a forest, near the river Malini writes a letter on a lotus leaf to Dushyanta feeling doubtful if he loved her."

Unlike the oleographs, this set was printed by Stengel & Co. in Germany, suggesting that cost-effective production of postcards was not possible at the Press. The image was reproduced as a black and white postcard by another large publisher, S. Mahadeo & Sons of Belgaum.[47]

Shakuntala Patra-lekhana.

Damayanti.

Figure 50. *Damayanti.* The Ravi Varma
Press Karla Series No. #830, c. 1905.
Coloured halftone, Divided back,
13.6 x 8.6 cm, 5.35 x 3.39 in.
[*Verso*] "Damayanti :– Being separated
from her husband Nala the fair
Damayanti enters her fathers place, yet
feeing deeply for her husband, she is
represented as sitting in a moon light,
her maid standing by her side."

Uptake for the postcard series seems to have been limited. At the end of 1903, remainders were to be found in D. B. Taraporevala & Sons Christmas List:[30] "Pictorial Post Cards have come to stay: as to that there is no particle of doubt. We have prepared a series of thirty Indian coloured Post Cards at considerable expense: they are sold at one anna each."[31]

Many Gerhardt cards are dated [18]'99 (Figures 3, 4, 45). Possibly unsigned ones like *Women Baking Bread* (see Introduction, Figure 1) and *Camp Life (Magistrate holding his court)* (Figure 48) may have been attempts by the Press to test the new postcard market and printing techniques. It is unlikely that any are earlier than Hoffmann's cards in the spring of 1898—I have yet to find one postmarked before 1900.[32]

After the Babajee Sakharam batch, Gerhardt does not seem to have created another series of signed postcards.[33] In fact, the Ravi Varma Press was a precarious enterprise in its first years, and the plague played a big role in contributing to the Varma brothers letting the Germans buy out their ownership by 1903.[34] As part of the final deal, Ravi Varma gave Schleicher rights to over 100 of his paintings and "mechanical

Birth of Shakuntala.

Mohini.

reproduction was used in India for the first time to popularize a leading artist."[35] The main product of the Press were "oleographs"—rich colour lithographs 14 by 20 inches or larger. At least 22 of the images were also published as postcards by the Press.

Shakuntala Patra-lekhana (also known as *Shakuntala Writing a Love Letter*, Figure 49) is one of Ravi Varma's best-known images.[36] It captures the dreamy heart of an adolescent girl. The forest and deer are conventions from 19th century European prints. So is the backdrop to *Damayanti* (Figure 50).[37] According to art historian Partha Mitter, Ravi Varma "shrewdly and confidently fused European and Indian elements"[38] and created a new "naturalistic iconography of Hindu gods."[39] It brought the epic religious scenes right into everyone's lives. Varma's contemporary Rabindranath Tagore (see *Calcutta*, Figure 20) wrote of Ravi Varma's paintings: "The secret of their appeal is in reminding us how precious our own culture is to us, restoring to us our inheritance."[40]

In *Birth of Shakuntala* (Figure 51), the forest sage Vishwamitra is violently covering his face as he is being confronted by his lover Menaka with their child. The sinews on the sage's legs, the flab on the baby make all three look like actual people (the swans in the background, on the other hand, were a staple of German reproductions).

FACING PAGE, LEFT

Figure 51. *Birth of Shakuntala.* The Ravi Varma Press Karla Series No. #829, c. 1905. Coloured halftone, Divided back, 13.85 x 8.9 cm, 5.45 x 3.50 in.

[*Verso*] "Birth of Shakuntala:– Menaka sent by Indra to distract sage Vishwamitra in his penances, succeeds in her mission and gets a child by him. While going to Indra-loka, she offers the child to Vishwamitra, who feeling penitent for his weakness tries to avoid Menaka and disowns the child."

FACING PAGE, RIGHT

Figure 52. *Mohini.* The Ravi-Varma-Press Karla Series No.#829, c. 1905. Coloured halftone, Divided back, 13.65 x 8.65 cm, 5.37 x 3.41 in.

[*Verso*] "Mohini :– the Goddess of beauty sitting on a swing."

Figure 53. *Victory of Indrajit.* The Ravi-Varma-Press Karla Series No. #817, c. 1905. Coloured halftone, Divided back, 13.65 x 8.7 cm, 5.37 x 3.43 in.

[*Verso*] "Victory of Indrajit: – Indrajit brings Indra as a captive before his father Ravana with the riches and nymphs of Indra-Loka."

Victory of Indrajit.

The archetypical *Mohini* (Figure 52), "The Goddess of Beauty sitting on a swing," is perfect and ordinary, ideal yet accessible. As Erwin Neumayer and Christine Schellenberger—pioneering Austrian researchers into the Ravi Varma Press—discovered, *Mohini* was based on photographs of Anjanibai Malpekar, a favourite later muse of Ravi Varma.[41]

Victory of Indrajit (Figure 53) combines a great moment in Hindu religious narrative with real faces and, here, a scantily-clad woman. Ravi Varma walked a fine line in more ways than one. He was the first painter to win the official Kaiser-i-Hind Medal in 1905, yet when Bal Ganghadar Tilak (Figure 42) was accused of fomenting the assassination of British officials, Ravi Varma painted his portrait, oleographs of which were printed by the Press.[42]

The Press turned more than one Ravi Varma painting into postcards. *Untitled* (Figure 54) shows a scene at the Karla railway station outside Mumbai where the Press was headquartered. On the platform, a barefoot man is holding a stick, another is smoking a hookah. A number of men and women, girls and boys have gathered. What is on the *charpai*-like platform before them? Could it be a painting? Fresh oleographs?

Ravi Varma died in 1906, and his death was commemorated not only by his press but also by another with *The Late Raja Ravi Varma* (Figure 55). Unfortunately, he did not live to see his Press become, for many decades, the largest in India.[43] Reproductions

Figure 54. *Untitled.* The Ravi Varma Press Series No. #816, c. 1905. Coloured halftone, Divided back, 13.8 x 8.7 cm, 5.43 x 3.43 in.

Figure 55. *The Late Raja Ravi Varma.* P.S. Joshi, Artu Publisher, Bombay. c. 1906. Collotype Divided back, 12.1 x 8.7 cm, 4.75 x 3.42 in.

[*Verso*] **Raja Ravi Varma.** This great Indian Artist was born on the 29th of April 1818 and died on the 2nd October 1906.

of his images (often unauthorized) remain ubiquitous. The Press flourished under Schleicher, who died in 1935, and then continued under his daughter, who married an Indian, until a fire in 1972 shut it down completely.

After many years of correspondence, the German postcard historian Helmfried Luers told me that he had found an article by a German publisher in India. It was based on an interview between Schleicher, on a visit to Germany in 1906, and a paper industry trade journal.[44] In it Schleicher says that one reason he was so successful was that the desire for freedom had become so strong that Indians preferred to work either with local firms, or with Germans in particular, whom they considered to be the most anti-British.[45] The more you look around the edges of postcards, the more you see.

Notes

18. E.M.J. Venniyoor, *Raja Ravi Varma: The Most Celebrated Painter of India (1848-1906)* (Bangalore: Parsam Mangharam, 2007), p. 14.

19. Erwin Neumayer and Christine Schelberger, *Raja Ravi Varma, Portrait of an Artist: The Diary of C. Raja Raja Varma* (Delhi: Oxford University Press, 2005), pp. x, xv.

20. Ibid., p. 20.

21. Ibid., p. 213.

22. Ibid., p. 4

23. Ibid., p. 266

24. Ibid., p. 3.

25. "This morning Ms Gerhardt suggested certain improvements in my painting of the Bhaji Tank…" on March 5, 1899 is another example (*The Diary*, p. 70).

26. *The Diary*, op. cit., p. 63.

27. January 14, 1899, op. cit., p. 63

28. *The Englishman*, Kolkata, Nov. 1, 1899.

29. *The Diary*, op. cit., p. 213.

30. *The Times of India*, Nov. 13, 1903, Special advertising insert.

31. Ibid. The ad continues: "Our designs in these include, besides an excellent series of general subjects, some remarkable building scenes. There is not a single Card which does not commend itself by beauty of design or charm of colour and skillful workmanship."

32. It is also possible that the series is after the signed cards, although the only sent version I know of, *Women Baking Bread* (Figure 1, Introduction) is dated November 1, 1905 (Michael Stokes Collection). There are also other candidates for earliest artist-signed cards, like W. Cooper, Bombay which seems to have published court-sized lithographic postcards in Mumbai around this period, or Franz Himmel [sp?] & Co. on behalf of Compagnie Comet

which had a colour halftone *Souvenir of East Indies* series postmarked at least as early as 1899. There are also German missionary cards postmarked 1898 in my collection.

33. Gerhardt sseems to have been active in the arts community, contributing live snakes (Green Tree Vipers and Brown Tree-Snakes) to the Bombay Natural History Society in 1900 (*The Times of India*, Dec. 12), and winning a prize for an oil painting of a shikar scene in 1905 (*The Bombay Gazette*, February 9).

34. *The Diary*, op. cit., p. 4.

35. Partha Mitter, *Art and Nationalism in Colonial India, 1850-1922: Occidental orientations* (Cambridge/New York: Cambridge University Press, 1994), p. 208.

36. S. Mahadeo & Sons in Belgaum, for example, produced a black and white version (Author's Collection).

37. Erwin Neumayer and Christine Schelberger et al., *Popular Indian Art: Raja Ravi Varma and the Printed Gods of India* (Oxford University Press, 2003), p. 37.

38. *Art and Nationalism*, op. cit., p. 210.

39. Ibid., p. 212.

40. Rabindranath Tagore, *Chhinna Patrabali*, 1893, quoted in Mitter, *Art and Nationalism*, p. 218.

41. *The Diary*, op. cit., p. 255.

42. *The Diary*, op. cit., p. 242.

43. *The Diary*, op. cit., p. xiv.

44. *Papier-Zeitung*, No. 57 , 19 July, 1906.

45. *Papier-Zeitung*, No. 79 (4 October) 1906, p. 3294.

46. *The Diary*, op. cit., p. 66

47. S. Mahadeo & Sons in Belgaum, for example, produced a black and white version (Author's Collection).

A Bombay Parbhu

M.V. DHURANDHAR

The greatest postcard artist of Mumbai, if not all India, was M.V. Dhurandhar (1867–1944). Unfortunately largely forgotten today, he was the first Indian head of the Sir Jamshedjee Jeejibhoy (J.J.) School of Arts and its star artist, one who merged Indian themes and sensibilities with Western art methods as fluidly as Ravi Varma. His postcard series of Mumbai residents from 1903 onwards make him, claims the historian Partha Mitter, the first Indian who signed and "designed postcards for a local manufacturer."[48]

Mahadev Vishwanath Dhurandhar was born in Kolhapur, some 250 miles south of Mumbai, and later in life looked much liked the man in *A Bombay Parbhu* (Figure 56). Originally a warrior tribe from Rajasthan, the Parbhus ruled the area that became Mumbai before the Portuguese and British arrived, and were now mainly successful doctors, lawyers and engineers. They were known for a devotion to poetry and art (there were about 4,000 Parbhus in Mumbai, a tenth of the size of the Parsi community).[49]

Dhurandhar's gift for painting was recognized early. Sent by his father to study at the new J.J. School of Art in 1890, he received a gold medal two years later for a painting at the Bombay Art Society. "My joy was beyond words; with Guru's grace and blessings, this painting won a prize of Rs. 50/- from J.N. Tata. At that time, I was the first Indian student artist to win a prize" M.V. Dhrurandhar.[50] (I read all this with great interest in Dhurandhar's autobiography, which my mother-in-law Rukmani Ramani tracked down in Mumbai and had translated by a Maharashtrian friend.)

Dhurandhar's Mumbai postcards are saucy and sassy. The twin outcasts in *Converted and Unconverted Pariah* (Figure 57) take on the fault lines between Indians and Europeans, upper and lower classes. *The Ayah* (Figure 58) shows a nanny with a pram on the "Queen's necklace" (see Figure 23) of Malabar beach, where Dhurandhar and other J.J. School students spent so much time sketching. The maid's employers could be the

Figure 56. *A Bombay Parbhu.* M.V. Dhurandhar [signed], Unknown Publisher, c. 1903. Chromo-halftone, Undivided back, 12.1 x 8.98 cm, 4.76 x 3.54 in.

Converted and unconverted Pariah

Figure 57. *Converted and unconverted Pariah.* M.V. Dhurandhar [signed], Unknown Publisher, c. 1905. Chromo-halftone, Undivided back, 13.95 x 9 cm, 5.49 x 3.54 in.

Figure 58. *The Ayah.* M.V. Dhurandhar [signed], Unknown Publisher, c. 1903. Chromo-halftone, Undivided back, 12.05 x 8.75 cm, 4.74 x 3.44 in.

FACING PAGE
Figure 59. *Parsee Ladies at Seaside.* M.V. Dhurandhar [signed], Unknown Publisher, c. 1903. Chromo-halftone, Undivided back, 12.1 x 8.7 cm, 4.76 x 3.43 in.

Postmarked Bombay Oct. 22, 1904 to "Mrs. Sherron 201 Leavesden Rd. Walford Herts, England"

[*Verso*] "Leave Here Feb. 14 for Home. John"

The Ayah

Parsee Ladies at Seaside

Parsee Ladies at Seaside (Figure 59), the daughter even more Westernized than her mother. "This is exactly like the Parsees here dress & gives a good idea of the lovely colors these women wear" wrote someone on the back of one card.[51]

Meanwhile, the *Telegraph Peon* (Figure 60) speeds by on the hippest thing in town, a bicycle.

Dhurandhar's postcards crystallize emerging characters like the *Railway Porter* (Figure 61) and *The Bombay Policeman* (Figure 62)—whose sun umbrella would soon be replaced with the *lathi* stick. *Pattawala (Office Peon)* (Figure 63) shows the company clerk striding out of the bazaar like a prince carrying the instruments of modernity. (The English "peon" is derived from the Spanish peón, meaning someone with little authority who executes menial tasks.)

Telegraph Peon

M.M.

Still waiting for a reply to my letter

23-2-04

Figure 60. *Telegraph Peon.* M.V. Dhurandhar [signed], Unknown Publisher, c. 1903. Chromo-halftone, Undivided back, 12.1 x 8.7 cm, 4.76 x 3.43 in. Copyright Michael Stokes Collection, Royal Society for Asian Affairs, London.

[*Recto*] "23-02-04. Still waiting for a reply to my letter, M.M."

Railway Porter

Figure 61. *Railway Porter.* M.V. Dhurandhar [signed],
Unknown Publisher, c. 1903. Chromo-halftone, Undivided back,
12.1 x 8.65 cm, 4.76 x 3.41 in.

[*Blindstamp recto*] Dr A. Mayr XXX House Apollo Bunder Station [?]
9-12-05 [*Blindstamp verso*] A.H.W. Rs. 0-1-0 [blue pencil] "24./12.05."

Postmarked Bombay 9 Dec. 1905. Addressed to "24.XII.1905. Herrn
Professor Josef Mayr. N. [?] Karlsburg, Maehren, Austria Europe.

[*Recto*] "Herzliche Grusse zum Weinachtsfeier" [Warm Greetings
for Christmas]

Like the backs of many Dhurandhar cards, this one bears the
blindstamp and price of A.H. Wheeler & Co., at 47 Hornby Road, a
bookstall chain and contractor for advertising on Indian Railways.
Their distribution network and relationship with the authorities
supports the idea that this was an official commission from the
postal service.

The Bombay Policeman

Figure 62. *The Bombay Policeman.*
M.V. Dhurandhar, Unknown Publisher, c. 1903.
Chromo-halftone, Undivided back, 12.1 x 8.7 cm,
4.76 x 3.43 in.

Postmarked May 14, 1903, Spencer's Buildings.
Addressed to Miss Olive McMillan, St. Augustine's,
Cliftonville, Margate England,:

[*Verso*] "May 14, Marble Halls, Nungumbaukum,
Madras. Note new address, hope you enjoyed
yourself at Dover. With Love, Mother."

Older characters were given new twists by Dhurandhar in postcard pairs. *Marwari* (Figure 64) shows a moneylender strutting through the public square, carrying the ominous red books he uses to chase debtors through the courts. *The Brahmin* (Figure 65), on the other hand, as the art historian Alan Life notes, is reluctantly shuffling from tradition to modernity.[52]

In one of my favourite cards, *Milkmaid* (Figure 66), the European city is draped like a gauze curtain behind the most traditional of village tasks. Alan Life writes that Dhurandhar's postcards of workers "infuse occupation with the potential for realization, the suspended moment with the unchanging conditions of life."[53] This is certainly true of the beautiful *Gardener (Mali)* (Figure 67), kneeling imperiously on the ground. *Street Sweepers* (Figure 68) conveys the glorious pleasure of wielding the broom on an empty street.

Figure 64. *Marwari.* M.V. Dhurandhar [signed], Unknown Publisher, c. 1903. Chromo-halftone, Undivided back, 12.1 x 8.8 cm, 4.76 x 3.46 in.

Postmarked May 6, 1905, Sea Post Office, Calcutta. Addressed to "Mrs. Johanna Roscher, VI. [6th District] Garbergasse 7, Vienna, Austria."

[*Verso*] "4/5 05 Karl Michael"

Figure 63. *Pattawala (Office Peon).* M.V. Dhurandhar [signed], Unknown Publisher, c. 1903. Chromo-halftone, Undivided back, 12.1 x 8.75 cm, 4.76 x 3.44 in.

Brahmin

Figure 65. *Brahmin.* M.V. Dhurandhar [signed], Unknown Publisher, c. 1903. Chromo-halftone, Undivided back, 12.1 x 8.7 cm, 4.76 x 3.43 in.

Milkmaid

Figure 66. *The Milkmaid.* M.V. Dhurandhar [signed], Unknown Publisher, c. 1903. Chromo-halftone, Undivided back, 12.1 x 8.7 cm, 4.76 x 3.43 in.
[*Blindstamp verso*] A.H.W. Rs. 0-1-0»

Gardener (Mali)

Figure 67. *Gardner (Mali).* M.V. Dhurandhar [signed], Unknown Publisher, c. 1903. Chromo-halftone, Undivided back, 11.95 x 8.75 cm, 4.70 x 3.44 in.

Postmarked Sea Post Office, Sept. 24, 1904. Addressed to "Mrs. Johanna Roscher, VI. [6th District] Garbergasse 7, Vienna, Austria"

[*Verso*] "Herzl. Grusse [Warmest Greetings] Karl Michael."

Street Sweepers

A Marwari Woman

Lessons in Music

ABOVE LEFT
Figure 68. *Street Sweepers.* M.V. Dhurandhar [signed], Unknown Publisher, c. 1905. Chromo-halftone, Undivided back, 13.95 x 9.05 cm, 5.49 x 3.56 in.

ABOVE RIGHT
Figure 69. *A Marwari Woman.* M.V. Dhurandhar [signed], Unknown Publisher, c. 1905. Chromo-halftone, Undivided back, 14 x 9 cm, 5.51 x 3.54 in.

Figure 70. *Lessons in Music.* M.V. Dhurandhar [signed], Unknown Publisher, c. 1905. Chromo-halftone, Undivided back, 13.95 x 9.05 cm, 5.49 x 3.56 in.

Like Ravi Varma, Dhurandhar spent a lot of time painting women. *A Marwari Woman* (Figure 69) features a character fully developed in her pose and gestures. *Lessons in Music* (Figure 70) was published around 1905, when Dhurandhar participated in the first Bombay Exhibition, official medal which he designed and received a Gold Medal for, in addition to other awards. It was the first time the Exhibition was sponsored by the Indian National Congress party—which in turn led to rumours, unfounded, of a "boycott" by Europeans.[54] The smug teacher is reclining with his sitar, as if not letting his student play. She is challenging him. They are too close for Indian comfort.

Hindu Girl of the Period (Figure 71) speaks to a new assertive urban woman overcoming outdated strictures. Dhurandhar once sent this postcard as a New Year's greeting card to a former mentor. (I found it at the home of the late Michael Stokes, a collector in Kent who amassed a collection that, early in my collecting career, dazzled me with all the Gerhardts and Dhurandhars I did not have.)

Hindu Girl of the Period

Figure 71. *Hindu Girl of the Period.* M.V. Dhurandhar [signed], Unknown Publisher, c. 1905. Chromo-halftone, Undivided back, 14 x 9 cm, 5.51 x 3.54 in. Copyright Michael Stokes Collection, Royal Society for Asian Affairs, London.
This particular card was sent by Dhurandhar to E. Greenwood, the Teacher of Elementary Drawing at the J.J. School of Art, after he had retired in England.

[*Verso*] "To E Greenwood Esq. [uire] A happy Christmas and a Happy New Year from M.V. Dhurandhar"

1 Young maid Servant.

१ तरुण दासी.   १ तरुण दासी.

2 At First Sight.

२ प्रथमदर्शन.   २ प्रथमदर्शन

3 How Sweet you are!

३ आलिंगन.   अ

6 What is this

६ એ શું?   ६ हें काय?

7 False defence.

७ ખોટો બચાવ.   ७ खोटावचाव.

8 Dismissed.

८ કાઢી મુક્રી.   ८ रजा वि

4 Hush! My wife! My wife!

5 Wife enraged.

युप. म्हारी स्त्री! म्हारी स्त्री! ४ चुप बायको! बायको.

५ पत्नीप्रकोप.   ५ पत्नीप्रकोप.

9 Reconciliation at last.

10 New maid-servant.

नाभनुं.   ९ मनधरणी.

१० नवी दासी.   १० नवी दासी.

Figure 72 (1) *Young maid Servant.* M.V. Dhurandhar, Lakshmi Art Printing Works, Dadar, Mumbai, *Coquettish Maid Servant* Series, 1907. Halftone, Divided back, 14.25 x 8.4 cm, 5.61 x 3.31 in.

Figure 73 (2) *At First Sight.* M.V. Dhurandhar, Lakshmi Art Printing Works, Dadar, Mumbai, *Coquettish Maid Servant* Series, 1907. Halftone, Divided back, 14.25 x 8.4 cm, 5.61 x 3.31 in.

Figure 74 (3) *How Sweet you are!* M.V. Dhurandhar, Lakshmi Art Printing Works, Dadar, Mumbai, *Coquettish Maid Servant* Series, 1907. Halftone, Divided back, 14 x 8.4 cm, 5.51 x 3.31 in.

Figure 75 (4) *Hush! My wife! My wife!* M.V. Dhurandhar, Lakshmi Art Printing Works, Dadar, Mumbai, *Coquettish Maid Servant* Series, 1907. Halftone, Divided back, 14 x 8.5 cm, 5.51 x 3.35 in.

Figure 76 (5) *Wife enraged.* M.V. Dhurandhar, Lakshmi Art Printing Works, Dadar, Mumbai, *Coquettish Maid Servant* Series, 1907. Halftone, Divided back, 14 x 8.9 cm, 5.54 x 3.50 in.

Figure 77 (6) *What is this* M.V. Dhurandhar, Lakshmi Art Printing Works, Dadar, Mumbai, *Coquettish Maid Servant* Series, 1907. Halftone, Divided back, 14.1 x 8.4 cm, 5.55 x 3.31 in.

Figure 78 (7) *False defense.* M.V. Dhurandhar, Lakshmi Art Printing Works, Dadar, Mumbai, *Coquettish Maid Servant* Series, 1907. Halftone, Divided back, 14.05 x 8.45 cm, 5.53 x 3.33 in.

Figure 79 (8) *Dismissed.* M.V. Dhurandhar, Lakshmi Art Printing Works, Dadar, Mumbai, *Coquettish Maid Servant* Series, 1907. Halftone, Divided back, 14.2 x 8.4 cm, 5.59 x 3.31 in.

Figure 80 (9) *Reconciliation at last.* M.V. Dhurandhar, Lakshmi Art Printing Works, Dadar, Mumbai, *Coquettish Maid Servant* Series, 1907. Halftone, Divided back, 14.1 x 8.3 cm, 5.55 x 3.27 in.

Figure 81 (10) *New maid-servant.* M.V. Dhurandhar, Lakshmi Art Printing Works, Dadar, Mumbai, *Coquettish Maid Servant* Series, 1907. Halftone, Divided back, 14.025 x 8.4 cm, 5.52 x 3.31 in.

Dhurandhar published at least 66 coloured postcards in four series between 1903 and 1905, two of which were court-sized (very similar to Gerhardt's output). The cards were printed in Germany using the chromo-halftone process "where drawn details are replaced by color lithographic formulas of shades and tints combined with a black ink halftone screen,"[55] a process Dhurandhar seems to have preferred.[56] There is the possibility that the series was commissioned by the Indian Postal Service.[57] Dhurandhar's postcards always seem to have been sponsored or commissioned by someone, including many product advertising postcards.[58]

The most interesting of his later postcards were printed by The Lakshmi Art Printing Press. The Press belonged to Dadasaheb Phalke (1870–1944), a businessman who once worked at the Ravi Varma Press and had been a student at the J.J. School. Dhurandhar's work for Lakshmi Arts included at least two sets of narrative postcards. They prefigure the type of storytelling for which Phalke was famous; by 1912 he turned his attention to the moving pictures and became the father of Indian cinema.[59]

The ten-card series *Coquettish Maid Servant* (Figures 72–81) features titles in English, Gujarati and Hindi. All communities could understand this story of a pretty young maid who comes to work in a middle-class home. The husband is seduced. His wife finds out (note the telltale imprint of flour from the maid's hand in Figure 74). She fires the maid. The couple reconciles and hires a much older maid. Common sense pays handsome dividends.

A second Lakshmi Art set, *Good Boy, Bad Boy* celebrates the virtues of studying and responsibility versus sloth and waste, again the essential moral ingredients of Phalke's popular silent films.

Dhurandhar is said to have produced 5,000 drawings and paintings during his lifetime.[60] By 1944, he had received every conceivable honour, from Rao Bahadur—bestowed by the Viceroy—to fellowship in the Royal Society of Arts in London. An author who used Dhurandhar's images in *The People of Bombay* wrote that of all the Bombay Parbhus, Dhurandhar was among the most luminous of surnames.[61]

Unfortunately, Dhurandhar does not speak of postcards in his autobiography. He does however speak of the many bureaucratic struggles at the school: "even those bitter memories till today are blood-curdling,"[62] and of how his first wife was lost to the plague when "due to some unavoidable reason she was not inoculated." He continues, "I was very upset after my wife's death. But within 13 days, my elder brother Balwantrao began to press me to marry again. I was sad and depressed . . . So I told the truth to that gentleman, 'I don't want to get married now.' And I was spared of this ordeal for some time."[63]

Notes

48. Partha Mitter, *Art and Nationalism in Colonial India, 1850-1922: Occidental Orientations*, p. 90, quoted in Allan Life, "Picture Postcards by M.V. Dhurandhar: Scenes and Types of India–with a Difference," in *Visual Resources*, Vol. XVII, p. 404.

49. W.E. Gladstone Solomon, *The Women of the Ajanta Caves*, (New York: Frank-Maurice Inc., 1926), p. 48.

50. M.V. Dhurandhar, "The First Prize Won in the Exhibition of Bombay Art Society," in *Forty Years in the Temple of Art*. A medal he won in 1895 at the Bombay Art Exhibition elicited congratulations from Ravi Varma.

51. *Parsee Ladies at Seaside*, a different version of Figure 60, 14 x 9 cm in the Author's Collection.

52. Allan Life, "Picture Postcards by M.V. Dhurandhar: Scenes and Types of India–with a Difference," in *Visual Resources*, Vol. XVII, p. 406.

53. Ibid., p. 406.

54. Gold Medal, *The Bombay Gazette*, Feb. 7, 1905. That year Dhurandhar also won a prize for his design of "a modeled frieze in relief" in the Applied Arts category, and was Commended for his painting "Assault on Shahista Khan" (*The Bombay Gazette*, Feb. 3, 1905). Rumours of a European boycott were contained in a letter from "Disappointed" to the Editor, *The Bombay Gazette*, Jan. 14, 1905.

55. Howard Woody, "International Postcards Their History, Production and Distribution (Circa 1895 to 1915)," in Christraud M. Geary and Virgina-Lee Webb, *Delivering Views: Distant Cultures in Early Postcards* (Washington D.C.: Smithsonian Institution, 1998), p. 18.

56. M.V. Dhurandhar, op. cit. p. 24, He writes ". . . the sad aspect was that, in those days, nobody knew the art of the half-tone process. So in both these publications, my pictures were printed by lithography. Naturally, those printed pictures were not at all to my satisfaction."

57. Phone conversation with Nimai Chatterjee, London 2007, followed up by email correspondence with Partha Mitter, June 21, 2015.

58. There are dozens of these commercial cards by Dhurandhar, most of them printed by Indian publishers (about a dozen are in the author's collection). Other Mumbai painters like A.H. Muller also produced advertising cards based on Hindu themes.

59. Dhurandhar's cooperation with authors also extended to authors like Purushottama Visrama Mavaji for whom he illustrated *The Cloud Messenger*, Kalidasa's epic poem, printed by The Lakshmi Art Printing Works in 1910.

60. Allan Life, op. cit., p. 404. Dhurandhar postcards are dated at least to 1910.

61. Percival Strip and Olivia Strip, *The Peoples of Bombay*, (Bombay: Thacker & Co., 1944), p. 16.

62. M.V. Dhurandhar, op. cit., p. 42.

63. Ibid., pp. 25–27.

LA POSTE AU CACHEMIRE.

K.F. Editeurs - Paris.

Kashmir

Kashmir is border country. Today it is split between India and Pakistan; during the Raj it lay between British and Princely India, the cool and the hot, between European mountain metaphysics and the gigantic Himalayas overwhelming all preconceptions. Today its beauty is divided by a militarized "Line of Control," an unrecognized boundary that keeps open the wound of Partition. I know much of the western side of this line, the part under Pakistani control, but the eastern, Indian side I have accessed only through (moving) pictures and postcards.

The earliest postcard of Kashmir, from about 1900, may be the fanciful *La Poste Au Cachemire* [*The Kashmir Post*] (Figure 1). It shows the triumphant delivery of mail in this most autonomous of princely states ruled by a capricious Maharajah. The first postcards of Kashmir with wide distribution were made by the photographer Fred Bremner. Soon after opening a studio in Lahore in 1902 he was told by a doctor that he had a fatal heart condition.[1] He responded by taking a trip to the valleys in *View at Soonamurg* (Figure 2) in the belief that—here he quotes the local saying—"once you have seen Kashmir you can die happy."[2] During his visit he made a number of albumen photographs, many of which he published as postcards, starting in 1903.[3] Bremner writes in his autobiography *My Forty Years in India* (1940):

The country with which one is inclined to compare Kashmir is Switzerland, which certainly has many charms of lake and mountain scenery; but Switzerland is without the charm of Oriental life, the quaint manners and customs of the people, the free and easy way of living, whether in a house-boat on the river and lakes, or going through the side valleys, which all add to the attractions of a trip to the Valley of Kashmir... I may state that it was in a house-boat that I rigged up a small apartment as a dark room and did all the developing of my plates which were 12 x 10 ins. something different in size compared to a pocket camera.[4]

Figure 1. *La Poste Au Cachemire* [*The Kashmir Post*].
Kunzli Freres Editeurs, Zurich/Paris, c. 1900. Lithograph,
Undivided back, 14 x 8.9 cm, 5.51 x 3.50 in.

The Kashmir State flag is on top and insignia with
Hindi and Urdu letters at the bottom. (See *Introduction*,
Figure 4, for more information on this series.)

VIEW AT SOONAMURG.

Figure 2. *View at Soonamurg.* Bremner, Lahore, 1903. Collotype, Undivided back, 13.7 x 8.9 cm, 5.39 x 3.50 in.

Postmarked Dec. 19, 1903, and sent to Mr. Harington, Bath, England: "Simla 16.12.03. Thank you so much for sending the very pretty pictures cards of Bath. They don't get them up half as well out here! Best Love, Gracie."

Figure 3. *A Houseboat at Baramulla, Kashmir.* Lambert, Kashmir, c. 1910. Coloured halftone, Divided back, 13.9 x 8.85 cm, 5.47 x 3.48 in.

Houseboats were apparently popular among foreigners because the Maharajah usually did not permit them to build their own residences. [*Verso, Handwritten*] : "Apparently of 'early [18]90's [vintage].' The same type of boat prevails in 1929. Besides, it the cook boat for a crew of 6-8, their families and general services. A shikara propelled by lotus-leaf heart-shaped paddles for short trips, accompanies a house-boat. It is flat-bottomed & recalls gondolas to some. Passengers sit in the middle under awnings & curtains, on cushions flat on the bottom. A house-boat has drawing room, dining room, & 2 or three sleeping rooms each with 'bath.' This one probably accommodates the 3 on roof. Some are very large or palatial."

A Houseboat at Baramulla, Kashmir   *Lambert, Kashmir*

A Houseboat at Baramulla, Kashmir (Figure 3) shows one such vessel with tourists on the roof. One of the most popular Bremner images developed in a houseboat was used in the postcard *Specimens of Kashmir Carving* (Figure 4).[5] The density of the collotype deepens one's appreciation of the woodworker's lifework.

Another person picked out by Bremner's camera was *A Typical Yarkundi* (Figure 5), a Central Asian trader who made his way across the slippery, winding routes of the Hindu Kush, Karakoram and Himalayan mountain ranges into Kashmir's valleys. Bremner often situates individuals in their environment, unlike the studio portraits favoured at the time, bringing a documentary sensibility to what are still carefully composed photographic postcards, like *Pastoral View, Scinde Valley, Kashmir* (Figure 6).

In *A Mountain Cottage, Kashmir* (Figure 7) seven people are each doing their specific task around the home. A personal Bremner favourite, shown here in a later sepia postcard,[6] was *Rope Bridges, Jhelum River, Kashmir* (Figure 8). Wandering through Kashmir, he wrote that,

*. . . the eye may sometimes rest on a figure slowly gliding through mid-air with no apparent support whatever. . . One of the bridges is merely a single rope made of tough twisted cowhide and secured at both banks of the river. The passenger is seated in a small suspended cradle. He then lets himself go and his own impetus carries him fully half-way over and he is pulled across the remaining distance by a smaller guiding rope."[7]

Figure 4. *Specimens of Kashmir Carving.* Bremner, Lahore and Quetta, Lahore, 1903. Collotype, Undivided back, 13.95 x 8.9 cm, 5.49 x 3.50 in.

This postcard was also titled *Specimens of Walnut and Copper Carving, Kashmir.*

Sent to J.A.S. Lrydell [?] Esq., Lindisfarne, 24 Belmont Park, London S.E. England, Postmarked Rawalpindi 21 Oct. 1903 [?]

[*Recto, handwritten*] "Do you remember watching these people working when we were all in Kashmir together? Oct. 21 M.A.G. [?]..."

SPECIMENS OF KASHMIR CARVING.

Bremner, Lahore.

A TYPICAL YARKUNDI.

LEFT
LEFT

Figure 5. *A Typical Yarkundi. Bremner, Lahore,* Lahore, 1903. Collotype, Undivided back, 13.85 x 8.9 cm, 5.45 x 3.50 in.

Postmarked Ferozepur, Nov. [?] 1910, and sent to Master Robert A.K. Anderson, c/o Miss Phayre Davies, 92 Manor Park, London S.E. [*Recto*] "Ferozpore – 17.11.10. Thanks for last mail. Have been v. [very] busy so no time. Hope you are all well. & going strong. All well here Much Love – Dad."

BELOW

Figure 6. *Pastoral View, Scinde Valley, Kashmir. Bremner, Lahore and Quetta,* Lahore, 1903. Collotype, Undivided back, 13.95 x 8.8 cm, 5.49 x 3.46 in.

FACING PAGE, ABOVE

Figure 7. *A Mountain Cottage, Kashmir.* Fred Bremner, Lahore, 1903. Collotype, Undivided back, 14 x 8.8 cm, 5.51 x 3.46 in.

Postmarked March 03, 1906, and sent to J.A.S. Lrydell [?], London, England, [*Recto*] "Dear old boy Do you remember seeing houses just like this when we were in Cachmere? This is pretty I think. M.A.J. Sept. 30"

This may be the very cottage where Bremner had an indelible experience: "I never spent such a night. The melting snow was trickling on to the bed through apertures in the ceiling. Rats were running about, and in a far corner there happened to be a fowl cackling away from time to time. In the morning I found it had laid the largest egg I ever saw. Needless to say I had it for breakfast."[12]

FACING PAGE, BELOW

Figure 8. *Rope Bridges, Jhelum River, Kashmir. F. Bremner, Photographer, Simla and Lahore.,* c. 1910. Halftone, Divided back, 13.8 x 8.75 cm, 5.43 x 3.44 in.

This uncorrected image gives some sense of how postcards can age in different colour tones, to each its own terroir.

F Bremner—Lahore and Quetta

Pastoral View, Scinde Valley, Kashmir.

Bremner, Lahore.

A Mountain Cottage, Kashmir.

Rope Bridges, Jhelum River, (Kashmir)

Pundit Priest, Kashmir.

A Village Belle, Kashmir.

The village bells at noon were gaily ringing

ABOVE

Figure 9. *Pundit Priest, Kashmir.* Clifton & Co. from a photograph by Fred Bremner, Lahore, c. 1903. Collotype, Undivided back, 13.4 x 9 cm, 5.28 x 3.54 in.

BELOW

Figure 10. *A Village Belle.* Clifton & Co. from a photograph by Fred Bremner, Mumbai, c. 1905. Collotype, Undivided back, 13.95 x 8.8 cm, 5.49 x 3.46 in.

[*Recto*] "The village bells at noon were gaily ringing'."

[*Verso*] Postmarked Madras, October 6, 1908 and addressed to Miss G. Arden, c/o S.C. Gesten [?] Esq. 3 Port Trust Building, Strand Road, Calcutta. s/s "Nizam" Madras 8-10-08 "My dear Edie:- Having many things to write you, I would not write with paper and ink; but I trust to come unto you and speak to you face to face. Love to ma & yourself and the others from your affectly [affectionately] Frank."

FACING PAGE, LEFT

Figure 11. *Kashmir Nautch Girl.* Clifton & Co. from a photograph by Fred Bremner, Mumbai, c. 1905. Collotype, Undivided back, 12.9 x 8.9 cm, 5.08 x 3.50 in.

FACING PAGE, RIGHT

Figure 12. *Kashmiri Nautch Girl.* Clifton & Co. from a photograph by Fred Bremner, Lahore, c. 1903. Collotype, Undivided back, 13.9 x 8.95 cm, 5.47 x 3.52 in.

The hard to read postcard was written by Oscar on a houseboat in Srinagar on Sept. 24, 1904, postmarked there the same day, and sent to Mrs. C. Kauffmann [nee von Nordeck] in Melsungen, Kassel, Germany, postmarked Oct. 15, 1904.

Kashmir Nautch Girl.

KASHMIRI NAUTCH GIRL.

The wide distribution of Bremner's Kashmir images was facilitated by Clifton & Co.'s publication of many of them, including *Pundit Priest* (Figure 9), a learned Hindu Brahmin "seen in prayer on the banks of the Jhelum."[8] *A Village Belle, Kashmir* (Figure 10) has been embellished and annotated by the sender on the front: "The village bells at noon were gaily ringing", and on the back, Frank has much to add that "I would not write with paper and ink."

Another portrait *Kashmir Nautch Girl* in Clifton's version (Figure 11) and *Kashmiri Nautch Girl* (Figure 12) in Bremner's work– the "I" speaks to the regional Punjab market Bremner was addressing, compared to Clifton's all-India market. The image owes its strength to the detail of the embroidery and fabric, the sharp contrast of the white cuffs on the dancer's wrists and the folds of her garment. Even her nail polish is visible. The cleaner, divided back Clifton view—in contrast to Bremner's vignette style—benefits the image. There was a quick switch, within a few years after 1900, to cleaner, less fussy postcards which yield space to the photograph.

The same woman, again wearing the *pheran* or traditional dress of Kashmiri women, is featured in another collotype, *Much extolled Beauty in Kashmir* (Figure 13). Note the identical earrings and what is now probably a watch on her left wrist. The importance of dress and jewellery for Kashmiri *nautch* girls also figures in the more unusual collotype by Srinagar-based Mahatta & Co., *Kashmir beauty* (Figure 14). The pink seems to billow both outward from the frame and upward to the woman's face.

84 Much extolled Beauty in Kashmir.

Mahatta & Co. No. C 14   Kashmir beauty

Mahatta & Co. No. 1   First Bridge, Srinagar

ABOVE LEFT

Figure 13. *Much extolled Beauty in Kashmir. Views of India Series.* [Archaeological] Photo-Works of India, Delhi c. 1910. Collotype, Divided back, 14 x 13.95 cm, 5.51 x 3.49 in.

This firm was also known as Jadu Kissen's [or] The Archaeological Photographic Works of India, based in Srinagar and Delhi, and named after its proprietor, a one-time photographer to the Dept. of Archaeology.

ABOVE RIGHT

Figure 14. *Kashmir beauty.* Mahatta & Co. # C 14, Srinagar, c. 1905. Coloured collotype, Divided back, 13.9 x 8.8 cm, 5.47 x 3.46 in.

Figure 15. *First Bridge, Srinagar.* Mahatta & Co. # C 14, Srinagar, c. 1905. Coloured collotype, Divided back, 13.5 x 8.85 cm, 5.31 x 3.48 in.

Note the rare misaligned colour printing at the right horizontal edge.

Figure 16. *Untitled.* Mahatta-Srinagar (blindstamp, back) #21 [pencilled], Srinagar, c. 1940. Real photo postcard, Divided back, 13.2 x 8.2 cm, 5.20 x 3.23 in.

Figure 17. *Mar Nala, Srinagar (Kashmir).* The "AQUARELLE" Series No. 1. Hartmann (likely printed by Raphael Tuck & Sons), London, c. 1904. Coloured halftone, Divided back, 13.9 x 8.8 cm, 5.47 x 3.46 in.

This particular one, with the carefully placed stamp, was sent by Ernest L. of the XIIth Hussars in Deccan to Miss Marcineau in France on July 22nd 1909:

[*Verso*] "Dear Marealle, I hope that you are quite well; it is a considerable time since I had a letter from you."

Figure 18. *Nanga Parbat (Kashmir). The "AQUARELLE" Series No. 5.* Hartmann (likely printed by Raphael Tuck & Sons), c. 1904. Coloured Halftone, Divided back, 13.7 x 8.9 cm, 5.39 x 3.50 in.

Figure 19. *Tuckt of Sunamon.* Raphael Tuck & Sons #7089, London, c. 1905. Coloured halftone, Divided back, 13.85 x 8.75 cm, 5.45 x 3.44 in.

[*Verso*] "**The Tuckt [Takht] of Sunaman** is an ancient Hindu Temple and a prominent landmark, situated on an eminence overlooking the town of Srinagar, one of the chief cities of Kashmir. The picture shows this hill viewed from the Dhal lake, the summer resort of the ancient Delhi kings. The boat woman is depicted wearing the native costume of Kashmir, and the method is shown in which fruit and vegetables are brought from the floating gardens to the mainland."

The Tuck's cards are signed by F.G. Parbury, a name which does not appear on any other Tuck India series. He might have been an amateur who visited Kashmir and returned with paintings that caught Tuck's attention or a postcard artist working from a photograph.

Figure 20. *Ancient Temple on the Takht Hill B.C. 200 Kashmir.* The Archaeological Photographic Works of India, Delhi, c. 1905. Coloured collotype, Divided back, 14 x 8.75 cm, 5.51 x 3.44 in.

Postmarked 24.10.1910, and sent to Miss. Ruth E. Clark , 802 Mulberry in Scranton, Pennsylvania, USA.

[*Verso*] "Did you climb up the Takht I Suliman? I did this time & had such a fine view. It was not a hard climb either. I wonder what you will do Xmas! I hope you will have a good time & be happy & make everyone else happy – as you always do. With heaps of love, yours affectionately, Auntie Carrie."

Jadu Kissen's Archaeological Photographic Works of India, Cashmere Gate, Delhi, was originally archaeological photographer to the Government of Punjab, had an office in Simla (1912),[13] and published many archaeologically-themed postcards.

After Bremner's postcard production blossomed between 1903 and 1905,[9] the production of Kashmiri postcards was increasingly taken over by local photographers like Mahatta & Co., established in 1915 in Srinagar's Bund area and soon the leading postcard publisher of Kashmir (it survives to this day in Delhi). *Mahatta & Co No 1. First Bridge, Srinagar* (Figure 15), also a collotype, seems earlier than 1915; later Mahatta output was largely black and white real photo postcards like the striking—but slightly insipid—postcard from a later era, *Untitled* (Figure 16).

In contrast to Mahatta and Bremner's, Tucks and British amateur artists took a painterly approach to Kashmir. The first British Kashmir postcard series was probably printed by Tuck's; though not an Oilette, it also uses a halftone colour printing process. An early experiment, the set of six aquarelles all have distinctive signboard titles. The delicate view of wooden-framed buildings in *Mar Nala, Srinagar, Kashmir* (Figure 17) has been both stamped and signed on the front, a reminder of how deliberate a ritual was sending a postcard.

The fifth card in the series, *Nanga Parbat (Kashmir)* (Figure 18), is one of the only peaks shown in early postcards that is not in today's Indian sector but largely on the Pakistani side. I first glimpsed it while flying between the mountains in a Fokker

Figure 21. *Kashmir Srinagar.* Raphael Tuck & Sons #7089, London, c. 1905. Coloured halftone, Divided back, 13.85 x 8.65 cm, 5.45 x 3.41 in.

[*Verso*] "**Srinagar** (the Venice of the East) in the beautiful and famous vale of Kashmir, is one of the chief cities of that native State. It was founded during the sixth century, and is a picturesque wooden-built town, situated on both sides of the Upper Jhelum. Autumn tints here are most beautiful, the distant snow-capped mountains making a fine background for the brilliant yellow of the fading poplars and the vivid crimson of the Chenar trees."

turboprop plane to Gilgit and Skardu for UNICEF Pakistan in my twenties. I saw it again on a day-long walk up to a village in Astor Valley, off the age-old road to Srinagar from Punjab that is now blocked by army check posts and mines. I had to eat pine nuts every hour or so to make it to the thousands feet high steep hillside, but no one else minded. The baked potato I was served by villagers when I nearly collapsed on top remains the most deliciously nourishing food I have ever eaten. Similarly, the months I spent in Muzaffarabad, Skardu and Hunza valleys and other peripheral extensions of the Maharajah's dominions (sometime sealed by little more than an annual token tribute from a petty ruler) made me conscious of how much absolute beauty and absolute suffering commingle in Kashmir.

Among Tuck's first official India Oilette sets in 1905 was one devoted to Kashmir[10] which demonstrates the superior colour and line handling of the Oilette. *Takt of Sunamon* (Figure 19) neatly separates three viewing planes to dramatize the height of a temple overlooking Srinagar—shown in close-up in Jadu Kissen's *Ancient Temple on the Takht Hill B.C. 200 Kashmir* (Figure 20). *Kashmir Srinagar* (Figure 21) uses the warm colours of autumn leaves, rendered in the thick brush strokes of old Dutch masters that the firm was known for reproducing so well. The repeat use of an image title in its own little frame, like the Aquarelle series and almost nowhere else on Tuck's India cards, links the two sets and reiterates the remoteness of Kashmiri images.

The most popular Tuck's view, *A Street Scene in Srinagar City* (Figure 22), suggests something slightly mysterious going on among the shrouded men on the street. Their dark colouring may have to do more with the colourists' fantasy than reality, for

Figure 22. *A Street Scene in Srinagar City.* Raphael Tuck & Sons #9311, London, c. 1905. Coloured Halftone, Divided back, 13.8 x 8.8 cm, 5.43 x 3.46 in.

[*Verso*] "**Srinagar** is the capital of the native state of Kashmir in Northern India. Its streets are of the usual regular patterns of primitive houses of wood, light, flimsy structures with mud roofs. The chief occupations of the inhabitants are silver-working, carpet-weaving, and the manufacture of paper and leather. The population in 1901 was 122,618." An unsigned, pencilled message on the back of the card dated 21/3/12 reads, "Dear Molly I was very Pleased to receive postcards from you and very glad to know you are quite well and getting an on alright in your situation, but very sorry to hear you have had the influenza. I know what it is myself. I was in bed a fortnight with it when I was in service-"

Kashmiri men and women can be as fair as Europeans, a point emphasized in *A Cashmere Lady* (Figure 23).

Many a British amateur painted Kashmir's vistas on postcards as well. One was the anonymous E. E. whose *Six Artistic Views of Kashmir* were printed at the unusual size of 6 by 3 inches around 1910. (They were one of the first sets of postcards I ever bought, and in the twenty years since, only very occasionally see a card or two from it, reminding me of how much output has been lost, and how much there is left for a collector to find). When I opened the dark green envelope, they felt quite untouched and included *Kradyal Canal, Srinagar, Kashmir* (Figure 24) and *Temple, Chenar Bagh, Kashmir* (Figure 25). Another amateur, a "Miss L. Barne of Madras" (Chennai), inspired by Impressionism perhaps, left us with *Shopping on the Dal Lake* (Figure 26).

Figure 23. *A Cashmere Lady. The Times of India*, Mumbai, c. 1930. Coloured halftone, Divided back, 13.9 x 8.8 cm, 5.47 x 3.46 in.

A particularly well-done postcard is *North Colonnade, Martand, Kashmir* (Figure 27) by W. Poole. Poole was a professional painter, and manages to capture the once imposing nature of this 6th century temple on a plateau overlooking Kashmir valley. As a contemporary author wrote, "the ruins although noble and massive do not show to great advantage,"[11] but Poole's trimming of the structure also seen in Bremner's *Martund Temple, Kashmir* (Figure 28) manages to restore to them something of their lost dignity. The colonnades carry the shattered weight of a pre-Islamic past, one which still reverberates in the misfortunes of Kashmiri Muslims and Hindus.

Figure 27. *North Colonnade, Martand, Kashmir.* W. Poole [signed], Thacker, Spink & Co., Simla, c. 1910. Coloured halftone, Divided back, 13.9 x 8.85 cm, 5.47 x 3.48 in.

BELOW
Figure 28. *Martund Temple, Kashmir.* Fred Bremner, Lahore and Quetta, 1903. Collotype, Undivided back, 13.75 x 8.8 cm, 5.41 x 3.46 in.

Martund Temple, Kashmir.

Despite the grandeur of Kashmir's landscapes, most of the population lived in frightening poverty. Famines, floods and epidemics were frequent. Men were generally peasant tenants who spent generations passing much of their surplus to the Maharajah —or another ruler—and his officials. *Study of a Kashmiri Man* (Figure 29), with its lines around the man's eyes, gives some sense of the lives of most inhabitants of the magical state. Women, in fact, toiled even harder than men (see Figures 1, 7, 17, 24), something more directly recognized in the prolific British illustrator E.H. Hardy's *Pounding Grain in Kashmir* (Figure 30).

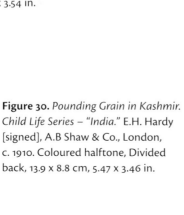

Figure 29. *Study of a Kashmiri Man.*
Unknown publisher (R. Holmes?),
c. 1910. Sepia collotype, Divided back,
13.95 x 9 cm, 5.49 x 3.54 in.

Figure 30. *Pounding Grain in Kashmir.*
Child Life Series – "India." E.H. Hardy
[signed], A.B Shaw & Co., London,
c. 1910. Coloured halftone, Divided
back, 13.9 x 8.8 cm, 5.47 x 3.46 in.

Some of the nicer Kashmiri postcards combine photography and colour. H.A. Mirza & Co.'s *The City and the Mosque of Shah – Hamadan, Srinagar (Kashmir)* (Figure 31) shows the broad sweep of the Jhelum, with a 14th century wooden mosque, often rebuilt after fires, looming over houseboats and riverside homes. *The Residency, Srinagar (Kashmir)* (Figure 32), where the British representative to the Maharajah lived, is one of the firm's most successful postcards, with a faux sunset set off by the building and poplar trees, while the pink highlights dance on the flowers and people loaf about on the verandah.

Nanga Parbat meaning Naked Peak is the 9th highest mountain in the world and among the most difficult to climb. Twenty years into my collecting career, an unexpected set of high quality real photo postcards appeared on auction. They were from the Nanga Parbat expeditions sent by the Germans in the 1930s, the Nazi-sponsored one led by Willy Merkl in *Deutsche Himalaya-Expedition 1934 zum Naga Parbat (8120 m)* (Figure 33). Climbing the highest mountains in search of mountain

The City and the Mosque of Shah - Hamadan, Srinagar (Kashmir).

The Presidency, Srinagar (Kashmir).

Figure 31. *The City and the Mosque of Shah – Hamadan, Srinagar (Kashmir).* H.A. Mirza & Sons, Delhi, c. 1910. Coloured collotype, Divided back, 14.1 x 9.2 cm, 5.55 x 3.62 in.

Figure 32. *The Presidency. Srinagar (Kashmir).* H.A. Mirza & Sons, Delhi, c. 1910. Coloured collotype, Divided back, 14.1 x 9 cm, 5.55 x 3.54 in.

Deutsche
Himalaya-
Expediton 1934
zum Nanga Parbat
(8120 m)

Aufn. W. Merkl

Figure 33. *Deutsche Himalaya-Expedition 1934 zum Naga Parbat (8120 m).* [signed] Aufr, [Auffuhrer [Sponsor] W. Merkl, c. 1932. Real photo postcard, Divided back, 13.9 x 9 cm, 5.47 x 3.54 in.

The cancellation on the back, on January 17, 1932 is from "Munchen, Hauptstadt der Bewegung" by which is meant Munich's role in the origins of the Nazi movement during the Beer Putsch in 1923. It also exhorts bicyclists not to hang on to moving vehicles ("Radfahrer! Nicht anhaengen an Fahrzeuge!") Addressed to Ilse Unfug, Ingolstadt [German7], Kupferstr. 3 II.

"Pasing [Rasing?] 17.1.1932,

[Dear Ilse, For your birthday tomorrow, we send you our Best Wishes and Blessings. May the heavens grant your parents recovery on this day. In response to your New Years greetings we send you best wishes and many thanks. These days dear Karl is here with us. This way the kids are occupied again. How are your father and mother? Hopefully better. Have you heard any news from Grandpa Rosenhem (included above). News? One again all the best and best wishes to your father and mother and best wishes for recovery. Yours thankfully [unclear] Jettel, Karl, Helga and Kurti.]

idolatry to replace Christendom was part of the Nazi ethos. Later German expeditions and secret missions tried to locate the original "homeland" of the Aryan people in the Himalayas. A lot was staked on climbing a mountain that the British had not been able to conquer. *Himalaja: Nanga Parbat 8125 Meter Hauptgipfel* [*Main Peak*] (Figure 34) and *Himalaya: Nanga Parbat 8125 Meter In Gletschebruch* [*Glacier Canyon*] (Figure 35) speak of the hope the climbers had as they raised funds and popularized an expedition whose progression presaged, for the Germans, World War II. The 1934 expedition led to a disaster with three prominent mountaineers including Merkl and Sherpas being killed. Another foray in 1937 led to even more deaths (it was not until 1953 that the Austrian Herman Buhl became the first man to reach the top).

The camera pulling back in *Himalaya Nanga Parbat 8125 Meter von der "Marchenwiese" aus* [*from "Fairy Meadows"*] (Figure 36) gives a better approximation of the spectacular setting for a meadow that, in the spring, is bursting with wild flowers and wild promise.

Figure 34. *Himalaja: Nanga Parbat 8125 Meter Hauptgipfel* [*Main Peak*]. Deutsche Himalajafahrt 1934 [German Himalaya Expedition 1934], c. 1934. Real photo postcard, Divided back, 14.9 x 10.6 cm, 5.87 x 3.17 in.

[*Verso*] "Nanga Parbat, Lager VI, 6955 m Blick auf den Sudpfeiler des Hauptgipfels [Nanga Parbat, Camp 6, 6,955 meters, View of the Southern arrow of the Main Peak].

Figure 35. *Himalaya: Nanga Parbat 8125 Meter In Gletschebruch* [*Glacier Canyon*]. Deutsche Himalajafahrt 1934 [German Himalaya Expedition 1934], c. 1934. Real photo postcard, Divided back, 14.9 x 10.7 cm, 5.87 x 3.21 in.

[*Verso*] "Nanga Parbat. Auf dem unteren Rakiotgletscher. Schneebruecke ueber eine 60 m tiefe Spalte." [Nanga Parbat. On the lower Rakiot glacier. Snowbridge over a 60m deep cleft].

*Himalaja:Nanga Parbat 8125 Meter
von der „Märchenwiese" aus*

Figure 36. *Himalaya Nanga Parbat 8125 Meter von der
"Marchenwiese" aus* [*Himalayas: Nanga Parbat 8,125 meters
from "Fairy Meadows"*]. Deutsche Himalajafahrt 1934
[German Himalaya Expedition 1934], c. 1934. Real photo
postcard, Divided back, 15.9 x 10.55 cm, 6.26 x 3.15 in.

[*Verso*] "Nanga Parbat. Auf dem unteren Rakiotgletscher.
Schneebruecke ueber eine 60 m tiefe Spalte." [Nanga Parbat.
On the lower Rakiot glacier. Snowbridge over a 60m
deep cleft].

Notes

1. Fred Bremner, *My Forty Years in India*, Banff Scotland,
   1940, p. 43. Bremner did not know that his heart was
   perfectly fine until he returned from his trip to Kashmir
   and received a second opinion (given how seriously he
   took his work, one wonders whether he really believed
   the first doctor).

2. Ibid., p. 43.

3. I have only one possibly court-sized Bremner card, but
   it seems to have been cut, and Bremner cards are postmarked, beginning at the end of 1902.

4. Bremmer, op. cit., 1940, p. 45.

5. Ibid. Bremner in his autobiography, where he called it
   "Kashmiri at Work, Specimens of Carving, walnut wood."

6. The rope bridge and the woodcarver were selected by
   Bremner for his autobiography, *My Forty Years in India*.

7. Bremner, op. cit., 1940, p. 45.

8. Bremner, op. cit., 1940, p. 46.

9. Bremner produced postcards with at least a dozen different
   imprints, from Bremner, Quetta to Bremner, Lahore,
   Bremner, Lahore and Quetta, F. Bremner, Photographer,
   Lahore and later F. Bremner, Photographers, Simla and
   Lahore. I have close to 200 Bremner cards, and there are
   probably a few hundred distinct ones.

10. Byatt gives the date of 1905 for the *Wide Wide World Series*
    cards numbered 7000-7500 (p. 294). The Kashmir cards
    are numbered 7089.

11. Arthur Neve, *The Tourists Guide to Kashmir, Skardo, Etc.*,
    18th edition, revised by Dr. E.F. Neve. Civil and Military
    Gazette Press, Lahore, ca. 1942, p. 59.

12. Bremmer, op. cit., 1940, p. 51.

13. *Thacker's Indian Directory*, 1892, 1912.

Clock Tower chandni Chowk, Delhi

Delhi

If Kolkata was the original "first city" of the Raj, Mumbai would become its business centre after 1900, and Delhi the legislative capital soon after that. Postcards served as signposts to the reassertion of Delhi's imperial role before the British completed their conquest of India in 1857. Like other cities, it also had a leading postcard publisher, H. A. Mirza & Sons and, separately, a singular postcard artist, Mortimer Menpes. H. A. Mirza & Sons dominated the market for Delhi postcards between about 1900 to the 1930s.[1] A professional photographer since the 1890s,[2] Mirza kept shop in the commercial heart of the city, *Clock Tower Chandni Chowk, Delhi* (Figure 1). The firm published postcards from at least 1903, when *Street Scene, Delhi* (Figure 2) was mailed to Chicago. Both *Bird's Eye View The City with Juma Masjid [Mosque]* (Figure 3) and *Juma Masjid, Delhi with a scene of annual Friday Prayer Meeting* (Figure 4) articulate a Muslim point-of-view[3] in the former Mughal capital. *Juma Masjid* (Figure 4) was made from a photograph taken at Eid prayers, showing one of the larger collections of people (about 25,000) in Indian postcards.

Old Delhi made for postcards like *The Well at Sultan Nizamuddeen. Delhi* (Figure 5) in honour of Shaikh Nizamuddin Auliya (1236–1325), a Sufi saint who arrived long before the Mughals and preached a religion of love and mysticism. Mirza was not the only one with a religious preoccupation. Jadu Kissen, also of Delhi (see Figure 20, Kashmir), offered *Hindu Colonnade of Pillars of Pure Hindu Architecture Belonging to the 9th or 10th Century, Delhi* (Figure 6) to remind us of the origins of some of these buildings.

Figure 1. *Clock Tower Chandni Chowk, Delhi. Built by Delhi Municipality at a Cost of R [Rupees] 28000, after the Mutiny, 1857 A.D.* H.A. Mirza & Sons, Delhi, c. 1905. Coloured collotype, Divided back, 13.8 x 8.9 cm, 5.43 x 3.50 in.

STREET SCENE, DELHI.

H. A. Mirza, Photographer, Delhi.

Figure 2. *Street Scene, Delhi.* H.A. Mirza, Delhi, c. 1903. Coloured collotype, Undivided back, 13.85 x 9.1 cm, 5.43 x 3.58 in.

Postmarked Jaipur November? 22, 1903? and Chicago Dec. 21, 1903, addressed to Mr. Dan Gutmann, 3653 Michigan Avenue in Chicago:

[*Recto*] "Delhi, India, Nov. 21 Dear Dan;- Little boys ride camels here and have monkeys to play with. How would you like to live in India? Remember me to everybody. Uncle Mannie."

Birds Eye View - The City with Juma Masjid, Delhi.
Commenced in 1644 A. D. by the Emperor Shahjahan and completed by him in 1658 A. D.
Is said to have employed a daily average of 5000 workmen.

Figure 3. *Bird's Eye View The City with Juma Masjid [Mosque]. Commenced in 1644 A.D. by the Emperor Shahjahan, and completed by him in 1658 A.D., the construction is said to have employed a daily average of 5,000 workmen.* H.A. Mirza & Sons, Delhi, c. 1905. Coloured collotype, Divided back, 13.6 x 8.95 cm, 5.35 x 3.52 in.

Juma Masjid, Delhi, with a scene of annual Friday Prayer-Meeting.
Commenced in 1644 A. D. by the Emperor Shahjahan and completed by him in 1658 A. D.
Is said to have employed a daily average of 5000 workmen.

Figure 4. *Juma Masjid, Delhi with a scene of annual Friday Prayer Meeting. Commenced in 1644 A.D. by the Emperor Shahjahan, and completed by him in 1658 A.D. Is said to have employed a daily average of 5,000 workmen.* H.A. Mirza & Sons #18272, Delhi, c. 1905. Coloured collotype, Divided back, 13.65 x 8.95 cm, 5.37 x 3.52 in.

At the back of the mosque and foreground of the image, separated by a cloth and stick barrier, is the women's section.

Even the former rulers were put on postcards: note how in *Group of Mughal Emperors* and *Group of Mughal Empresses* (Figure 7 and 8)[4] the emperors are more fully-featured than the empresses. Mirza postcards *Alauddeen Gate, a Partial View, Delhi* (Figure 9) and *Kutub Minar Delhi* (Figure 10) restored the destroyed and decaying city with polished tints from printers like Stengel & Co. Much like Tuck's sanitization of the exotic, Mirza and others offered a Mughal phantasmagoria. Jadu Kissen's *The Saman Burj* (Figure 11), for example, used hand-tinted detail to evoke the candle-lit splendours of a glorious past.

Figure 5. *The Well at Sultan Nizamuddeen. Delhi.* H.A. Mirza & Sons, Delhi, c. 1905. Collotype, Divided back, 13.9 x 8.9 cm, 5.46 x 3.50 in.

Figure 6. *Hindu Colonnade of Pillars of Pure Hindu Architecture Belonging to the 9th or 10th Century, Delhi.* The Archaeological Photo-Works of India, Delhi, c. 1905. Coloured collotype, Divided back, 13.8 x 8.75 cm, 5.43 x 3.44 in.

GROUP OF MOGUL EMPERORS

Figure 7. *Group of Mogul Emperors.* The Phototype Co., Mumbai, c. 1905. Collotype, Divided back, 3.85 x 8.95 cm, 5.45 x 3.52 in.

From Top Left to Top Right, First Row] Sultan Muhammad Mirza Badshah, Sultan Jalaluddin Miran Shah, Ameer Taimoor Raza Jaqraan Saani; [Second Row] Nooruddin Jehangir Badshah, Jalaluddin Akbar Badshah, Naseeruddin Humayun Badshah; [Third Row] Muhammad Farrukh Sher Bahadur Badshah, Moizadajjahan Dar Shah, Bahadur Shah Awwal Badshah; [Fourth

Figure 8. *Group of Mogul Empresses.* The Phototype Co., Mumbai, c. 1905. Collotype, Divided back, 13.6 x 8.9 cm, 5.35 x 3.50 in.

[From Top Left to Top Right, First Row] Jamila Khatoon W/o [Wife of] Muhammad Mirza, Nagina Khatoon W/o Jalaluddin Miran Shah, Sakina Khatoon W/o Ameer Taimoor; [Second Row] Akhtar Zamani W/o Alamgir, Moti Mahal Begum W/o Akbar Kuldan, Ruqayyah Sultan W/o Humayun; [Third Row] Akhtar Tabaan W/o Farrukh Sher, Maa Khatoon W/o Moinuddin, Ashraf Zamani W/o Bahadur Shah; [Fourth Row] Qudsia Begum W/o Shah Alam, Behroz Khatoon W/o Alamgir Saani, Sikandar Sultan W/o Alam Shah.

Alauddeen Gate, a Partial View, Delhi.
Built by Alaudin Khilji in 1310 A. D.

Kutub Minar, Delhi.
Commenced by Kutbuddin-Ibak in 1200 and completed by his successor Shamsuddin Altamash in 1220 A. D.
It contains 379 stairs & is 238 Feet 1 inch in height.

Tuck's represented Delhi's grandeur with the mysterious *Delhi. Old Fort* (Figure 12) and *Delhi (Fort) Lahore Gate* (Figure 13). Throughout the region, going back to ancient Indus times, city gates faced their population's most significant trading partners and were named after them; thus there is a Delhi gate in Lahore and a Kabul gate in Peshawar (See Figure 7, *North-West Frontier Province*). Delhi, Agra and Lahore seemed particularly well connected in this way.

One of the most popular postcards of the city among the British was *Cashmere Gate. Delhi* (Figure 14). This is where their final assault commenced on September 14, 1857, and the dying John Nicholson "stormed the breach in the Kashmir bastion and bought Delhi for ever with British blood" as a Tuck's caption put it. In Figure 14, the crude stress is on the red blood. This gate, so central to the legend of the British Raj, even

THE SAMAN BURJ OR THE PRINCESS' BOUDOIR, RICHLY INLAID WITH MOSAIC WORK, DELHI.

FACING PAGE, ABOVE

Figure 9. *Alauddeen Gate, a Partial View, Delhi. Built by Alaudin Khilji 1310 A.D.* The Phototype Co., Mumbai, c. 1905. Coloured collotype, Divided back, 13.95 x 8.85 cm, 5.49 x 3.48 in.

FACING PAGE, BELOW

Figure 10. *Kutub Minar, Delhi. Commenced by Kutbuddin-Ibak in 1200 and completed by his successor Shamsuddin Altamash in 1220 A. D. it contains 379 stairs & is 238 feet 1 inch in height.* H.A. Mirza & Sons, Delhi, c. 1905. Coloured collotype, Divided back, 13.7 x 8.95 cm, 5.39 x 3.52 in.

At the time, it was the tallest standing brick tower in the world.

Figure 11. *The Saman Burj or the Princess Boudoir, Richly Inlaid with Mosaic Work, Delhi.* The Archaeological Photo-Works of India, Delhi, c. 1905. Coloured collotype, Divided back, 13.85 x 8.85 cm, 5 .54 x 3.48 in.

H.A. Mirza offered a black and white version of the same image as *Interior Scale of Justice Fort Delhi.*

Figure 12. *Delhi. Old Fort.* Raphael Tuck & Sons #8983, London, c. 1905. Coloured halftone, Divided back, 13.9 x 8.85 cm, 5.47 x 3.48 in.

[*Verso*] "**Old Fort**. Between the Mosque and the Jumna river stands the Fort – the ancient stronghold and palace of the Mogul emperor. A towering wall of red sandstone encloses it, moated and battlemented."

Figure 13. *Delhi (Fort) Lahore Gate.* Raphael Tuck & Sons #8983, London, c. 1905. Coloured halftone, Divided back, 13.9 x 8.9 cm, 5.47 x 3.50 in.

[*Verso*] "**Lahore Gate**. To reach the ancient stronghold of the Mughal emperors, you pass under the great Lahore Gate. Its massiveness lightened by domes and arches, gilt and marble on top of it. You come then to barracks and commissariat stores and Tommy Atkins, exchange in a few steps ancient romance for modern reality."

serves to separate the Viceroy Lord Curzon and his wife in *Delhi, Jan. 1, 1903* (Figure 15), on a postcard published to celebrate the proclamation of King Edward VII as Emperor of India. It was the first Coronation Darbar since 1877, when Queen Victoria was proclaimed Empress of India. The 1903 Darbar was one of the greatest single events during the Raj era even if the new King, like his mother, chose not to attend. This permitted Lord Curzon to be "the man who pulled the strings"[5] in the words of Mortimer Menpes, the Darbar's artist-in-residence and the man responsible, ultimately, for what are among the finest European artist-signed postcards of India.

Figure 14. *Cashmere Gate. Delhi.* Unknown firm, c. 1905. Coloured halftone, Divided back, 13.15 x 8.5 cm, 5.18 x 3.35 in.

Figure 15. *Delhi, Jan. 1, 1903....* Royal Chain Postcards, London, c. 1903. Coloured halftone, Divided back, 13.9 x 8.85 cm [?], 5.47 x 3.48 in.

[Recto] *"King Edward was today proclaimed Emperor of India. Lord Curzon, whose photograph and that of his wife are shown here, represented the King. The scene was one of unexampled splendour and was deeply impressive even to the Indian Princes, accustomed as they are to scenes of magnificence. The Kashmir Gate, shown here, is that against which Lieuts. Salkeld and Home, in the memorable siege during the Mutiny, placed the powder-bags, under a storm of fire, which bust the gates and enabled the storming of Delhi to be commenced."*

Menpes (1860–1938) was an Australian 'painter, etcher, raconteur and rifle-shot,'[6] close
to the exiled American James MacNeil Whistler (1834–1903). Whistler was the most
admired painter in the English-speaking world at the time,[7] a man who promoted
the credo of "art for art's sake." Menpes once ran a printing press for Whistler, and
shared the older man's fascination with all things Japanese,[8] often scrimmaging
through European markets for special Japanese papers on his behalf.[9] Like Hoffmann,
Dhurandhar and Gerhardt, Menpes was very familiar with the printing process. Like
Dhurandhar, his images were also used in books like the illustrated volume *Darbar*
which he co-wrote with his daughter Dorothy. This book included about 100 prints from
his paintings, a dozen of which were selected for publicity postcards by the publisher
A. & C. Black & Co. of London.

Figure 16. *A Tailor.* Mortimer Menpes [signed], A. & C. Black Ltd.
India. Series No. 24, London, c. 1905. Coloured halftone, Divided back,
13.75 x 8.85 cm, 5.41 x 3.48 in.

A Black Ltd. was a well-established, high-end book publisher known for a
patented three-colour printing process.

The first image in *Darbar* is the postcard *A Tailor* (Figure 16). The second, *A Belle of Northern India* (Figure 17), uses the partially hidden face of the woman to electrify the view, catching the viewer in the very act of looking. *A Rajput of Rajgarh* (Figure 18) shown as an ageing warrior is given life by dazzling colour that rises to his shoulders. Menpes wrote, *India surpassed my wildest expectations; the scenes I saw fired my brain, quickened my pulses, and filled my soul with a mad and eager longing to paint, paint, paint, now and at once. But alas! My colour box did not hold such pigment; the brightest colours in my tubes appeared but dull and faded, and would not nearly correspond to the glowing tones of earth and sky, houses and shops, and of the ever changing multitudes that thronged and filled the streets about me.*[10]

A Rajput of Rajgarh.

FACING PAGE

Figure 17. *A Belle of Northern India.* Raphael Tuck & Sons Series III #9966, London, c. 1908. Coloured halftone, Divided back, 13.6 x 8.7 cm, 5.35 x 3.43 in.

[*Verso*] "*A Belle of Northern India*. The women of Delhi and district are, to the Western eye, rather more pleasing than those of many other parts of India. They often effect a swinging bell-shaped skirt of striking colour and are decorated profusely with armlets and anklets that jingle rhythmically with their stride."

In Flora Ann Steel's book *India*, also a collaboration with Mortimer Menpes, the same image was titled *Late Afternoon*.

Figure 18. *A Rajput of Rajgarh. India. Series No. 24.* Mortimer Menpes [signed], A. & C. Black Ltd., London, c. 1905. Coloured halftone, Divided back, 13.9 x 8.9 cm, 5.47 x 3.50 in.

A Street Scene, Delhi.

Oilette

Oilette

Mid-day, Delhi.

Menpes's versatility is manifest in *A Street Scene, Delhi* (Figure 19), part of a 12 card series of his Darbar paintings published by Tuck & Sons (Menpes was one of the few artists to work with more than one publisher). This time, instead of colours, fine lines dominate, just as they do in *Mid-day Delhi* (Figure 20), where a quilted tree is harmoniously balanced with shades of orange.

"Never have so many cameras been together,"[11] wrote Dorothy Menpes of the Darbar. *Watching the Pageant, Delhi* (Figure 21) has the woman again gently lifting her *dupatta* to look back at the "cameraman." All eyes are on us, including those of a little boy. Menpes once again reverses the roles of the artist seeing and the person being seen, all within the casualness of a photographic moment. Postcards like this are, for me, deliciously entangled morsels of reflection.

Eight years later, over 80,000 people gathered for the third *Coronation Darbar 1911 – Delhi* (Figure 22). Some 12,000 British and Indian officials, 20,000 troops on parade,

FACING PAGE, LEFT

Figure 19. *A Street Scene, Delhi.* Mortimer Menpes [signed], Raphael Tuck & Sons #9966, London, c. 1908. Coloured halftone, Divided back, 13.7 x 8.7 cm, 5.39 x 3.43 in.

[*Verso*] "A Street Scene, Delhi. To pass through the streets of Delhi, threading one's way through its countless denizens – men, women, children, bulls, camels, oxen, etc. – is to walk in a dreamland. The kaleidoscope of colour, the indescribable colour, the dust or mud, according to season, all blend to the sense and become a lasting impression upon the mind of the beholder."

FACING PAGE, RIGHT

Figure 20. *Mid-day Delhi.* Mortimer Menpes [signed], Raphael Tuck & Sons #9967, London, c. 1908. Coloured halftone, Divided back, 13.95 x 8.9 cm, 5.49 x 3.50 in.

[*Verso*] "Mid-day Delhi. The great native city of Delhi is one of the most historic and fascinating places of the East. The bazaars have an interest quite their own; its narrow lanes, encumbered with camels, oxen and other animals, crowded with a chattering multitude in vivid raiment are unique."

Figure 21. *Watching the Pageant.* Mortimer Menpes [signed], Raphael Tuck & Sons #9967, London, c. 1908. Coloured halftone, Divided back, 13.7 x 8.85 cm, 5.39 x 3.48 in.

[*Verso*] "Watching the Pageant, Delhi. The great Delhi Durbar is known by means of the vernacular press to the inhabitants of the remotest parts of India. At Delhi those native women, who are not deterred from viewing the spectacle by caste or religious restrictions, are in this instance perhaps the most fortunate."

Watching the Pageant, Delhi.

Coronation Durbar 1911 - Delhi.
His Imperial The King & Her Majesty the Queen Durbar Time.

Figure 22. *Coronation Darbar 1911 – Delhi. His Imperial The King & Her Majesty the Queen Durbar Time.* H.A. Mirza & Sons, Delhi, c. 1911. Coloured collotype, Divided back, 13.9 x 8.95 cm, 5.47 x 3.52 in.

THE IMPERIAL. DELHI. DURBAR.

Figure 23. *The Imperial Delhi Durbar.* A. Vivian Mansell & Co. "Royalty" Series, Fine Art Publishers, London, c. 1911. Coloured halftone, Divided back, 13.95 x 8.85 cm, 5.49 x 3.48 in.

Delhi   The Viceroy announcing the boons granted by H. M. The King Emperor

Figure 24. *Delhi The Viceroy announcing the boons granted by H.M. The King Emperor.* Unknown Publisher, c. 1911. Collotype, Divided back, 14 x 9.05 cm, 5.51 x 3.56 in.

Coronation Day, Delhi Durbar

Figure 25. *Coronation Day, Delhi Durbar.* H.A. Mirza & Sons, Delhi, c. 1911. Coloured collotype, Divided back, 13.75 x 8.9 cm, 5.41 x 3.50 in.

Figure 26. [*Welcome to India Long Live King Emperor*]. Unknown Publisher, c. 1911. Real photo postcard, Divided back, 13.8 x 8.75 cm, 5.43 x 3.44 in.

[*Verso, Handwritten*] "[no.] 1. . . . tonight for the second time & I bought these [postcards], mind it was just like buying gold, but they are real good ones, no. 1 is the gateway through which the King & Queen will pass through tomorrow, the 7th of Dec. 1911. No. 2, is the King's camp, which looks a splendid show, it's a pity you could not come out here & have a good look around here, it is a splendid sight, there was a mishap in this Camp last Sunday, 6 tents were burnt down & yesterday the reception tent at the fort was burned down also, ..."

and 50,000 members of the general public attended.[12] This time postcard-crazy
King George V and Queen Mary did go to India (see Chapter 3) for *The Imperial
Delhi Durbar* (Figure 23). Indeed, George V contributed to making it a milestone on
the road to modern India. He surprised everyone by announcing the relocation of the
imperial capital from Kolkata to Delhi, upsetting two centuries of Bengal's precedence
within the Raj, a the move that was nearly overturned by Parliament. The transfer of
the capital was intended to shift focus from the growing anti-colonial movement in
Bengal and to acknowledge the importance of other parts of the subcontinent, ruled
more easily from a central and northern capital. (The King also mollified Bengalis by
annulling Bengal's extremely unpopular partition by Lord Curzon in 1905). *Delhi The
Viceroy announcing the boons granted by H.M. The King Emperor* (Figure 24) indicates
the importance these proclamations had for people at the time.

The British were legitimizing their role and the changes by wrapping themselves
in the cloak of the renovated Mughals. The unusual *Coronation Day, Delhi Durbar*
(Figure 25) represents the paradox by using an Indian design to frame the Darbar's
pageantry. Publisher Moorli Dhur & Sons in Ambala would have provided the pattern
for the card.[13] Another photo postcard from the event shows a ceremonial Indian gate,
Welcome to India Long Live King Emperor (Figure 26).

I only know a bit of modern Delhi, enough to be struck by how similar it seems to Islamabad as a government city. The same great Mughal fort, tombs and city gates as Lahore; the same plush cantonment and government officers' residential areas; the same fashionable shopping strips; the same Punjabi jokes in clubs and drawing rooms. Black and white Delhi real photo postcards like *Connaught Place, New Delhi* (Figure 27) or *Central Assembly Hall – New Delhi* (Figure 28) from the 1930s and 1940s of *new* Delhi seem to me like the polished photographs and plans of Islamabad in the 1960s and 1970s, proclaiming the future to be just a postcard away.

No.634.   CENTRAL ASSEMBLY HALL - NEW DELHI   JOHNNY STORES POSTCARDS

FACING PAGE
Figure 27. *Connaught Circle.* c. 1940. Real photo postcard, Divided back, 13.5 x 8.9 cm, 5.31 x 3.50 in.

Figure 28. *Central Assembly Hall – New Delhi.* Johnny Stores, Karachi, c. 1927. Real photo postcard, Divided back, 13.95 x 8.65 cm, 5.49 x 3.41 in.

One owner of this card, not postmarked, wrote on the back: "Parliament Building, New Delhi cribbed from the Colosseum at Rome".

THE TAJ

AGRA

A hundred forty miles south of Delhi is the city of Agra, on the Yamuna river, a city whose fortunes were intimately tied to those of the Mughal Emperors. Bereft of political import during the Raj, its Mughal edifices still spawned an outsized postcard presence. When exactly did Agra's most famous building, the Taj Mahal, turn into the global symbol of India?

"No other [building] is so consistently admired for a beauty that is seen as both feminine and regal," writes scholar Giles Tilotson.[14] The Taj acquired this status in about 1900, when its iconic view stabilized into the symmetrical, full frontal we are accustomed to in *The Taj Mahal, Agra* (Figure 29). Other early Taj postcards like *Taj Mahal in Agra* (Figure 30) are made from perspectives that did not survive the canonization of the Taj view. Interestingly, Tilotson goes on to say that the idea of the Taj as the Indian national symbol "was largely foreign in origin,"[15] and foreigners apparently even chose the name "Taj,"[16] all of which, if true, would have been made possible at least in part by a deluge of Taj postcards from nearly every publisher at the time.

The story of the Taj even spread in 1909 to an American pair of advertising postcards, *Mumtaz-i-Mahal* (Figure 31) and *Emperor Shah Jehan* (Figure 32). On the top of both cards is the tomb of the 17th century Emperor Shah Jehan's beloved wife and mother of fourteen children, Arjmand Banu Begam. On the bottom, "from an ivory miniature" with a splash of red, is an embossed portrait of her as Mumtaz-i-Mahal—"the Exalted One of the Palace." After describing "a dream in marble, designed by Titans and finished by Jewellers," the caption on the back of this card ends with: *"India Tea now links that ancient land of mystery and romance with this new world of the West . . .".* (Note, however, that these faces, as my friend Robert Del Bonta points out, are actually based on engravings of the last Mughal Emperor Bahadur Shah Zafar and his wife Zeenat Mahal.)

FACING PAGE, ABOVE
Figure 29. *The Taj Mahal, Agra.* Raphael Tuck & Sons #7237, London, c. 1905. Coloured halftone, Divided back, 13.7 x 8.8 cm, 5.39 x 3.46 in.

[*Verso*] "The Taj Mahal. A dream of Oriental splendor, fashioned as the last resting place for the "Exalted One of the Palace," the wife of Shah Jehan. "If there is a heaven on earth, it is this, it is this."

FACING PAGE, BELOW
Figure 30. *Taj Mahal in Agra. Series 755 India No. 1*, Budapest?, C & A Co., c. 1905. Coloured halftone, Divided back, 13.9 x 8.85 cm, 5.47 x 3.48 in.

[*Recto*] "I.H.T.T. Keplet [sp?] 1.1.1909."

Figure 31. *Mumtaz-I-Mahal.* "*The Exalted one of the Palace.*" (*from an ivory miniature*). *The Taj. Tomb of Mumtaz-i-Mahal. Built by the Emperor Shah Jehan.* India Tea Growers Postcard, USA, 1909. Lithograph, Undivided back, 13.9 x 8.8 cm, 5.47 x 3.46 in.

[*Verso*] Postmarked St. Louis, Missouri, Oct. 1, 1910 and sent to Mrs. W.M. Trane, Trowbridge, Ill. [Illinois], "Mumtaz-I-Mahal – 'The Exalted One of the Palace' – Empress of the Great Mogul Emperor Shah Jehan. Married A.D. 1615, died 1620. Her late resting place is 'the exquisite mausoleum The Taj Mahal, a dream in marble, designed by Titans and finished by Jewellers'."

"The days of Oriental splendor are past and India is now a land of commercial activity. India Tea now links that ancient land of mystery and romance with this new world of the West, for India Tea, the best the world produces, can now be had in the most remote towns and villages in the United States. India Tea is sold by: –[Blindstamped] R. M. Bingsman Trowbridge, Ill. [Illinois]."

THE TAJ,
Tomb of
Mumtaz-i-Mahal.
Built by the
Emperor
Shah Jehan.

EMPEROR SHAH JEHAN
(From an ivory minature)
Born A. D. 1592, died 1666.

[over

Figure 32. *Emperor Shah Jehan. The Taj. Tomb of Mumtaz-i-Mahal. Built by the Emperor Shah Jehan. "The Exalted one of the Palace." (from an ivory miniature).* India Tea Growers Postcard, USA, 1909. Lithograph, Undivided back, 13.8 x 8.75 cm, 5.43 x 3.44 in.

Postmarked St. Louis, Missouri, Nov. 22, 1910 and sent to Mrs. Lafe Spencer, Louisville, Ill.

[*Verso*] "Mumtaz-I-Mahal – 'The Exalted One of the Palace' – Empress of the Great Mogul Emperor Shah Jehan. Married A.D. 1615, died 1620. Her late resting place is 'the exquisite mausoleum The Taj Mahal, a dream in marble, designed by Titans and finished by Jewellers.'

"The days of Oriental splendor are past and India is now a land of commercial activity. India Tea now links that ancient land of mystery and romance with this new world of the West, for India Tea, the best the world produces, can now be had in the most remote towns and villages in the United States. India Tea is sold by: –[Blindstamped] S M Dailey Louisville Ill. [Illinois]."

Figure 33. *Delhi Gate. Agra Fort.* #8945 *Agra Series II*, Raphael Tuck & Sons, London, c. 1905. Embossed coloured halftone, Divided back, 14 x 8.9 cm, 5.51 x 3.50 in.

[*Verso*] "**Delhi Gate, Agra Fort**. The Fort has a circuit of over a mile. Its walls are of red sandstone nearly 70 feet high. There are two entrances, the Delhi Gate being on the West. Crossing the drawbridge and passing over the outer and Inner archways of the Delhi Gate, a somewhat steep slope leads to another gate with dome and battlements and two octagonal towers, one of which is shown in the picture."

Figure 34. *The Moti Musjid [Mosque], Agra.* #7237 *Agra*, Raphael Tuck & Sons, London, c. 1905. Coloured halftone, Divided back, 13.8 x 8.75 cm, 5.43 x 3.44 in.

[*Verso*] "**The Moti Musjid**. The Moti Musjid or Pearl Mosque, designed by the Moghal Emperor, Shah Jehan, 1625-58, glistens as the sun gleams on the dazzling white marble. It is the purest, the most elegant of Indian mosques, and was used as a hospital during the Mutiny."

According to the dean of 19th century Indian art historians, James Fergusson, the Moti Musjid was "one of the purest and most elegant of buildings in its class to be found anywhere."[19]

The Taj, among other things, was also associated with the spread of packaged tea brands, first in the West, and later in the subcontinent as well. Even today in Pakistan, the Taj is something of a symbol, with the same crumbly white faux-marble replicas for sale in tourist and local bazaars as in India. We had one in Vienna and then brought it to Pakistan where it took root in the living room before slowly crumbling away.

Agra was (and still is) full of magnificent Mughal buildings besides the Taj. Some of my Tuck favourites include *Delhi Gate, Agra Fort* (Figure 33) and the arches of *The Moti Musjid, Agra* (Figure 34). The *Exterior of Zenana, Agra* (Figure 35) was redesigned as a Seasons Greeting and advertising card for tea salesmen. Then there is the luminescent *Entrance to Akbar's Tomb, Agra* (Figure 36) with its echoes of Persia, and the squat symmetry of the memorial in honour of Mumtaz Mahal's grandfather, by H.A. Mirza & Sons, *Tomb of Itmad-u-Daoula, Agra* (Figure 37).

Figure 35. *Exterior of Zenana, Agra. #7237 Agra.* Raphael Tuck & Sons, London, c. 1905. Coloured halftone, Divided back, 13.7 x 8.8 cm, 5.39 x 3.46 in.

[*Verso*] "**Exterior of Zenana, Agra**. Here white marble pavilions look out on delicate inlaid pillars and finely perforated screen's thence across the Jumna. Here the ladies of Shah Jehan's court once dreamed of a world beyond the confines of a zenana."

This card was blindstamped in the back by K.D. Dinshaw, Edward Building, Grant Road, Bombay, and bears a Mumbai postmark with an illegible date; it was probably sold as stamped to collectors.

BELOW LEFT

Figure 36. *Entrance to Akbar's Tomb, Agra. #8946 Agra Series II.* Raphael Tuck & Sons, London, c. 1905. Coloured halftone, Divided back, 13.9 x 8.85 cm, 5.47 x 3.48 in.

[*Verso*] "**Entrance to Akbar's Tomb, Agra**. The Mausoleum of the Emperor Akbar who reigned 1488-1518 A.D. is some distance from the cantonment at Agra. On the way to it is a sculptured horse to commemorate a favourite of the Emperor. The mausoleum is of red sandstone and white marble and the cenotaph itself is of white marble surrounded by a lattice-work screen of the same material. Through this the sighing winds whisper a continual requiem over the great Emperor."

BELOW RIGHT

Figure 37. *Tomb of Itmad-u-Daoula, Agra. Was an Wazir of the Emperor Jehangir. This Building built during the reign of Jahanghir 1628 A.D.* H.A. Mirza & Sons, Delhi, c. 1911. Coloured collotype, Divided back, 14 x 8.95 cm, 5.51 x 3.52in.

The Tomb of Itmad-ud-Doula, Agra.
Was an Wazir of the Emperor Jahangir. This Building built during the reign of Jahangir in 1628 A. D.

SIMLA.
VICEREGAL LODGE.

SIMLA

```
[Shimla]
```

When the shift of India's capital from Kolkata to Delhi was announced in 1911, things got even better for what was already the summer capital of the Raj. Simla (as it was then known), located in the Himalayan foothills on the route to Kashmir some 300 miles from Delhi, let the British be themselves, and dwell in homes like *Simla. Viceregal Lodge* (Figure 38) or *The Snowdon Residence of H.E. The C. in – Chief, Simla* (Figure 39). The *Upper Mall with Church and Post Office, Simla* (Figure 40) is an almost entirely European looking place. "Like our Scotland ah!" wrote one sender on a snow-filled view;[17] so miraculous was this white stuff compared to the hot plains, it was relished separately on *Icicles, Simla* (Figure 41).

Simla meant recuperation, like the long diagonal in *Walker Hospital, Simla* (Figure 42), which offers the eye the pleasure of drifting off to an endless healthy future. How enticing was the comfort of *Grand Hotel, Simla* (Figure 43)!

There was, sadly, another side that sometimes came through in Simla postcards. Note the boy carrying wood in the foreground of *Simla View from Cart Road* (Figure 44). A more realistic appraisal of the beast-of-burden work that, as I remembered from Murree, permanently disfigured so many people in the hills, is acknowledged in *Simla Timber Coolie* (Figure 45). When people from the surrounding hills made it into Simla postcards, they were often defined by the services they could render, as in *Simla. Coolie Women with Children* (Figure 46).

Figure 38. *Simla. Viceregal Lodge.* #8968 *Simla Series II.* Raphael Tuck & Sons, London, c. 1905. Coloured halftone, Divided back, 13.9 x 8.8 cm, 5.47 x 3.46 in.

[*Verso*] "**Viceregal Lodge**. The summer residence of the Viceroy. It is a beautiful building, and has fine gardens and lovely walks upon the hills and magnificent scenery."

The Snowdown Residence of H. E. The C.in - Chief, Simla.

Figure 39. *The Snowdon Residence of H.E. The C. in – Chief, Simla.* H.A. Mirza & Sons, Delhi, c. 1910. Coloured collotype, Divided back, 14.15 x 8.85 cm, 5.57 x 3.48 in.

Upper Mall with Church and Post Office, Simla.

Figure 40. *Upper Mall with Church and Post Office, Simla.* H.A. Mirza & Sons, Delhi, c. 1910. Coloured collotype, Divided back, 14.15 x 8.9 cm, 5.57 x 3.50 in.

Icicles, Simla.

Figure 41. *Icicles, Simla.* Unknown publisher, c. 1910. Collotype, Divided back, 13.9 x 8.8 cm, 5.47 x 3.46 in.

Figure 42. *Walker Hospital, Simla.* H.A. Mirza & Sons, Delhi, c. 1910. Coloured collotype, Divided back, 14.2 x 9.15 cm, 5.59 x 3.60 in.

Opened in 1902, it provided 20 beds for Europeans, and was meant to be self-supporting. Patients paid Rs. 5 per day for their care. "Lady Franklin's Free Bed Fund," named after the wife of the Inspector-General of Health provided for poor Europeans.[20] Mr. Franklin had seen the need for the hospital after a visit to Ripon Hospital in Simla. Originally meant for Indians but by 1899 overflowing with Europeans.

Figure 43. *Grand Hotel, Simla.* The Archaeological Photo-Works of India, Delhi, c. 1908. Coloured collotype, Divided back, 13.85 x 8.75 cm, 5.45 x 3.44 in.

Postmarked Simla, Oct. 29, 1908 to Mrs. Taylor, Bath, England.
[*Verso*] "29. Oct. Simla. 5:30 p.m. W. just home from office & have had no time to write—asks me to write his expenses & send our love—both well. Though W. has spent (?) his time playing tennis—very cold. Lovely weather. Love to S. & all. With thanks for her letters in haste. V. A.C.O.D."

SIMLA.
VIEW FROM THE CART ROAD.

SIMLA TIMBER COOLIE.

ABOVE

Figure 44. *Simla View from Cart Road. #8968 Simla Series II.* Raphael Tuck & Sons, London, c. 1905. Coloured halftone, Divided back, 13.75 x 8.8 cm, 5.41 x 3.46 in.

[*Verso*] "**View from the Cart Road**. Simla is in the mountainous region of the Punjab, on the southern slopes of the Himalayas. The town is beautifully laid out and the scenery is magnificent."

Figure 45. *Simla Timber Coolie.* Bourne & Shepherd, c. 1905. Coloured collotype, Divided back, 13.65 x 8.85 cm, 5.37 x 3.48 in.

Kolkata-based Bourne and Shepherd was one of the oldest photographic studios in India, and certainly the most famous, having built its reputation on the albumen photography of Samuel Bourne during the 1860s. It also had a studio in Simla, and while much less of a presence in the postcard market, it did publish a handful of unusual coloured postcards like this one.

Simla. - Coolie Women with Children.

Figure 46. *Simla. – Coolie Women with Children.* Unknown publisher, c. 1905. Collotype, Divided back, 13.85 x 8.9 cm, 5.45 x 3.50 in.

[*Verso*] "just like them thought you would like to see them Tat ta [goodbye]"

Figure 47. *The Jakko Temple, Simla.* H.A. Mirza & Sons, Delhi, c. 1910. Coloured collotype, Divided back, 14 x 8.95 cm, 5.51 x 3.52 in.

Edward Buck tells the story of Charles de Russet, son of a local French photographer and merchant. Charles dropped out of the nearby Bishop Cotton School at the age of seventeen. He came to sit under a Jakko temple tree with the monkeys for two years. Accepted by the monkey and other *fakirs* in the area, he became known as the "leopard *fakir*" because of the headdress he wore as he wandered through the bazaar. He later retired to another temple, and is said to have forgotten how to speak French. An expert on mystics who interviewed him in 1892 said he lived "idle, happy and contented, without any anxiety about the morrow."[21]

The Jakku Temple, Simla.

Lakkar Bazar, Simla.

Figure 48. *Lakker Bazaar, Simla.* H.A. Mirza & Sons, Delhi, c. 1910. Coloured collotype, Divided back, 14.15 x 9.05 cm, 5.57 x 3.56 in.

IN THE SIMLA BAZAR.

Figure 49. *In the Simla Bazaar*. W.P. [signed W. Poole], Thacker,
Spink & Co, Simla, c. 1910. Coloured halftone, Divided back,
13.85 x 8.85cm, 5.45 x 3.48 in.

The Jakko Temple, Simla (Figure 47) was home to a renowned *fakir* who led a troop of monkeys that would descend into the *Lakker Bazaar. Simla* (Figure 48), causing havoc for merchants and customers alike. Edward Buck, Simla's official Raj historian, might have used a watercolour postcard like *In the Simla Bazaar* (Figure 49) to opine on the great divide in the perception of Shimla between Indian and European people: "The bustle, closeness, smells, pariah dogs, unowned children of the kennel, and all the attraction of the bazaar are to them more pleasing than the majestic tranquillity of mountains and valley and far-off plain."[18] What Simla offered depended on the desires one brought to it.

Notes

1. http://tasveergharindia.net/cmsdesk/essay/114/index_3.html, accessed August 18, 2011.

2. Photo 472/2(8) British Library, India Office Library.

3. The Dutch council in Jeddah used Mirza postcards of Mecca to report on Islam's holiest city in 1908 (Ali Asani, and Carney E. S. Gavin, *Through the lens of Mirza of Delhi: The Debbas Album of Early-Twentieth-Century Photographs of Pilgrimage Sites* in *Mecca and Medina*, in *Muqarnas Online* Vol. 15, 1998, p. 179).

4. The same postcard were also published by P.S., Oriental Publishing House, Mumbai.

5. Dorothy and Mortimer Menpes, *The Darbar* (London: Adam & Charles Black, 1903), p. 203.

6. For an interesting article, see *Two Colonials in London's Bohemia*, Australian National Library, http://www.nla.gov.au/pub/nlanews/2003/sep03/article4.html.

7. *Palaces in the Night: The urban landscapes in Whistler's prints*, Fitzwilliam Museum, p. 1. He was himself an experienced printer.

8. Menpes made a voyage to Japan in 1887, and came back to build a Japanese-inspired house outside London that greatly displeased Whistler.

9. *Palaces in the Night*, op. cit., 'Paper,' p. 3.

10. Menpes, Dorothy and Mortimer, *World Pictures*, p. 207. The earliest numbered Darbar card by Tuck's is actually a black and white collotype like *Sculptured Arch & Iron Pillar* from the "Delhi Durbar" Souvenir series numbered 920 (Author's collection).

11. *The Durbar*, op. cit., p. 60.

12. *Coronation Darbar Delhi 1911 Program*, p. 40.

13. I have seen only one other card like this, with the same patterns, *Imperial Procession from Fort to Camp, Delhi*, also from Moorli Dhur & Sons.

14. Giles Tilotson, *Taj Mahal*, Cambridge, Harvard University Press, 2008, p. 1.

15. Ibid., p. 6.

16. Ibid., p. 6.

17. *Town Hall, Simla*, postcard sent from Simla and dated Sept. 20, 1909, Author's Collection.

18. Edward Buck, *Simla, Past and Present* (Bombay, Times Press, 1925), p. 186.

19. James Fergusson, *Indian Architecture 2*, 317 quoted in Murrays *Handbook of India Burma and Ceylon*, p. 267.

20. Edward Buck, op. cit., p. 92.

21. Ibid., p. 191 quoting John C. Oman, in *Mystics, Ascetics and Saints of India* (1894).

LAHORE.
CENTRAL MUSEUM.

Lahore

Lahore was a principal city of the Raj. The capital of Punjab, gateway to the northwest, it offered a blend of Muslim, Sikh and Hindu traditions. Rudyard Kipling's *Kim* is set here. His father John Lockwood founded and worked at the *Lahore Central Museum* (Figure 1). Outside the museum stands *Lahore, Kim's Gun* (Figure 2), where, as the first sentence of the novel (1901) goes, "He sat, in defiance of municipal orders, astride the gun Zam-Zammah on her brick platform opposite the old Aijab Ghar—the Wonder House, as the natives call the Lahore Museum."[1]

This was also the city of my father's family, the "hometown" we went to each December for a month to the bungalow and garden at 5 Queen's Road. In Lahore, every memory is vivid, whether watching from the roof as the British Council in the adjacent bungalow was under attack, or spending time at the first English bookstore I ever knew, Ferozsons on the Mall (its supply of Enid Blyton books was plentiful).

Kipling began his working life as a newspaperman for six years in Lahore and wrote some of his most memorable stories here, including the original version of *The City of Dreadful Night*. It described the view on a drug-laced August night in the centre of the walled city from the minaret of *Lahore Wazir Khan's Mosque. (Outer Part)* (Figure 3).[2] The young Kipling apparently took a stroll here one evening after his working day at the *Civil and Military Gazette* in which the story first appeared.[3] The scene, looking away from the mosque from the right rear minaret is captured by *The Golden Mosque, Lahore* (Figure 4), and, from a closer angle and different colour scheme,

Figure 1. *Lahore. Central Museum. Lahore Series II. No. 8966.* Raphael Tuck & Sons, London, c. 1905. Coloured halftone, Divided back, 13.9 x 8.8 cm, 5.47 x 3.46 in.

[*Verso*] "**Central Museum, Lahore**. This is perhaps the most effective of all the public buildings in Lahore. The foundation stone was laid in 1890, by the Duke of Clarence, eldest son of King Edward VII. It contains specimens of the antiquities, arts, manufactures and products of the Punjab."

Note that the original Aijab Ghar is a little further along the Mall, at the original Punjab Exhibition building opened in 1864.

The Phototype Co., Bombay.

Lahore, Zamzama Gun

Figure 2. *Lahore Zamzama Gun.*
The Phototype Co., Mumbai, c. 1902.
Collotype, Undivided back,
13.6 x 8.95 cm, 5.35 x 3.52 in.

Kim's second sentence continues: "Who hold Zam-Zammah, that 'fire breathing dragon," holds the Punjab, for the great green bronze piece, is always first of the conqueror's loot."

LAHORE.
WAZIR KHAN'S MOSQUE. (OUTER PART)

Figure 3. *Lahore. Wazir Khan's Mosque (outer Part). Lahore Series I. No. 8965.* Raphael Tuck & Sons, London, c. 1905. Embossed coloured halftone, Divided back, 13.9 x 8.85 cm, 5.47 x 3.48 in.

[*Verso*] "**Wazir Khan's Mosque (Outer Part) Lahore**. This beautiful mosque was built in 1634 by Hakim Alau-ud-din, Governor of the Punjab under Shah Jehan[.] Over the noble entrance is written in Persian :– 'Remove thy heart

from the gardens of the world and note that this building is the true home of man.' From the gallery round the minaret in the picture there is a fine view over the City of Lahore."

The minaret offering the views here and in Figure 4 is hidden except for its tip behind the gated doorway; from there you see the view down the adjacent street in Figures 4 and 6.

Figure 4. *The Golden Mosque, Lahore.* K.C. Mehra & Sons, Peshawar, c. 1905. Coloured halftone, Divided back, 13.9 x 8.85 cm, 5.47 x 3.48 in.

Figure 5. *Lahore. The Golden Mosque. Lahore Series I, No. 8965.* Raphael Tuck & Sons, London, c. 1905. Coloured halftone, Divided back, 13.8 x 8.9 cm, 5.43 x 3.50 in.

[*Verso*] "**Golden Mosque, Lahore**. This mosque has three gilt domes and was built in 1753 by Bikhari Khan, a favourite of the widow of Mir Mannu, who governed Lahore a short time after her husband's death. He is said to have displeased the lady, and her female attendants beat him to death. The mosque is picturesquely located at the junction of two streets. In a courtyard behind is a large well with steps descending to the water."

in *Lahore.Golden Mosque* (Figure 5). The view from the other side of this minaret is *Panoramic View of Lahore* (Figure 6). "Is it possible to climb to the top of the great Minars," asks the narrator, "and thence to look down on the city?"[4] to find:

Dore might have drawn it! Zola could describe it – this spectacle of sleeping thousands in the moonlight and the shadow of the Moon. The rooftops are crammed with men, women and children; and the air is full of undistinguishable noises. They are restless in the City of Dreadful Night; and small wonder. The marvel is that they can even breathe.[5]

Climbing the minaret, looking down on the naked rooftops, reminds me of the time my father took me all around the inner city and showed me the little homes and

PANORAMIC VIEW OF LAHORE.

Figure 6. *Panoramic View of Lahore. Taraporevala's Elite Series No. 45.* D.B. Taporevala & Sons, Mumbai, c. 1903?. Collotype, Undivided back, 13.9 x 8.9 cm, 5.47 x 3.50 in.

This photograph was actually taken by Samuel Bourne on a visit to Lahore in 1864.[9]

The Central Model School, Lahore.

Figure 7. *The Central Model School, Lahore.* K.C. Mehra & Sons, Peshawar, c. 1908. Coloured halftone, Divided back, 13.85 x 8.9 cm, 5.45 x 3.50 in.

Figure 8. *Ranjit Singh's Tomb, Lahore.* Moorli Dhur & Sons [?] No. 21, c. 1908. Coloured collotype, Divided back, 13.75 x 12.9 cm, 5.41 x 5.08 in.

Figure 9. *General View Shah Masjid and Ranjit Singh Samad, Lahore (India).* Coloured collotype, H.A. Mirza & Sons, Delhi, c. 1908. Divided back, 14.05 x 9 cm, 5 .53 x 3.54 in.

alleyways they once lived in, seven siblings and eight uncles. Once he walked me a few blocks out of the walled city to the *Central Model School* (Figure 7) where, one day as a 6-year-old, he appeared for the entrance exams and got in, all without telling his father.

The dominant presence in the city when the British took control in 1848 was not the Mughals, but the Sikhs. A five hundred-year-old religion combining Hinduism and Islam, with Punjabi founding Gurus, at its height during the reign of Maharajah Ranjit Singh (1780-1839), the Sikh Empire stretched from Afghanistan to Kashmir and was governed from Lahore. After Ranjit Singh died in 1839, the realm quickly fell victim to intrigue and invasion. *Ranjit Singh's Tomb* (Figure 8) was still under construction when the British also made Lahore their capital of Punjab.

LAHORE.
ROYAL MOSQUE. (INNER PART)

Figure 12. *Eid Mubarak.* Mushtaq [signed], H. Ghulam Mohd & Sons, Lahore, c. 1940. Lithograph, Divided back, 13.8 x 8.75 cm, 5.43 x 3.44 in.

[*Verso, Handwritten*] Addressed to Thomas W. Mele Esq. 1715 E 30th St., Baltimore, MD, USA. "New Year and Christmas" [Pre-printed "Eid" is struck through and replaced with "New Year & Christmas" to complete Greeting Card]. "From: Bashir Ahmad University Chemical Laboratories. Lahore. INDIA, Nov. 21, 1942."

For a long time, I thought that this card, which I bought at a show in the US, was sent by a distant relative who went to Germany in the 1920s to learn chemistry and came back and worked in various chemical firms in Lahore, but now think this was probably a different Bashir Ahmad.

Maharajah Ranjit Singh was buried adjacent to what was then the largest mosque in the world, as seen in *General View Shah Masjid and Ranjit Singh Samad, Lahore* (Figure 9) and *Lahore. Royal Mosque. (Inner Part)* (Figure 10). This compares to the real photo postcard from around 1940 of Eid prayers at the mosque, *Untitled* (Figure 11). Note the four missing cupolas on each corner, which were not fixed until after 1942. My own memories of coming here year after year for Eid, when we lived in Vienna and Islamabad, with a cohort of thirty uncles and cousins of every degree, are closer to Tuck's view. They remind me of the 8mm Kodachrome movies my father liked to shoot on these occasions that rendered the colours in similar tones, days when sweets abounded and oodles of colourful Pakistani money was pressed into our hands.

Which brings me to my favourite Eid postcard—they started becoming popular in the 1920s in Lahore and Mumbai. *Eid Mubarak* (Figure 12) is by Ghulam Mohammed & Sons, a major Lahore printer of lithographs and posters. Unexpectedly, in this fine composition by the artist Mushtaq, a woman is actually driving the camel.

The Huzuri Bagh, Lahore (Figure 13), facing directly across from the mosque entrance, is where Ranjit Singh held court through much of his reign, retreating to underground chambers in the summer. Today the square where the Tomb, the Mosque and the Fort all face each other is illuminated at night, allowing oneself to be transported all the more easily on a walk into the past.

The Lahore that the British built along the Mall, one end of which started near the Badshahi Mosque, was frequently the work of Sikh architects. Bhai Ram Singh designed the Lahore Museum; a lifelong protégé of John Lockwood Kipling, he brought about the distinctive style of *The Chief's College, Lahore* (Figure 14), now known as Aitcheson College.

Figure 13. *The Huzuri Bagh, Lahore.* K.C. Mehra & Sons (Stengel & Co. No. B 2122 *verso*), Peshawar, c. 1908. Coloured halftone, Undivided back, 13.85 x 8.85 cm, 5.45 x 3.48 in.

Figure 14. *The Chief's College, Lahore.* K.C. Mehra & Sons (Stengel & Co. B 2122 *verso*), Peshawar, c. 1908. Coloured halftone, Divided back, 13.8 x 8.95 cm, 5.43 x 3.52 in.

Figure 15. *The School of Art* [hand corrected *Government College*], *Lahore.* Bremner no. 105, Lahore, c. 1903. Collotype, Undivided back, 13.9 x 8.85 cm, 5.47 x 3.48 in.

Postmarked December 1903 to Dr. Brae Kenburg, "Oakfield" 21 Lueramore Road, London, England.

[*Recto*] "17.12.03 Our best wishes to you and Mrs. BK for a very happy new year. Trust you both and the ch[ild] are well & flourishing. Much Love from Mrs. S. to Mrs. B.G.S."

Figure 16. *Fire near Ry. [Railway]*
Station – Lahore. Moorli Dhur &
Sons (Stengel No. 6557 *Verso*) Ph.
By Thom. Bell, Ambala, c. 1905.
Collotype, Divided back,
13.7 x 8.8 cm, 5.39 x 3.46 in.

Figure 17. *Dhobi. (Washingman.).*
Moorli Dhur & Sons, Ambala, c. 1908.
Coloured halftone, Divided back,
13.85 x 8.75 cm, 5.45 x 3.44 in.

Opened in 1890, it was an architectural commission where "after much deliberation
it was resolved that the Colonel [Samuel Jacobs] should be asked to adapt his plans to
accommodate the elevations and architectural features prepared by Bhai Ram Singh."[6]
These Lahore architects developed an architectural blend of local and European styles
no less novel than the Indo-Sarcenic of Mumbai.

Unlike most other places in this book, Lahore did not have a leading local postcard
publisher. Many of the postcards chosen here are from the series by Peshawar-based
K.C. Mehra & Sons, which I consider closest to the memories I have of an empty
Mall Road and the much emptier streets of the 1960s and 1970s. The city's earliest
commercial publisher was probably Bremner, who occasionally mislabelled a card,
like *The School of Art, Lahore*, hand corrected by the sender to *Government College*
(Figure 15).[7] Government College, with the main church-like building completed in
1877, is where many of the architects and builders of the city, future rulers of Pakistan
and Nobel laureates from India and Pakistan would study, as well as my father, who,
like many of his friends, was a die-hard old "Ravian," as alumni named themselves
after the Ravi river that flows by Lahore.

Lahore may not have had a dominant postcard publisher because Moorli Dhur & Sons,
at Ambala railway junction 130 miles away, dominated the Punjab market by 1910.
Perhaps because of its distribution clout, it published atypical postcards like the newsy
Fire near Ry. Station – Lahore (Figure 16) following an earthquake that damaged a
number of structures in the city of 180,000 on April 5, 1905. It offered postcards of
domestic help too, including *Dhobi. (Washingman.)* (Figure 17) with the cane pattern,

white cloth and man neatly framed together very nicely. The Ambala firm also published a series of humorous Raj postcards that shed insight into colonial life. For example, there are few intimations of relations between Europeans and Indians in other media, with *How We Make Love in the East* (Figure 18) a startling exception. "Stay quiet about it," says the sweeper in Hindu-Urdu. "Sure," replies the soldier.

Another card begs the question of who is enjoying himself in *The Wonderful Art of Taking Things Easy* (Figure 19). The servant when Sahib is away? Or has Sahib gone native?

The man sprawled on a lounge chair in *Not so bad . . .* (Figure 20) is flush with drink despite empty pockets lined with the names of the domestic staff he has not paid this

Figure 18. *How We Make Love in the East.* G.E. McCulloch [signed], Moorli Dhur & Sons (Stengel No. 1644 *verso*], Ambala, c. 1908. Coloured halftone, Divided back, 13.85 x 8.75 cm, 5.45 x 3.44 in.

[*Verso*] "Ask Winter what this means. I'm no scholar."

Figure 19. *The Wonderful Art of Taking Things Easy.* G.W. Strong [signed], Moorli Dhur & Sons, Ambala, c. 1908. Lithograph, Divided back, 13.8 x 8.75 cm, 5.43 x 3.44 in.

Postmarked Trimulgherry, 23 Sept. 1910 (?) and addressed to Mr. and Mrs. A. Barnes, 67 Frog Road (?), St. Denys, Southhampton, Hanks. England. [*Verso*] "Left cancela [tion] India. Dear Both (?), I hope you and boys are quite well. Thought you would like a card. After all this time, this is a punka boy, lazing down and pulling the punka, in hot weather to keep us cool. Taking things easy you know. The Hot. Weather is now over thank goodness & we can now breathe, Kind regards from Billie."

Figure 20. *Not so bad. eh? what !! A bit rough at the end of the month though.* GWS [signed], Moorli Dhur & Sons (Stengel No. 1202 *verso*), Ambala, c. 1908. Coloured halftone, Divided back, 13.6 x 8.85 cm, 5.35 x 3.48 in.

This postcard has a pre-printed message "Dear _____ Not so bad, eh? What !! A bit rough at the end of the month though. Yours _____."

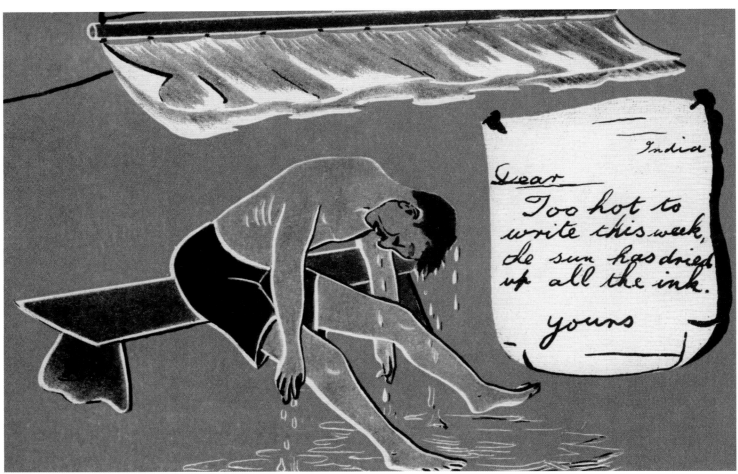

Figure 21. *Too hot to write this week, the sun has dried up all the ink.* Moorli Dhur & Sons, Ambala, c. 1908. Coloured halftone, Divided back, 13.6 x 8.9 cm, 5.35 x 3.50 in.

Figure 22. *Lahore. Chief Court. Punjab. Lahore Series II. No. 8966.* Raphael Tuck & Sons, London, c. 1905. Coloured halftone, Divided back, 13.9 x 8.8 cm, 5.47 x 3.46 in.

[*Verso*] "**Chief Court, Lahore**. This fine building is in the late Pathan style of the 14th century. Between the Court and the Cathedral is a statue of Lord Lawrence who was Chief Commissioner and Lieut. Governor of the Punjab 1853–59."

Figure 23. *Lahore. Punjab Club. Lahore Series II. No. 8966.* Raphael Tuck & Sons, London, c. 1905. Coloured halftone, Divided back, 13.8 x 8.85 cm, 5.43 x 3.48 in.

[*Verso*] "**Punjab Club, Lahore**. There are many fine buildings in the modern part of the City of Lahore, while the picturesque old town with its balconies, projecting oriel windows, and irregular buildings will delight the artist. The stately Punjab Club is on the west side of the Mall, going east from Charing Cross where the Jubilee statue of Queen Victoria stands at the crossroads."

Figure 24. *Lahore. Shalimar Garden. Lahore Series I. No. 896.* Raphael Tuck & Sons, London, c. 1905. Coloured halftone, Divided back, 13.9 x 8.7 cm, 5.47 x 3.43 in.

[*Verso*] "**Shalimar Garden, Lahore.** These gardens were laid out in 1637 by order of Shah Jehan. They are divided into three parts on different levels. The whole extent is about three parts on different levels. The whole extent is about 80 acres and with its tanks and fountains and flower beds it is a very pretty place."

Figure 25. *The Shalamar Garden, No. 2, Lahore. Lahore Series I. No. 896.* Raphael Tuck & Sons, London, c. 1905. Coloured halftone, Divided back, 13.85 x 8.9 cm, 5.45 x 3.50 in.

month. Being out of money for alcohol seems to have had much resonance among expatriates. So does another pre-printed message card *Too Hot to write this week, the sun has dried up all the ink* (Figure 21).

Tuck's Lahore postcards included *Lahore. Chief Court* (Figure 22), which the caption declares to be of the "late Pathan style of the 14th century" (whatever that means). It was inaugurated in 1888, and served well as a Maharajah's palace in the Hollywood film *Bhowani Junction* (1956). It was filmed just as my grandfather became a judge here, and uncles and great-uncles argued cases and talked politics and Pakistan started moving from martial law to martial law.

As one drives from the High Court around mid-Mall towards the Upper Mall, one passes what was *The Punjab Club* (Figure 23), now a civil service college, and then further along, towards Shahdara, one comes to the delicate *Shalimar Garden* (Figure 24) in Tuck's view, or Mehra's *The Shalamar Garden, No. 2, Lahore* (Figure 25). Still not in very good shape, with fitful attempts by every government to restore one pavilion or another, yet still enchanting with giant banyan trees and fountains that gush for dignitaries, it is a cradle of fond memories for myself and millions more.

There is a copy of the Shalimar Gardens in Srinagar, built by the same Emperor, just as there is a *Delhi Gate. Lahore* (Figure 26), a gate that seems happy to wait out history and the resumption of trade across the border. For me it is still the place to go to, park your car, buy a soft drink and start ducking through the passageways on the way to Wazir Khan's Mosque and the glorious perch on its minaret.

Figure 26. *Delhi Gate. Lahore.* K.C. Mehra & Sons, Peshawar, c. 1910. Coloured halftone, Divided back, 13.85 x 8.95 cm, 5.45 x 3.52 in.

AMRITSAR

Although they ruled from Lahore, the Sikh religious capital was 30 miles to the east in Amritsar. About half the size of Lahore then, and after the railway line was built in 1880 only a brief ride away, Amritsar is dominated by the four hundred-year-old Golden Temple in *Birdseye View – Amritsar* (Figure 27). The Golden Temple is the central place of pilgrimage for Sikhs, where the holy book *Guru Granth Sahib* is kept. *Golden Temple (Amritsar)* (Figure 28) uses a familiar over-the-water shot of the "Temple of God," while *Golden Temple, Amritsur.* (Figure 29) shows the "white

Birdseye View — Amritsar.

Figure 27. *Birdseye View – Amritsar.* D.A. Ahuja & Sons No. 301, Yangon, c. 1908. Coloured halftone, Divided back, 13.85 x 8.95 cm, 5.45 x 3.52 in.

Postmark unclear, possibly Delhi. Sent to Mr. Oetis [sp?] Hale, 70 Wisconsin St., Oakland Alameda Ct. California, U.S.A.

"Amritsar, India, December 22, 1912. Dear Mr. Hale. From Peshawar I came to Amritsar, a city of 200000 and the

religious capital of the Sikhs, one of the prominent sects in India. Amritsar is situated in a fine level country. The great attraction here is the Golden Temple built on the inside of an artificial pond called the Sacred Tank in which the people bathe. There are also other large tanks in this city as well as in other cities. Very sincerely, H.S. Nagel [sp?]."

Golden Temple, Amritsar.

Figure 28. *Golden Temple (Amritsar).*
D.A. Ahuja & Sons No. 21, Yangon,
c. 1908. Coloured halftone, Divided
back, 13.85 x 9.1 cm, 5.45 x 3.58 in.

[Verso, Not postmarked] "you haven't got
this one before have you Lovie. I hope
you will like these Best Love xxx."

D.A. Ahuja offered a number of India
shots (see *Benares*).

GOLDEN TEMPLE, AMRITSUR.

Figure 29. *Golden Temple Amritsur.*
Unknown Firm, c. 1905. Coloured
collotype, Undivided back,
13.85 x 9.2 cm, 5.45 x 3.62 in.

marble causeway 204 ft. long, flanked on either side by gilded standard lamps" that leads to the repository.[8]

The temple itself was guarded by *Sikh Akalis at Amritsar* (Figure 30), one of the best in Tuck's *Native Life in India* series, a cool contrast of blue and marble and one of the first postcards I really liked.

A postcard with a theme found at other places as well, *Amritsar – Lover Walk Jhansi* (Figure 31) refers to the secluded public area in many towns and cantonments where men and women could walk, flirt and, if it was dark enough, even kiss.

SIKH AKALIS AT AMRITSAR.

Amritsar — Lover Walk Ihansi

Figure 30. *Sikh Akalis at Amritsar. Native Life in India Series IV. No. 9311.* Raphael Tuck & Sons, London, c. 1905. Coloured collotype, Divided back, 13.75 x 8.8 cm, 5.41 x 3.46 ins.

[*Verso*] "**The Sikh Akalis** are one section of the famous 'fakirs' or native priests of India. Unlike many of these fakirs, their enthusiasm is of an active nature, and in times past, when the Sikhs were engaged in warfare, they frequently led the advancing army in person fighting with great bravery and considerable disregard of their life."

Figure 31. *Amritsar – Lover Walk Jhansi.* Unknown firm, No. 29980 [*Verso*], c. 1905. Collotype, Divided back, 13.8 x 8.75 cm, 5.43 x 3.44 in.

MURREE

Murree was the summer capital of Punjab from 1863 until 1876, after which this hill station on the edge of the Himalayas was frozen in time until 1947. In the 1960s, by virtue of being an hour's drive from Pakistan's new capital in Islamabad, it started to flourish again. Murree was also home to one of my favourite postcard publishers, Baljee (as a war photographer see *North-West Frontier Province*).

Coloured collotypes like *Murree. Bazaar (Summer)* (Figure 32) finely blend large albumen photography—you can still see the titles in the glass negatives—and stencilled colours to give them the feel of magic lantern slides in candle-lit rooms like those we inhabited in Murree guest houses where the electricity often failed for hours. I see this carved hillside and remember walking down to the Mall from Kashmir Point day after day to see if the new issue of *Melody Maker*, already six-months-old by sea from London, was in so that we could check the pop charts.

Figure 32. *Murree. Bazaar (Summer).* D. Baljee & Co., Murree and Rawalpindi, 719 [*Verso*], c. 1905. Coloured collotype, Divided back, 13.95 x 9.05 cm, 5.49 x 3.56 in.

A single image that from the Church on the Mall, for a long time open to Europeans only, down to the native bazaars, encapsulates the colonial state.

Figure 33. *On the Ashleigh Road Murree.* D. Baljee & Co., 736 [*Verso*], Murree and Rawalpindi, c. 1905. Coloured collotype, Divided back, 14 x 9.1 cm, 5.51 x 3.58 in.

BELOW
Figure 34. *Dungagali from Nathia Road (Snow).* D. Baljee & Co., Murree and Rawalpindi, 750 [*Verso*], c. 1905. Coloured collotype, Divided back, 13.95 x 9.05 cm, 5.49 x 3.56 in.

[*Verso, Handwritten*] "I need not tell you how sorry I am for not being able to send you any cards, so I hope it will not be so again. Am very pleased to say that I have received papers alright."

Figure 35. *Post Office, Cherat.* D. Baljee & Co., Murree and Rawalpindi, 750 [*Verso*], c. 1905. Coloured collotype, Divided back, 13.95 x 9 cm, 5.49 x 3.54 in.

[*Verso, Not postmarked*] "I. Nasirabad India 10/8/11 Dear Miss Stacey I am so very pleased to let you know that I am quite well again, after an illness of two".

On the Ashleigh Road Murree (Figure 33) is a deep view with a glazed mist effect. *Dungagali from Nathia Road (Snow)* (Figure 34) expertly plays off white, blue and greens. Baljee coloured postcards are pretty hard to come by, but one of his postcards seemed to have played well on an all India level. *Post Office, Cherat* (Figure 35) shows a hill station even more remote than Murree, in Frontier Province near the "Black Mountains," now too a tendril of the postal service.

Notes

1. Rudyard Kipling, *Kim*, (London: Penguin Classics), p. 49.
2. See Kipling Papers, PRS.K52 A15/888, Bancroft Library, University of California, Berkeley and also "The Bhang Maker", *Civil and Military Gazette* Vol. VIII, Oct.-Dec. 1889.
3. "The City of Dreadful Night," in Rudyard Kipling, *Life's Handicap* (London: Penguin Classics), p. 286.
4. Ibid.
5. Ibid.
6. Parvaiz Vandal and Sajida Vandal, *The Raj, Lahore and Bhai Ram Singh*, (Lahore: Topical Publishing, 2006), p. 172.
7. In another example, *The Golden Temple* became *The Golden Mosque* in a subsequent printing. The earliest Lahore postcards traced thus far are German missionary cards from 1898.
8. *A Handbook for Traveller's in India, Burma & Ceylon*, 15th Edition (London: John Murray, 1932), p. 337.
9. Bourne, Samuel, "Ten Weeks with Cameras in the Himalayas," in *The British Journal of Photography*, February 15, 1874, p. 69.

Nusserwanjee & Co., Karachi

THE ERSKIN WHARF, HARBOUR KARACHI

Karachi

The western province of Sindh was part of Bombay Presidency until 1936, a sleepy backwater until an irrigation project along the lower Indus in 1932 started the transformation of Karachi into one of the world's largest cities. To be sure, Karachi saw initial growth in the late 19th century, like Mumbai, with the export of agricultural goods through the port as seen in *The Erskin Wharf, Harbour Karachi* (Figure 1) or *A View of Grain Shipping, Kimari* (Figure 2).

A 1903 postcard of the city's main business thoroughfare, *Elphinstone Street, Karachi* (Figure 3), shows an emptiness unimaginable today. Few Karachiites would believe that another very popular early postcard showed the *Alligators at Mughar Pier, Karachi* (Figure 4). Maghar Pier is an ancient grove and home to a unique species of short-nosed crocodile (Hindus and Muslims still congregate here to make offerings). *Tombs Maghar Pier, Karachi* (Figure 5) and *Relics of Ancient Tombs Maghar Pier Karachi* (Figure 6) shows some of the elaborate carved sandstone graves that dot the deserts around Karachi, many of which remain to be explained by archaeologists.

Karachi's iconic building is *Frere Hall* (Figure 7), opened in 1865, a hybrid of Arab and European styles made out of a local tan limestone common to most major Karachi buildings of the period. It echoed the world of Sindh's first administrator, Sir Bartle Frere. He designed it, and later as the Governor of Bombay Presidency, fostered the Indo-Saracenic style that Frere Hall previews (see *Mumbai*, Figures 3-5, 7, 8). The people gathered around the statue of Queen Victoria are similar to the cosmopolitan threads that were coming together in the evenings on Malabar Beach (see *Mumbai*, Figure 22).

Figure 1. *The Erskin Wharf, Harbour Karachi.* Nuserwanjee & Co., c. 1903. Coloured collotype, Undivided back, 13.85 x 9 cm, 5.45 x 3.54 in.

Postmarked Kolkata [?] May 30, 1909. Addressed to Dr. Mrs. Pearson, 30 Half Moon Lake, Herne Hill, London England SE. [*Verso*] "I have been here Trust you are both well April 30 1909 Your Loving Brother Alf India"

A View of Grain Shipping, Kimari.

Figure 2. *A View of Grain Shipping, Kimari.* Byramjee Eduljee., c. 1903. Collotype, Divided back, 13.95 x 8.8 cm, 5.49 x 3.46 in.

Bremner, Lahore and Quetta

Elphinstone Street, Karachi.

Figure 3. *Elphinstone Street, Karachi.* Bremner, Lahore and Quetta, c. 1902. Collotype, Undivided back, 13.95 x 8.95 cm, 5.49 x 3.52 in.

R.Jalbhoy Karachi.

ALIGATORS AT MAGHAR PIR, KARACHI.

Figure 4. *Alligators at Mughar Pier, Karachi.* R. Jalbhoy, Karachi, c. 1905. Collotype, Undivided back, 13.8 x 8.75 cm, 5.43 x 3.44 in.

Photographer R. Jalbhoy & Sons offered a number of postcards of the crocodiles, of which this the most ferocious. A popular tale had a British officer walking across their backs without incident.

Figure 5. *Tombs, Maghar Pier, Karachi.*
R. Jalbhoy, Karachi, c. 1905. Coloured
collotype, Divided back (no line),
13.95 x 8.85 cm, 5.49 x 3.48 in.

Can R. Jalbhoy be one of the men sitting
on the tombs? People often brought
bodies from far away to be buried in the
sanctity of Maghir Pir.

Figure 6. *Relics of Ancient Tombs,
Maghar Pier, Karachi.* Johnny Stores,
Karachi, c. 1920. Real photo postcard,
Divided back, 13.9 x 8.8 cm,
5.47 x 3.46 in.

Figure 7. *Frere Hall.* M.G. Shahani &
Co., Karachi, c. 1905. Coloured halftone,
Divided back, 14.05 x 9.25 cm,
5.53 x 3.64 in.

When we were living in Islamabad, going to Karachi was like going to New York. The uncle with whom we stayed looked like a Hollywood star in sunglasses. There was real ice cream and a warm ocean. Years later, as I came down for work with UNICEF in a limestone Clifton mansion, I ate Goan and Madrasi and Hyderabadi and Bengali food, and realized that Karachi, unexpectedly in 1947, had became a sanctuary for Muslims from all over India. It was a global city, like Mumbai, within the subcontinent— sandwiched between East and West. *Frere Hall* (Figure 7), on the way to and from Clifton, always struck me as a place where two pieces of a puzzle have been perfectly forced together, Muslim pillars carved into the belly of a Church.

Another early colour postcard shows *Government House* (Figure 8), just across the street from Frere Hall, built by the British conqueror of Sindh, Sir Charles Napier in the 1840s. Now it is the heavily guarded residence of Sindh's Governor. Across the busy street, behind sandstone gates still untouched by time, is the *Sind Club* (Figure 9), a place where the Raj unashamedly lives on and where I could visit relatives and the fathers of friends who had chosen to spend their final years by occupying air-conditioned rooms on monthly rent.

Government House.

Figure 8. *Government House.* M.G. Shahani & Co., Karachi, c. 1905. Coloured halftone, Divided back, 13.8 x 9.1 cm cm, 5.43 x 3.58 in.

Sind Club.

Figure 9. *Sind Club.* M.G. Shahani & Co., Karachi, c. 1905. Coloured halftone, Divided back, 13.8 x 9 cm, 5.43 x 3.54 in.

Figure 10. *Karachi, Eduljee Dinshaw Charity Hospital.* Moorli Dhur & Sons, Ambala, c. 1903. Coloured collotype, Divided back, 13.9 x 8.85 cm, 5.47 x 3.48 in.

BELOW
Figure 11. *Kothari Parade and Lady Lloyd Pier.* M.G. Shahani & Co., Karachi, c. 1905. Coloured halftone, Divided back, 14 x 9.2 cm, 5.51 x 3.62 in.

Kothari Parade and Lady Lloyd Pier.

Early Karachi postcards featured new buildings like the ethereal *Karachi, Eduljee Dinshaw Charity Hospital* (Figure 10). Another celebrates *Kothari Parade and Lady Lloyd Pier.* (Figure 11, opened 1887), a civic donation by a Parsee businessman. Behind it, a walkway named after the wife of the Viceroy stretches towards the Arabian Sea.

Clifton Karachi (Figure 12) and *Maha Shivratri Hindu Festival Clifton Karachi* (Figure 13), while not quite as intimate with the beach as Malabar Beach postcards, also reflect people creating new social spaces on the waterfront.

Figure 12. *Clifton Karachi.* Johnny Stores, Karachi, c. 1920. Real photo postcard, Divided back, 14.05 x 8.8 cm, 5.53 x 3.46 in.

Figure 13. *Maha Shivrati Hindu Festival Clifton Karachi.* Johnny Stores, Karachi, c. 1920. Real photo postcard, Divided back, 13.85 x 9 cm, 5.45 x 3.54 in.

New creative types emerged in this city as well, whether *A Young Indian Actor* (Figure 14) or *Miss Buchwa Jan of Karachi* (Figure 15). Buchwa Jan is leafing through an album of photographs of what look like British officials, acknowledging her foreign admirers, quite the opposite of *An Indian Family, Karachi* (Figure 16). They might have lived in *Native Town, Karachi* (Figure 17), roughly equivalent to the walled city in Lahore.

Karachi was home to one distinctive postcard publisher, S.S. Brij Basi & Sons, which, after its founding in 1915, would become one of the most successful all-India publishers of visual media (the firm relocated to Delhi after 1947 and still flourishes).

Figure 14. *A young Indian Actor.*
Rewachand Motumal & Sons, Karachi,
c. 1905. Coloured collotype, Divided
back, 14.1 x 8.9 cm, 5.55 x 3.50 in.

Figure 15. *Miss Buchwa Jan, Karachi.*
Rewachand Motumal & Sons,
Karachi, c. 1905. Collotype, Divided
back, 13.8 x 8.8 cm, 5.43 x 3.46 in.

Figure 16. *An Indian Family, Karachi.* R. Jalbhoy, Karachi, c. 1905.
Collotype, Divided back, 13.8 x 8.8 cm, 5.43 x 3.46 in.

Note the real shoes on the sitters.

Figure 17. *Native Town.* R. Jalbhoy, Karachi, c. 1905.
Collotype, Divided back, 13.7 x 8.7 cm, 5.39 x 3.43 in.

Shri Hanuman ji.

S.S. Brij Basi & Sons,
Bunder Road, Karachi.

Printed in Germany

Figure 18. *Shri Hanuman ji.* S.S. Brij Basi
& Sons, Karachi, c. 1928. Coloured real
photograph of painting, Divided back,
13.75 x 8.8 cm, 5.41 x 3.46 in.

Like the Ravi Varma Press, they sold devotional images, this time in the Nathdvara style inspired by Rajasthani folk art. There was a long tradition of hand painting by individual artists and clan workshops. The postcards were printed on bromide paper in Germany in 1928, starting with *Lord Krishna* (Figure 18), the sparkle and hand-tints possibly added in Karachi. Christopher Pinney invokes the "mytho-poetic world of natural beauty"[1] to describe them. *Shri Hanuman ji* (Figure 19) and *Ram and Tulsidas' Meeting* (Figure 20) are also signed by the great Nathdvara painter Ghasiram, who, like many of his colleagues, initially resisted mass-reproduction but later came to see it as economically beneficial. Brij Basi postcards are less colourful than Ravi Varma ones even as they too incorporate the tropes of photographic realism. Like Tuck's, Brij Basi were supremely self-confident – "other pictures in the market cannot even be compared to the shadow of our quality pictures,"[2] went one ad. I tend to agree (for more Brij Basi cards, see *Independence*, Figures 28, 30 and 34).

Figure 19. *Ram and Tulsidas' Meeting.*
S.S. Brij Basi & Sons, Karachi, c. 1928.
Coloured real photograph of painting,
Divided back, 13.3 x 8.7 cm, 5.24 x 3.43 in.

Figure 20. *Lord Krishna.* S.S. Brij Basi & Sons, Karachi, c. 1928. Coloured real photograph of painting, Divided back, 13.8 x 8.65 cm, 5.43 x 3.41 in.

[*Verso, pencil*] "A god" [*Verso, blindstamped*] C.A. Rangamathanh, Glass and Picture Merchants, 143 Devancha Anjali St. [?] P.T. Madras.

Brij Basi claimed that "Pictures listed below are printed in a famous German workshop and are by photographic machines and the paper used is very good quality, thick and glossy. Further they are printed in attractive colours and have a 'wonderful brightness'."[3]

SINDH

The province of Sindh, on both banks of the Indus river stretching four hundred miles north of Karachi, was much older than its later capital. How old, precisely, was settled in 1924 with the discovery of the ancient metropolis of Mohenjo-daro in central Sindh. *Excavations on the Stupa Mound, Mohenjodaro* (Figure 21) and *First Street peopled to show its width* (Figure 22) are from original photographs taken by the Archaeological Survey of India teams excavating here after the first promising trenches sunk by the

Excavations on the Stupa Mound, Mohenjodaro.

Figure 21. *Excavations on the Stupa Mound, Mohenjodaro.* Archaeological Survey of India?, c. 1935. Halftone, Divided back, 14 x 8.85 cm, 5.51 x 3.48 in.

John Marshall, who led the work here, wrote: "A considerable number of buildings separated from each other by streets and lanes have been excavated in the southern portion of the stupa mound... The terrain here descends more or less abruptly to the south, where a narrow valley cut by rain separates this area from another, Area L, immediately to the south of it. No definite connection has yet been established between the two areas by excavation."[4]

First Street peopled to show its width, Mohenjodaro.

Figure 22. *First Street peopled to show its width, Mohenjodaro.* Archaeological Survey of India?, c. 1935. Halftone, Divided back, 14 x 8.9 cm, 5.51 x 3.50 in.

archaeologist Rakhaldas Banerji in the winter of 1922–23. Today we take the ancient Indus Valley civilization for granted, equal in scope and antiquity to ancient Egypt and Mesopotamia. But this was contrary to received 19th century European opinion – India's firmly dated history was pushed backed 2,000 years by these discoveries. Planned cities with advanced sanitation, beautiful seals and sumptuous jewellery in 2500 BCE were a big shift in historical and political perspective. Being able to show the greatness of ancient India added to the desire for freedom[5] (the British had little equivalent to show during their Bronze Age).

My first visit to Mohenjo-daro was as a teenager, when we came as guests of a feudal lord and were allowed to recklessly dig for an hour on an unexcavated mound of unknown antiquity (I still have pottery fragments from that visit). Mohenjo-daro was a stunningly eerie city that way. That visit, together with many to the other Indus city in Punjab, Harappa, sparked a lifelong fascination with ancient Indus culture that included my starting a website on the subject over twenty years ago. The absolute lack of knowledge regarding the 'original' Indian urban culture that came up in Sindh was far too intriguing for me not to investigate. There is no information about the name of a single ruler, nor does a single word from its language survive. Its script remains undecipherable despite years of scholarly effort. There must be strong connections to Hinduism and its reverence for water – Mohenjo-daro is a city of wells and a Great Bath – but what were they?

Persian Wheels, all over Indus (Figure 23) speaks to the resilience of age-old methods. "Persian" is a misnomer; the traditional waterwheel method of lifting water probably comes from the area; it went to Persia and then came back centuries later under a new name.

Figure 23. *Persian Wheels, all over Indus.* R. Jalbhoy, Karachi, c. 1905. Halftone, Divided back, 13.9 x 8.7 cm, 5.47 x 3.43 in.

Figure 24. *On the Indus, Looking Towards Sukkur Bridge.* Fred Bremner, Lahore and Quetta, c. 1903. Collotype, Undivided back, 14 x 8.85 cm, 5.51 x 3.48 in.

The photograph behind the postcards was probably shot on inauguration day, March 25, 1889. To set up this shot would have taken Fred Bremner's compositional skills and the dexterity of boatmen whose livelihoods were about to be much diminished by the trains seen behind them.

Figure 25. *Landsdowne Bridge, Sukkur.* Moorli Dhur & Sons, Ambala, c. 1908. Coloured halftone, Divided back, 13.9 x 8.8 cm, 5.47 x 3.46 in.

LLOYDS BARRAGE – SUKKUR

Figure 26. *Lloyds Barrage – Sukkur.* New Book Co., Bombay, c. 1940. Real photo postcard, Divided back, 13.95 x 8.95 cm, 5.49 x 3.52 in.

SADH BELA BUILT IN THE INDUS – SUKKUR

Figure 27. *Sadh Bela Built in the Indus – Sukkur.* New Book Co., Bombay, c. 1940. Real photo postcard, Divided back, 13.9 x 8.9 cm, 5.47 x 3.50 in.

Bremner's *On the Indus, Looking Towards Sukkur Bridge* (Figure 24) is a fine contrast between old and new. In the foreground is a fisherman's boat, of the same type that was used in ancient Indus times. Long geometric poles reach like straws outside the frame. In the distance are the steel girders of the Landsdowne Bridge, inaugurated on March 25th, 1889. *Landsdowne Bridge, Sukkur* (Figure 25), was the longest cantilever bridge in the world, at the time, permitting railway traffic to go straight over the northern head of the Indus river.

The biggest structural change to the area however came with the opening of *Lloyds Barrage – Sukkur* (Figure 26) in 1932, then the largest irrigation project in history, bringing over 6 million acres under cultivation through a series of canals, some of which are longer and larger than the Suez Canal.

Sadh Bela Built in the Indus – Sukkur (Figure 27) is a small island with a Hindu temple on it that looked much like this when I visited it, drawn by stories of events in 1947 when many Hindu families took refuge here before returning to their homes. Now the community to support the temple had shrunk so much that the priest pressed a booklet from the library into my hands, as if saying that I should take it, for it may not last here.

Among the oldest people in the province were the *Hindoo Fakirs* (Figure 28) in a postcard also found in the Prince of Wales album, see *Bombay*). *Fakirs* are often isolated from their surroundings by photographers, the focus on their long hair, sparse clothing, body paint and piercings. Instead, Bremner shows them with the instruments they used to offer music, poetry and spiritual guidance, woven into the social tapestry of food and shelter that sustained them.

Figure 28. *Hindoo Fakirs.*
Bremner No. 44, Quetta, c. 1903.
Collotype, Undivided back,
13.95 x 9.05 cm, 5.49 x 3.56 in.

Then there were those who were evolving: the *Natives of Sindh (Amil Rage)*
(Figure 29). Every person in this literate Hindu caste of officials and traders in
Hyderabad is wearing at least one Western article.

Shikarpore Bazaar (Figure 30) shows a wealthy town not far from Sukkur dominated
by families who made a living trading with relatives in Kandahar, Afghanistan. The
British rarely ventured into Shikarpur judging from the limited imagery and writings
about it they left behind. The bazaar is captivating. Once you walk in, is there a way
out? If Karachi postcards pushed the new and modern, ones of Sindh captured the
historical shafts through which the present travelled.

Figure 29. *Natives of Sind (Amil Rage.).* Bremner No. 44, Quetta,
c. 1903. Collotype, Undivided back, 13.9 x 8.95 cm, 5.47 x 3.52 in.

Postmarked Karachi, Nov. 11, 1904. Addressed to Miss Vasey, Edwardes
Road, Rawal Pindi. [*Recto*] "Choose your particular fancy C.W."

Figure 30. *Shikarpore Bazaar.* Bremner, Lahore, c. 1903. Collotype,
Divided back, 13.9 x 8.9 cm, 5.47 x 3.50 in.

This striking image was also published in a 1924 issue of *National
Geographic Magazine.*[6]

BALOCHISTAN

West of Sindh, a British official, Sir Robert Sandeman (1835–1892) cobbled together the vast arid areas bordering western Iran and southern Afghanistan. The mound of Quetta ("fort") was obtained on lease by Sandeman from the Khan of Kalat in 1876, a man who had long paid tribute to the ruler of Afghanistan. Sandeman made Quetta the capital of eight hundred thousand tribesmen and farmers scattered over an area larger than the British Isles. Welcome to "British Baluchistan."

Fred Bremner moved his studio to Quetta from Karachi in the early 1890s and seems to have been the area's first postcard publisher as well. One of his earliest cards, a composite of three photographs called *Armed Afghan Tribes* (Figure 31), combined words and figures to spark fascination. These were the men that the British in India most feared, having fought two bloody wars in Afghanistan—one in 1842 (lost), another in 1878-1880 (won at great cost). Afghans were taken to be the toughest of all fighters the British had to deal with.[7]

Bremner, Quetta.

ARMED AFGHAN TRIBES.

Figure 31. *Armed Afghan Tribes.* Fred Bremner, Quetta, c. 1902. Collotype, Undivided back, 13.9 x 8.95 cm, 5.47 x 3.52 in.

Postmarked Dec. 22, 1902, Madhopur. Addressed to Captain H. Stemson, Sheffield, England.

[*Recto*] "With our warm regards, wishing you a Happy and bright year. Wishing you are all well Madhopur, near Pathankote."

Bremner chose the same triptych for his autobiography *My Forty Years in India* (1940).

Another Bremner standard was *Baluchistan (Brahui) Tribes* (Figure 32). The long tresses of Balochi tribesman were a novel sight to newcomers. Brahuis were the dominant Balochi tribe, distinct from Pathans in the Northwest Frontier and other parts of Balochistan. They spoke a Dravidian language similar to those used in South India today (and, archaeologists speculate, related to the still unknown language spoken in ancient Mohenjo-daro). The nominal ruler of the Brahui factions was the *Khan of Kalat and Sirdars, Baluchistan* (Figure 33), shown here in a postcard probably published soon after a March 6th, 1906 meeting between Sir Henry MacMahon (1862–1949), later Chief Commissioner of Baluchistan, and Mir Mahmud of Kalat.

BALUGHISTAN (BRAHUI) TRIBES.

Khan of Kalat and Sirdars, Baluchistan.

Figure 32. *Baluchistan (Brahui) Tribes.* Bremner, Quetta, c. 1903. Collotype, Undivided back, 13.85 x 8.9 cm, 5.45 x 3.50 in.

[*Recto, Handwritten*] "Some handsome types! Don't you think so?"

BELOW
Figure 33. *Khan of Kalat and Sirdars, Baluchistan.* Bremner, Lahore and Quetta, c. 1902. Collotype, Undivided back, 14.1 x 9 cm, 5.55 x 3.54 in.

Mir Mahmud had taken over after his father, Khudadad Khan, had both his Prime Minister and his son executed for treachery in 1893.

Postmarked Quetta, March 7, 1906 and sent to Mr. Ralph Benton in Washington D.C., USA.

[*Recto*] "Quetta, Baluchistan Agency, British India, March 6, 1906.

"This chap, the one in the middle of the front row, and a lot of the other chiefs (sirdars) arrived today, to meet me – an'th'Prince uv Wails uv course! The place is full of gay costumed and strange looking people bent on the same errand! Your father, Frank Benton." The sender is apparently an American making fun of British accents with his spelling.

Figure 34. *Kalat. Kalat Miri & City Gate.* R.W. Rai & Sons, Quetta, c. 1905. Collotype, Divided back, 14.05 x 9.05 cm, 5.53 x 3.56 in.

Figure 35. *A Brahui Chief.* N. D. Batra, Quetta, c. 1905. Collotype, Divided back, 13.55 x 8.85 cm, 5.33 x 3.48 in.

This postcard also has the initials K.C.M. for K.C. Marrott, a Karachi photographer who seems to have supplied signed postcard images to a number of publishers.

Kalat. Kalat Miri & City Gate (Figure 34) is one of those postcards that seem to align, at least for me, with what we know of ancient Indus cities and gateways.

Balochis were a distinct postcard "type." *A Brahui Chief* (Figure 35) and others [8] have rulers next to them to measure their height, a privilege that befell few others during the Raj (the Andaman Islanders come to mind). Another postcard, *A Human Nest in Baluchistan* (Figure 36) used an odd but then common phrase [9] that put the area's residents at the margins of the human race.

To be sure, stereotypes were not exclusively negative. Bremner's favourite photograph of a Balochi, which he printed on a full page in his autobiography, was the *A Baluchi Shepherd* (Figure 37). He said he saw something of Jesus of Nazareth in the pastoral figure. [10]

Mullick Brothers ('Artistic Photography') on Bruce Road in Quetta [11] were competitors to Bremner, responsible for gripping portraits like *A Baluch Dwarf* (Figure 38). A stalwart image they offered of the province was *The Chapper Rift Baluchistan* (Figure 39); crossing this rift with a steel bridge was a much-feted 19th century engineering feat. [12]

Figure 36. *A Human Nest in Baluchistan.* Mullick Brothers, Quetta, c. 1905. Collotype, Divided back, 13.8 x 8.9 cm, 5.43 x 3.50 in.

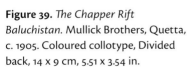

Figure 37. *A Baluchi Shepherd.* Bremner, Lahore, c. 1908. Collotype, Divided back, 13.8 x 8.7 cm, 5.43 x 3.43 in.

Postmarked Panjrai, May 25, 1907. Addressed to H. V. HEnshaw Esq., 200 Jameson Ave: Toronto Canada, from A. Alraham [sp?] Survey of India Quetta Baluchistan India. Another version of the card had this message: "A quaint looking object. The sheep are excellent eating."[13], a sentiment which Bremner shared: "Honestly I never tasted better [mutton] anywhere, not even Scotland."[14]

Figure 38. *A Baluch Dwarf.* Mullick Brothers, Quetta, c. 1905. *Mullick's Baluchistan Series, No. X.* Halftone, Divided back, 13.9 x 8.8 cm, 5.47 x 3.46 in.

Postmarked Manora, Karachi, April 9, 1909, and addressed to Miss Bella Mouer, 4 Weston Terrace, Weston St [?], Sheffield, England.
[*Verso*] "15.4.09 Manora. Dear Bella Pleased to say I am still keeping in good health and hope all at home are the same, also that the weather has taken a turn for the better so that you can go out more neal turn [sp?] Hoping you are keeping well. Percy"

Figure 39. *The Chapper Rift Baluchistan.* Mullick Brothers, Quetta, c. 1905. Coloured collotype, Divided back, 14 x 9 cm, 5.51 x 3.54 in.

Sandeman wanted to build a line to quickly move troops to the Afghan frontier in Chaman, 60 miles from Quetta. The route led over the Chopa Rift, "the shoulder of a mountain which has the appearance of being cracked from top to bottom."[15] The Louise Margaret Bridge over the Chopa Rift kept being washed away by floods and was abandoned in the 1940s.

Figure 40. *Khojak Tunnel.* Bremner, Lahore and Quetta, c. 1902. Collotype, Undivided back, 14.15 x 8.9 cm, 5.57 x 3.50 in.

Figure 41. *Khojak Tunnel.* K.C. Marrott, Karachi, c. 1905. Collotype, Divided back, 13.8 x 8.9 cm, 5.43 x 3.50 in.

Bremner writes: "When I went to visit that part of the country there was at work a party of about thirty British miners, who were helped by hundreds of Indians in the construction of what is known as the Khojak Tunnel, four miles in length, passing through the Khawaja range. These European miners were being handsomely paid. They were a somewhat rough lot, but from all accounts very kindly disposed. Usually they had on pay day what might be termed a "burst up" – quite jolly and revelling in drinking bottles of beer."

Figure 42. *Khojak Tunnel by the end Baluchistan.* Mullick Brothers (*verso* initialed K.C.M.), Quetta, c. 1905. Collotype, Divided back, 13.7 x 8.9 cm, 5.39 x 3.50 in.

Figure 43. *Bolan Railway, near Panir.* Bremner, Lahore, c. 1908. Collotype, Divided back, 13.75 x 8.8 cm, 5.41 x 3.46 in.

Indeed, the railways creeping through the province was a common postcard motif. The photograph for *Khojak Tunnel* (Figure 40) was probably taken on inauguration day in 1892. It shows the entrance to the tunnel that exits just before the Afghan border at Chaman. *Khojak Tunnel* (Figure 41) features the men who built it, some of them European miners brought here especially for the purpose. *Khojak Tunnel by the end Baluchistan* (Figure 42) with its gun slits reminds us of what a violent intrusion into the landscape and culture the railway line actually was. The fortified tunnel is almost 2.5 miles in length and passes through the mountains in *Bolan Railway, near Panir* (Figure 43). Apparently, as the two halves of the tunnel, each bored from one side, were coming together in the middle, the fit was not perfect and adjustments had to be made beneath the hill. Khojak station was named Shelabagh, or "Shela's garden" after a dancer who caught the workers' fancy.[16] As far as I know, she did not make it on to a postcard.

FRUIT MARKET, QUETTA.

Figure 44. *Fruit Market, Quetta.* Bremner, Lahore, c. 1903. Collotype, Undivided back, 13.55 x 8.85 cm, 5.33 x 3.48 in.

One of Bremner's most popular views was *Fruit Market, Quetta* (Figure 44).[17] Density, darkness and detail combine in the full collotype effect. Note the tiny markers of European presence like the [*Jab*]*bar Khan Fruit Seller* sign in the top left. The Urdu beneath also uses the English words "fruit seller." Between the grapes is a Victorian oil lamp.

Bruce Road, QUETTA (Figure 45) was the town's main commercial area, here on a busy day complete with five men watching the action from the rooftop in the foreground. It did not seem much larger when I spent a week in Quetta in 1991

Figure 45. *Bruce Road, QUETTA.* Mullick Brothers, Quetta, c. 1905. Collotype, Divided back, 13.5 x 8.8 cm, 5.31 x 3.46 in.

Figure 46. "*Earthquake Quetta 1935*" [pencilled on back]. Unknown Publisher, c. 1935. Real photo postcard, Divided back, 13.85 x 8.9 cm, 5.45 x 3.50 in.

driving around in a forty-year old Mercedes like the one we once had in Vienna, visiting old cemeteries and Parsee families who remembered pre-Partition days. In particular they remembered *that* day, May 31st, 1935, when one of the most devastating earthquakes of the Raj struck Quetta, killing almost 10,000 people. Whole street sides collapsed. Lost to posterity was Sandeman Memorial Hall in *"Earthquake in Quetta 1935"* (Figure 46). Built in 1899, it was another Taj-inspired structure, this one used to bring Balochi tribes together each year to mediate disputes. *The Residency, Quetta* (Figure 47), "one of the prettiest official residencies in India" according to the *Imperial Gazetteer*,[18] was also destroyed.

The Residency Quetta

Figure 47. *The Residency, Quetta.* Mullick Brothers, Photographers, Quetta, c. 1905. Coloured collotype, Divided back, 14.1 x 9 cm, 5.55 x 3.54 in.

The rulers of Kalat—one of whom, Mohammed Azam Jan Khan is shown in *The Khan of Kalat 1932* (Figure 48) —always had a difficult relationship with the British[19]. In 1947, the reigning Khan first chose not to join Pakistan, but was compelled by force to change his mind. Smaller civil wars have followed regularly, and the province remains the scene of a separatist struggle unfolding in the shadow of the conflicts in Afghanistan.

If Sindh reflects historical persistence, Balochistan, perhaps home to even older cultures, reflects historical endings. Travelling through the province by car, one passes by mound after abandoned mound by the side of the road, starting just outside Quetta at *The Hanna Pass Baluchistan* (Figure 49). Covered in sun-bleached mud, they are testimony to a time when there was much more water available, vegetation and towns bloomed, and a rich trade passed between Indus and western cities beyond the Balochi mountains.

Figure 48. *The Khan of Kalat Quetta 1932*
[*Verso in pencil*]. Unknown Publisher, 1932.
Real photo postcard, Divided back,
13.8 x 8.5 cm, 5.43 x 3.35 in.

The Hanna Pass Baluchistan

Figure 49. *The Hanna Pass Baluchistan.* Mullick Brothers, Photographers, Quetta, c. 1910. Coloured collotype, Divided back, 13.95 x 9 cm, 5.49 x 3.54 in.

Notes

1. Christoper Pinney, *'Photos of the Gods'* (London: Reaktion Books Ltd, 2004), p. 83.

2. Ibid., p. 90-91. Ghasiram was once accused of having been inspired by Ravi Varma postcards.

3. Pinney, op. cit., p. 86. The author cites and thanks L.S. Garg for making this information available to him.

4. John Marshall, *The Indus Civilization*, , Vol. I (London: Arthur Probsthain, 1931), p. 145.

5. See for example, Nayanjot Lahiri's *Finding Forgotten Cities*, Permanent Black, 2006.

6. *National Geographic*, November 1924. Together with an image of a Kashmiri *nautch* girl, it was reprinted by the same magazine in 2001. The images were purchased for the magazine by Maynard Owen Williams in India in 1920.

7. As Kipling put it "When you're wounded and left on Afghanistan's plains, And the women come out to cut up what remains, Jest roll to your rifle and blow out your brains."

8. For example, *Masori Bugti Baluch* in the author's collection.

9. Bremner also had his "A Human Nest," (Pathan Woman & Child), Bremner, Quetta, No. 20. A later Mullick Brothers real photo postcard of *A Human Nest . . .* was titled *After Their Days Work*, Baluchis Tribe.

10. Bremner had a very similar postcard with *In the Nishat Bagh, Kashmir.*

11. Mullick Brothers was founded in the 1890s and thrived as army photographers through the 1940s. Omar Khan, "War Photography in 19th Century India and Afghanistan," in *Reverie and Reality*, (San Francisco: Fine Arts Museums, 2003), p. 153.

12. For example, see *Scientific American Supplement*, No. 704, June 29, 1889.

13. Robert Scoales Collection, sent by H.J. (?) from Quetta on the 10th of August (?) 1904.

14. Fred Bremner, *My Forty Years in India*, Banff Scotland, 1940, p. 32.

15. *A Handbook for travellers in India, Burma, and Ceylon... etc.*, London/Calcutta, John Murray/Thacker, Spink & Co., 1926, pp. 272, 411.

16. "Owais Mughal," article in http://pakistaniat.com/2006/12/18/railways-khojak-tunnel accessed Sept. 18, 2010

17. Fourteen of 60 photographs in the Baluchistan section of the well-distributed compendium *The Bombay Presidency The United Provinces The Punjab, Etc. Their History, Commerce and Natural Resources* by Somerset Playne (1917–1920) were credited to Bremner including this one.

18. *Imperial gazetteer of India: Provincial series*, Baluchistan, Superintendent of Government Printing, Kolkata, 1908, p. 77.

19. The current Khan of Kalat is in exile in London.

Künstler-Postkarten v einer Weltreise № 7 Ges gesch.

DAS THOR VON JEYPORE.

Verlag von Jos. Heim, Wien IV.

Jeypore
[Jaipur]

Today's celebrity wedding destination, Jaipur, has a past firmly rooted in palaces, dancing girls, astronomy and the colour pink. Probably the earliest postcards of Jaipur, "one of the most beautiful cities in India"[1] according to Thomas Cook's century-old India guides, are in Joseph Hoffmann's 1898 India series (see Chapter 2). One is the luminous sandstone city gate, *The Gate of Jaipur* (Figure 1). A second, *Girl's School in Jaipur* (Figure 2), may have been intended to communicate the modernism of the city's rulers.[2]

Jaipur—the capital of the princely state of Rajasthan, was ruled by a family with a photographic tradition that reached deep into their palace, the Hawa Mahal (Figure 16). Maharajah Sawai Ram Singh II, who reigned from 1835 until 1880, produced collections that included the women in his *zenana* and "a set of rooms, courtyards, terraces and other areas reserved exclusively for women."[3] This photography was considered a highly progressive move, "completely without precedent."[4]

His son and successor, Sir Sawai Madho Singh (1862–1922) is dressed for the 1903 Coronation Darbar in *His Highness the Maharajah Sahib Bahadoor. Jaipur* (Figure 3).[5] This postcard is by the firm Gobind Ram and Oodey Ram, a father and son team that ran the pre-eminent Jaipur photography studio at the turn of the century. It had close royal connections[6] in a city with no major European-run studios. *Showroom and Workshop Gobind Ram and Oodey Ram, Artists, Jaipur* (Figure 4) is, in fact, one of the very rare such postcards showing a firm's place of business. Inside, portraits like *Snake Charmer* (Figure 5) were made, the soft floral backdrop reinforcing the sense of snakes emerging gracefully from their basket. The firm described itself as 'Artists' for good reason.

Figure 1. *Das Thor von Jeypore* [*The Gate of Jaipur*]. *Artist Cards from a World Tour 1898, #7.* Josef Hoffmann [signed], Joseph Heim, Vienna, Austria, 1898. Lithograph, Undivided back, 14 x 9.05 cm, 5.51 x 3.56 in.

Kunstler-Postkarten v einer Weltreise № 2 Ges gesch

MÄDCHENSCHULE IN JEYPORE.

Verlag von Jos Heim, W

Figure 2. *Madschenschule in Jeypore [Girl's School in Jaipur]. Artist Cards from a World Tour 1898, #2.* Josef Hoffmann [signed], Joseph Heim, Vienna, Austria, 1898. Lithograph, Undivided back, 14.15 x 9.01 cm, 5.57 x 3.55 in.

Postmarked Salzburg, Austria in 1899 to Miss Karolia Ziegler in Salzburg. [*Recto, in German*] "Liebste Lina, Einstweilen besten Dank fuer die mir gesandte Karte. Freute Mich, dass auch Du meiner noch nicht ganz vergessen hattest. Hoffentlich geht es dir samt deinen werten Eltern und Schwestern gut. Ob dir diese Karte gefaellt weiss ich nicht. Zum Schluss sei herzlich gegrusst von deiner Marie Nobhauer Grusse an deine wertern Eltern und Schwestern. Marie Neubauer." [Dearest Lina. Many thanks for the card you sent me. Made me happy that you have not completely forgotten me. Hopefully you and your parents and sister are doing well. I don't know if you will like this card. Finally many greetings from Marie Neubauer as well, and she too greets your parents and your sister.]

Gobindram Oodeyram, Artists, Jaipur.   H. H. The Maharaja of Jaipur

Figure 3. *His Highness the Maharajah Sahib Bahadoor. Jaipur.* Gobindram Oodeyram, Artists, Jaipur, c. 1905. Coloured collotype, Divided back, 13.85 x 8.8 cm, 5.45 x 3.46 in.

Sawai Madho Singh II, Maharajah of Jaipur (1880–1922), had five wives and no children with them, and sixty-five children with his concubines, an intentional strategy in order to preserve the ability to make his choice of heir by adoption from a noble family, which he did, just as he had been chosen by his father, the photographer Maharajah Sawai Ram Singh II.

Showroom and Workshop, Gobind Ram and Oodey Ram, Artists, Jaipur.

Figure 4. *Showroom and Workshop Gobind Ram and Oodey Ram, Artists, Jaipur.* Gobind Ram and Oodey Ram, Jaipur, c. 1905. Collotype, Undivided back, 14.1 x 8.85 cm, 5.55 x 3.48 in.

"The father-and-son team of Gobindram and Oodeyram became, in the late nineteenth century, the leading photographic firm in Jaipur," writes Sophie Gordon.[17] The firm lasted into the 1970s. Later postcards from around 1930 have Oodey Ram Badripershad, Artists, Photographers and Photo Dealers, Ajmer Road, Jaipur in electrotype on the back.

Gobindram Oodeyram, Jaipur.　　Snake Charmer.　Jaipur.

Figure 5. *Snake Charmer. Jaipur.* Gobindram Oodeyram, Jaipur, c. 1905. Collotype, Divided back, 14.05 x 8.8 cm, 5.53 x 3.46 in.

They probably came to postcards early[7] – the lithograph *D [P]assenger Cart* (Figure 6) seems to have been printed in India, a compelling glimpse of the rural poor in the sprawling state of Rajasthan during what were trying times. In 1900 for example, just as the plague debilitated Mumbai (Chapter 3), an unrelated famine claimed ten percent of Jaipur's population of 160,000. The billowing sacks that dwarf the driver in *Grain Cart* (Figure 7) seem to manifest preciousness in a time of scarcity.

One of the things I like best about the firm are the many postcards of traditional artisans and workers at task, whether in *Potter. Jaipur* (Figure 8), where the scene has remained unchanged for five thousand years (the potter's lineage may be equally old) or *Astronom (Jeshi) School teacher. Jaipur* (Figure 9).

DASSENGER CART.   G. &. O. JAIPUR

Figure 6. *Passenger Cart.* G. & O. [Gobind Ram Oodey Ram], Jaipur, c. 1902. Lithograph, Undivided back, 13 x 9.1 cm, 5.12 x 3.58 in.

Postmarked April 3 1905[?] in Cork (?) to Sister Mary Joseph at St. Mary's Convent, S. Ascot, Berkshire, England.

[*Verso*] "I am sorry I have not written before. I am having lovely painting lessons twice a week. That is all I do in the way of lessons. With best love from Frances."

There are also completely unexpected postcards, like *Elephant fight. Jaipur* (Figure 10), an event almost never photographed.[8]

One of the most interesting postcard albums I have is a paper reconstruction of an album put together by one S. Annlickar. Called *1901 – 1905 Few Paintings from Gobinda Ram & Ooday-Ram-Of Jaipur Postcards – & Photographs,* it turned up at an auction a decade ago,[9] and I seized it as homage to a great studio by a local rather than a foreign collector. It is as revealing of its owner's mind as the royal album (see *Bombay, Lahore*) is of its.

Figure 7. *Grain Cart.* G. & O. [Gobind Ram Oodey Ram], Jaipur, c. 1902.
Lithograph, Undivided back,
11.8 x 9 cm, 4.65 x 3.54 in.
[*Recto*] "Happy Xmas 1902."

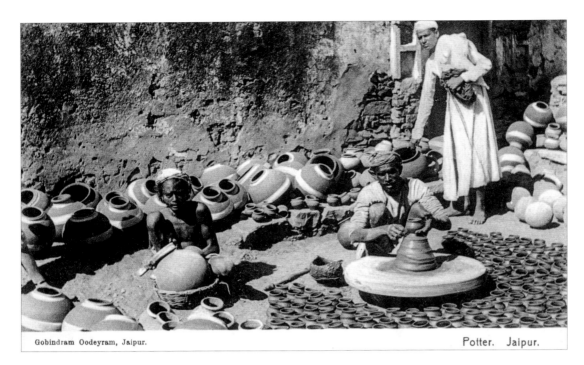

Gobindram Oodeyram, Jaipur.   Potter.   Jaipur.

Figure 8. *Potter. Jaipur.* Gobindram
Oodeyram, Jaipur. c. 1905. Collotype,
Divided back, 14 x 8.85 cm, 5.51 x 3.48 in.

Gobindram Oodeyram, Jaipur.   Astronom (Jeshi) School teacher. Jaipur.

Figure 9. *Astronom (Jeshi) School teacher.
Jaipur.* Gobindram Oodeyram, Jaipur,
c. 1905. Collotype, Divided back,
14.15 x 9.15 cm, 5.57 x 3.60 in.

Gobindram Oodeyram, Jaipur.

Elephant fight. Jaipur.

Figure 10. *Elephant Fight. Jaipur.*
Gobindram Oodeyram, Jaipur,
c. 1905. Collotype, Divided back,
14 x 8.8 cm, 5.51 x 3.46 in.

Figure 11. *Dancing Girls. Jaipur.*
Gobindram Oodeyram, Jaipur, c. 1905.
Coloured collotype, Undivided back,
13.65 x 8.9 cm, 5.37 x 3.50 in.

Part of the man holding the cloth
backdrop is visible on the left. The
association of Rajasthan and women
of pleasure was not helped when,
during Viceroy Curzon's reign, he had to
intervene in the matter of the Maharajah
of nearby Jodhpur embarking on "a
carnival of drinking and unnatural vice"[18]
that led to his removal when even his
own Sirdars rose in opposition.

Nautch

It opens with a postcard of "Krishna, his consort and cow," followed by a little child suckling a goat, the firm's storefront (Figure 4), and then *Dancing Girls. Jaipur* (Figure 11, here in a colour version)—among the most popular of the firm's postcards.[10] One of the reasons Sawai Ram Singh II may have wanted to highlight the respectable side of his zenana through photography had to do with the association of *nautch* girls with Jaipur.[11] Together with the religious postcards, *nautch* postcards are the dominant theme of the Annlickar album, and they were Gobind Ram and Oodey Ram staples. Uniquely, Annlickar distinguishes some postcards as "India Circulation," and others "Circulation Inland/Foreign." The album's 5th image, *Sleeping Hindoo woman* (Figure 12, later more widely called *Jaipur woman*), like the one before it also of "dancing girls," is labeled "India Circulation." The *nautch* postcard market segment crossed Indian and British lines. *Sleeping Hindoo Woman* is among the few examples of a woman lying down, bare foot to the sky, about as risqué as one could get at the time.

Gobindram Oodeyram, Jaipur.   Jaipur Woman.

Figure 12. *Sleeping Hindoo Woman.* Gobindram Oodeyram, Jaipur, c. 1905. Collotype, Divided back, 14 x 8.7 cm, 5.51 x 3.43 in.

A version of the postcard titled *Jaipur Woman*, postmarked in Oakland, California on May 11th, 1956 to a Miss Ruth Teiser, 932 Vallejo Street, San Francisco 11, California, has this typewritten message on the back "I've been told that you Americans have an old saying 'There's always room for one more.' I am hoping this is true of the GP Homecoming. G.O."

Figure 13. *Dancing Girls. Jaipur.*
Gobindram Oodeyram, Jaipur, c. 1905.
Coloured collotype, Divided back,
14.1 x 8.75 cm, 5.55 x 3.44 in.

Figure 14. *Dancing Girl – Jaipur.*
Gobind Ram & Oodey Ram #92, Jaipur,
c. 1910. Collotype, Divided back,
14.05 x 9.05 cm, 5.53 x 3.56 in.

The seventh image in S. Annlickar's album, and the first on a page of its own, is *Dancing Girls. Jaipur* (Figure 13, again in a colour version). It probably shows a mother and daughter. The older woman's face gives a sense of the tremendous wear of the profession, echoed in the revealing *Dancing Girl – Jaipur* (Figure 14).

My own favorite among Gobindram Oodeyram's *nautch* postcards is the striking *Maina Dancing Girls* (Figure 15). The pink colour in this and many others of the firm's postcards comes from the effort by Maharajah Sawai Ram Singh II to paint the

Gobindram Oodeyram, Jaipur.   Maina Dancing Girls. Jaipur.

Figure 15. *Maina Dancing Girls. Jaipur.* Gobindram Oodeyram, Jaipur, c. 1905. Hand-tinted collotype, Divided back, 14.15 x 9 cm, 5.57 x 3.54 in.

major buildings in the city pink. Apparently chosen to evoke Mughal sandstone and hospitality when the city was beautified in honour of Prince Albert's visit in 1876, the local oxide compound used turned out to be very durable and became the city's brand colour.[12] The firm used the same pink tint in their coloured carte-des-visites of *nautch* girls,[13] suggesting that it was added to the postcards in India. Sometimes the stencil could be a little off, as on the yellow cuffs around the horses legs in *A Jaipur Sardar* (Figure 16). The dyes probably came from Europe however, for the pink-red, green and gold hues look the same as those in French postcards.[14]

Gobindram Oodeyram. Jaipur.

A Jaipur Sardar.

Figure 16. *A Jaipur Sardar.* Gobindram Oodeyram, Jaipur, c. 1905. Coloured collotype, Divided back, 14.15 x 8.85 cm, 5.57 x 3.48 in.

Gobindram Oodeyram, Artists, Jaipur. Principal Palace Gate, Jaipur

Figure 17. *Principal Palace Gate, Jaipur.*
Gobindram Oodeyram, Jaipur, c. 1905.
Coloured collotype, Divided back,
13.8 x 8.85 cm, 5.43 x 3.48 in.

BELOW
Figure 18. *Female Chariot, Jaipur.*
Gobindram Oodeyram, Jaipur, c. 1905.
Coloured collotype, Divided back,
13.8 x 8.9 cm, 5.43 x 3.50 in.

The heavy curtains were used to hide
women of the *zenana* from the eyes
of strangers. Well-preserved colour
postcards like this are rare.

Gobindram Oodeyram, Artists, Jaipur. Female Chariot, Jaipur

There are also subtle uses of pink, like the little swabs in *Principal Palace Gate, Jaipur* (Figure 17) instead of the thick application in *Female Chariot, Jaipur* (Figure 18). More restrained and typical is *Manak Chowk, Jaipur* (Figure 19), where the building planes have been subject to a swoosh.

Tuck's nearly identical view– *Jeypore. Street Scene* (Figure 20) does not quite follow brand guidelines, and also shows how the halftone loses some of the collotype's crispness. Which was taken first? It is hard to tell—the season aside, the trees are at similar stages of growth. The variation of stalls in the foreground does not seem conclusive. Both shots would have been taken from the pink palace in *Jeypore. The Chowk and Hawa Mahal* (Figure 21). This was one of Tuck's most popular views in

Gobindram Oodeyram, Artists, Jaipur.   Manak Chowk, Jaipur

Figure 19. *Manak Chowk, Jaipur.* Gobindram Oodeyram, Artists, Jaipur, c. 1905. Coloured collotype, Divided back, 13.85 x 8.9 cm, 5.45 x 3.50 in.

Figure 20. *Jeypore. Street Scene.* Raphael Tuck & Sons #7023, London, c. 1905. Coloured halftone, Divided back, 5.43 x 3.44 in.

[*Verso*] "**Street Scene**. The city of Jeypore, situated 850 miles north-west of Calcutta, is handsomely and regularly built, and is the most important centre of Rajputana. It is comparatively of recent birth, being only founded in 1728. Amber, the ancient and now deserted capital, is five miles distant."

[*Verso continued from another card*] "hours, we want salt make Kings Rum [sp?], I will write you a long letter next week and let you know how I have been enjoying myself this Xmas I will close now with wishing you a very Happy New Year from yours always xx [kisses] Sincerely. xx G.E. Flanagan xxx."

JEYPORE. STREET SCENE.

JEYPORE. THE CHOWK AND HOWA MAHAL.

The Hawa Mahal, Jeypore.

Figure 21. *Jeypore. The Chowk and Hawa Mahal.* Raphael Tuck & Sons #7023, London, c. 1905. Coloured halftone, Divided back, 5.43 x 3.44 in.

[*Verso*] "**The Chowk and Hawa Mahal**. This is a picturesque and animated scene. The inhabitants of Jeypore are a busy people, and their bazaars are generally crowded. The continental business of Jeypore is chiefly banking and exchange, a capital of over 7,000,000 [sterling] being engaged."

Figure 22. *The Hawa Mahal. Jeypore.* c. 1905. Coloured halftone, Divided back, 14 x 8.9 cm, 5.51 x 3.50 in.

its Jaipur series. The red of the elephant coverings pulls the viewer's eye firmly to the life in the plaza below. Indeed, the square was all about looking. *The Hawa Mahal, Jeypore.* (Figure 22) was designed to allow women from the Maharajah's household to relieve their boredom by following the scene below.

When George and Mary came to Jaipur in November 1905—*Souvenir Card for the Prince and Princess of Wales visit to India in 1905-06* (Figure 23, see Chapter 3)—they sent their son Bertie, *My first tiger. Jaipur* (Figure 24). The triumph was probably carefully arranged by the Maharajah, but the Prince seems so much more human in the real photo-postcard.

Figure 23. *Souvenir Postcard in Commemoration of the Visit of Their Royal Highnesses the Prince and Princess of Wales visit to India in 1905-06. Dedicated by Special Permission to H.R.H. the Prince of Wales by His Royal Highness' most obedient servant, Raphael Tuck & Sons. Ltd.* Raphael Tuck & Sons #9153 "Souvenir Postcard," London, 1905. Coloured halftone, Divided back, 13.95 x 8.8 cm, 5.49 x 3.46 in.

A Tuck tour-de-force combining photography, painting and design elements. The Star of India is at the top, the royal vessel at the bottom.

Figure 24. *My first tiger. Jaipur.* 1905. Real photo postcard, Divided back, 13.65 x 8.75 cm, 5.37 x 3.44 in.

[Recto] "Jaipur. For dear Bertie with every good wish for Xmas & the New Year 1906 from yr [your] devoted Papa. My first tiger taken by Hamlett."

Credit: Postcard album compiled by King George V when Duke of York, 1905-6, The Royal Collection, RCIN 2587840, Windsor Castle.

Had the future George V visited Jaipur in the spring, he could have witnessed the annual *Sun procession – Jaipur* (Figure 25). Discontinued after 1949 when Rajasthan acceded to India, it celebrated the descent of the Maharajah's family from the sun goddess Surya. In fact, Jaipur's relationship to the heavens had many facets; from the laying of the main avenue on an East–West axis between "the gates of the sun and moon,"[15] (Figure 18) to Maharajah Sawai Ram Singh's personal fascination with astronomy. He had five observatories built across India in the 18th century, including ones in Varanasi and Delhi. When the *Astronomical Observatory – Jaipur* (Figure 26) was completed in 1734 it was the largest open-air observatory in the world and represented the junction of divine aspiration and terrestrial power (he had Jesuit priests from Europe check his astronomer's calculations). However, when the Maharajah died, the observatory fell into disrepair, and was not restored until 1901, when postcards like this helped make it into one of Jaipur's major attractions.

Gobind Ram & Oodey Ram, Jaipur

No. 16 - Sun procession - Jaipur.

Figure 25. *Sun procession – Jaipur.* Gobind Ram & Oodey Ram #10, Jaipur, c. 1910. Collotype, Divided back, 14 x 9 cm, 5.51 x 3.54 in.

Sent to Miss Rosemead in Sussex England.

[*Verso*] "3.3.32 Lahore. I hope you have received the air mail letter I sent off on Modaras with your birthday present. Am longing to get the mail this week to see if any more of you were silly enough to get chickenpox! Love from Mother."

Is the Maharajah in the picture? Sandria Freitag describes postcards like these by the firm invoking 'enacted space', referring to the relationship among different parts of the city expressed through processions and other programs.[19]

No. 19 - Astronomical Observatory - Jaipur.

Figure 26. *Astronomical Observatory – Jaipur.* Gobind Ram & Oodey Ram #19, Jaipur, c. 1910. Collotype, Divided back, 14 x 9 cm, 5.51 x 3.54 in.

The great Argentinean writer Julio Cortazar, who visited in the 1960s, described its marble instruments to track the sun as "an icy eroticism in the Jaipur night."[20]

Where did the Maharajahs actually end up? We might let Tuck's play the last card with the "picturesque" melancholy of *Jeypore. An Eastern Cemetery* (Figure 27). The caption celebrates the Rajputs as a "fine race [that] comes nearest in ideas, aspect, stature, demeanor, costume and equipage to those of European chivalry of the feudal times." The structures shown in this postcard are probably from Mandor near Jodhpur, and "contain the cenotaphs of the ruling chiefs of the country, erected in the spot where the funeral pyre consumed the remains of those who in former days seldom burned alone"[16]—a compromise between cremation and burial, traditional Hindu practices and Mughal tomb architecture.

JEYPORE. AN EASTERN CEMETERY.

Figure 27. *Jeypore. An Eastern Cemetery.* Raphael Tuck & Sons #7023, London, c. 1905. Coloured halftone, Divided back, 13.9 x 8.8 cm, 5.47 x 3.46 in.

[*Verso*] "**An Eastern Cemetery.** The cemeteries of Rajputana in which is situated the state of Jeypore, are as picturesque as all that surrounds the lives of the Rajputs. This fine race comes nearest in ideas, aspect, stature, demeanor, costume and equipage to those of European chivalry of the feudal times. The Rajput Princes claim to be descended from the Sun and Moon."

This card, blind stamped in Lucknow 7/3/12 from the G. Ammunition Column of the Royal Horse Artillery. The incomplete message continues in *Figure 14*, above: "My dear Molly received your cards & "Roster's [?] Football" last week, once again thanking you most kindly for your generosity in looking after me so, I shall not – forget – your"

Notes

1. *India, Burma and Ceylon. Information for Travellers and Residents,* (London: Thomas Cook and Son, 1923), p. 87.

2. Laura Weinstein, "Exposing the *Zenana*: Maharajah Sawai Ram Singh II's Photographs of Women in *Purdah*," in *History of Photography*, 34, 1, (London: Taylor and Francis, 2010), p. 7.

3. Ibid., p. 1.

4. Ibid.

5. The firm published the postcard *No. 1 – H.H. The Maharjah – Jaipur* showing Maharajah Sawai Madho Singh (Figure 3) as a teenager.

6. When Arch Duke Ferdinand of Austria visited in 1890 for example, the firm created the leather-bound album commemorating his visit. Numerous examples are given in Joachum Bautze's "Uncredited Photographs by Gobindram & Oodeyram," *Artibus Asiae*, Vol. 63, No. 2 (2003), pp. 223–246, although the author says that the firm was not attached to Maharajah Madho Singhji (1880-1922, p. 241).

7. Rare court-sized examples in the author's collection include a black and white small frame image of *His Highness the Majarajah of Udaipur*, signed G. & O. Jaipur and a similar *H.H. The Maharah of Jaipur*. I have not seen many court-sized G. & O. postcards, and Figure 4 is the only undivided back among the 18 different postcards in Annlickar's album.

8. Bautze, *op. cit.*, p. 22. He calls the postcard "a photographic re-edition" of an 18ᵗʰ century painting (p. 228).

9. It is labeled *Auction No – 3A (1) 2004.17.8* submitted by John Adams.

10. S. Annlickar's album is all black and white, suggesting that either the firm did not publish colour version of these collotypes till after 1905, the compiler did not like them, or they were too expensive. There are a total of 18 distinct postcards, six of which are religious, four *nautch*, and none of the Maharajah.

11. Laura Weinstein, op. cit.

12. http://www.2weekbackpack.com/Jaipur/Jaipur-Why-Painted-Pink-City.html

13. For example, http://www.bonhams.com/eur/auction/18061/lot/165/ seen July 4, 2011. **NAUTCH GIRLS** A pair of hand-coloured portraits showing *nautch* girls, carte-de-visite size on the cabinet cards of Gobind Ram and Oodey Ram of Jaipur, *coloured and heightened with gold over albumen prints, images approximately 95 x 62mm.,* 1870s (2).

14. See Leonard Pitt, *Postcards of Paris*, to compare colours. Another card of the same boy *Rajput feudal chief and his retainers – Jaipur* in Annlickar's album is labeled "Indian Circulation."

15. Edward Henry Nolan, *The Illustrated History of the British Empire in India and the East . . . to the suppression of the Sepoy Mutiny in 1859, . . .to the End of 1878* (1905 Edition), p. 303.

16. *The Rajputana Gazetteer, Volume 2* (Rajasthan: Superintendent of Government Printing, 1879), p. 262.

17. Sophie Gordon, "Checklist of the Exhibition," in Robert Flynn Johnson, *Nineteenth-Century Photographs of India from the Ehrenfeld Collection* (San Francisco: Fine Arts Museums, 2003), p. 175.

18. David Gilmour, *Curzon: Imperial Statesman* (New York: Farrar, Strauss and Giroux, 1994), p. 240.

19. Sandria Freitag, "Picturing Place in Popular Visual Culture," *Imagenaama*, I, 1, March-May 2013, pp. 40–41.

20. Julio Cortazar, *From the Observatory*, trans. Anne McLean (New York: Archipalego Books, 2011), p. 43.

A Group of School Girls

Madras

[Chennai]

Chennai is the city I know best in India, for this is where almost all my Tamil in-laws live, many of them women who, at different stages of their lives, could be staring at me from *A Group of School Girls* (Figure 1) or *A Little Brahmin Beauty, Madras* (Figure 2). Chennai is where my daughters spend their summers, and the intermingling of cultures is so well woven that my wife's family, before and after Partition, speaks English at the dinner table.

There is an immense energy contained within tradition, like the solidity of the thousand-year old *Madras Seven Pagodas* (Figure 3) in Mahabalipuram, or the 7th century Kapaleeshwaar Temple shown in *Siva Temple, Mylapore, Madras* (Figure 4), which has a *gopuram* or temple entrance like the one depicted on *Madras Entrance to Temple, Turi Kuli Kudram* (Figure 5). This was the first massive Hindu temple complex I ever visited. This was a real, living great bath. I found the tightly packed, multi-colour 3D gods colourful and satisfying, and the public celebrations of *Madras Hindu God Perumal Mahavellipuram* (Figure 6, at the city's major Vishnu temple) to be avoided. I much prefer a quiet little temple in an obscure corner of the city where one can hear the soft bells at dusk and the barefoot pitter-patter of supplicants, a moment evoked for me by *Wayside Temple. Madras* (Figure 7), with its majestic tree, shadows and children.

The modern story of South India starts with the battles embossed on *Lord Clive Boldly and Sincerely. Pondicherry Tanjore Arcot Hugli Calcutta Chandernapore Plassey* (Figure 8). Each is a place where Robert "Clive of India" (1725–1744) brought another

Figure 1. *A Group of School Girls.* Spencer & Co., Madras, c. 1902. Coloured collotype, Undivided back, 13.75 x 8.75 cm, 5.49 x 3.52 in.

Postmarked Kandy, Sri Lanka 12 11 1907 and sent to Mrs. C.B. Benson, 306 Warren Street, Hudson, N. Y., U.S.A.: [*Recto*] "Kandy Ceylon Feb. 10, 1907. So pleased to rec.[eive] your X'mas letter with its New year's greetings & was so interested in all that your wrote me.

Every word was of interest. I would write you a letter but have so little time as there is so much to see. These girls are from Madras, India. They were rings in their noses and in their toes. Burma and South India were most interesting and now the spicy breezes blow soft o'er Ceylon's Tale for us and we drive through Cinammon gardens, see the candle trees and breadfruit trees. . . Love to all. Yours as ever. S.E.D."

Figure 2. *A Little Brahmin Beauty, Madras.* Spencer & Co., Madras, c. 1905. Collotype, Divided back, 13.95 x 8.95 cm, 5.49 x 3.52 in.

BELOW

Figure 3. *Madras. Seven Pagodas.* Raphael Tuck & Co., London, Madras #8987, c. 1905. Embossed coloured halftone, Divided back, 13.8 x 8.65 cm, 5.43 x 3.41 in.

[*Verso*] "**Seven Pagodas**. Among the oldest remains in Southern India are these rock temples 35 miles from Madras believed to date back at least 1,300 years. Carved out of hardest granite they show no signs of decay. The people who made them must have been numerous and powerful, for their works are gigantic. Yet there is no city near which they could have inhabited, and from whose ruins we might get some trace of their history."

While we now believe that the temples date to the Pallava King Narasimharavan I around 630 CE, much about their origins remains obscure.

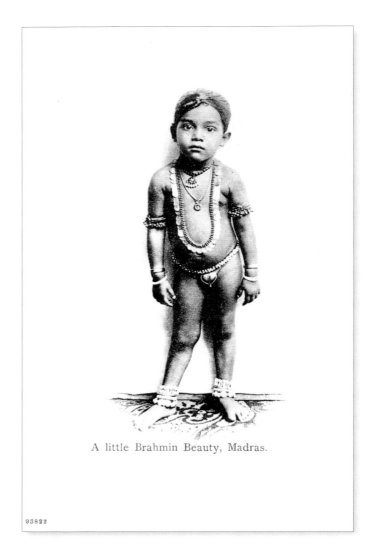

A little Brahmin Beauty, Madras.

93822

MADRAS.
SEVEN PAGODAS.

Figure 4. *Siva Temple, Mylapore, Madras.* Raphael Tuck & Co., London, c. 1905. Sepia collotype, Divided back, 13.8 x 8.65 cm, 5.45 x 3.44 in.

Figure 5. *Madras. Entrance to Temple Tiru Kuli Kundram.* Raphael Tuck & Co., London, Madras #8987, c. 1905. Embossed coloured halftone, Divided back, 13.85 x 8.75 cm, 5.45 x 3.44 in.

[*Verso*] "Entrance to Temple, Turi Kuli Kundram. The remains belonging to historic times are chiefly specimens of religious architecture. These temples and sculptures date back a thousand years and impress the imagination by the immense labour which has been devoted to their ornamental elaboration in most intractable materials."

Figure 6. *Madras. Hindu God Perumal Mahavellipuram.* Raphael Tuck & Co., London, Madras #8987, c. 1905. Embossed coloured halftone, Divided back, 13.85 x 8.75 cm, 5.45 x 3.44 in.

[*Verso*] The caption for this card is identical to Figure 5, suggesting lack of supply in the Tuck caption room.

kingdom or ruler into the British fold during the 18th century. The first two battles, particularly Pondicherry against the French in 1749, led to Madras passing into British hands.

View of Madras (Figure 9) by an early South Indian publisher, the German photography studio Wiele & Klein, shows the Marina along the beach where my elderly aunts like to congregate for an ice-cream in the evenings and the kids play with air guns. The shipping wharves in the fore-ground, rebuilt in 1885 and often washed away by storms, spoke to the ships docking far from the shallow shore. They were serviced – perilously, given traveller's reports – by the smaller boats in the lower right vignette, enlarged in *Masula Boat and Shipping* (Figure 10).

Figure 7. *Temple. Madras.*
Higginbotham & Co., Madras, c. 1920.
Real photo postcard, Divided back,
13.85 x 8.75 cm, 5.45 x 3.44 in.

BORN 1725 — DIED 1774
PONDICHERRY · TANJORE · ARCOT ·
HUGLI · CALCUTTA · CHANDERNAGORE ·
PLASSEY ·

Figure 8. *Lord Clive Boldly and Sincerely. Born 1725 – Died 1774 Pondicherry Tanjore Arcot Hugli Calcutta Chandernapore Plassey. Historical Series No. 54*, C.W. Faulkner & Co., c. 1901. Coloured lithograph, Undivided back, 13.9 x 8.8 cm, 5.47 x 3.46 in.

This rare card by British publisher C.W. Faulkner & Co. is a masterpiece of design, from the writing space to the coloured flag over the triton portrait,[5] the gold and silver, the sense of dignified restraint. Heraldic cards, designed by the English painter and sculptor Frederick Leighton (1830-1896), were an early specialty of Faulkner.

Figure 9. *View of Madras. Fisherman. Masulah Boat. Fishermen.* Wiele & Klein, Madras, No. 124, 97572, c. 1900. Collotype, Undivided back, court-sized 12.657 x 9.25 cm, 4.98 x 3.64 in.

Postmarked April 11, 1901, India. Addressed to Master Robert N.K. Auston? c/o Mrs. H. Nelson Davis Bronte Villa, Ler London SE England.

[*Verso*] "Dinapore, Bengal April 11, 01. Darling sonny – Very glad to hear you are well again. This is a picture of Madras harbour. Our ship lay right in front of this big house you see in the picture. It is getting very hot here but mother & I are both well. Much love from Daddy."

Wiele and Klein may go back to 1882, and were well established by 1890.[6] Most Wiele postcards were printed in Germany, even though the firm became one of the leading photo block process printers in India,[7] suggesting again that economies of scale in printing were greater than transportation costs.

Along the Marina in *Madras from the Pier* (Figure 11) is the *Senate House* (Figure 12), a squat brick-red hybrid that seizes the plot it is standing on. Chennai has always been a horizontal city, "its 600,000 inhabitants are spread over an area as extensive as that occupied by 6 million Londoners," declared the caption to *Madras. Nungumbakum Bridge* (Figure 13). I associate its palm-lined avenues with the colours of *Pycroft Road. Triplicane Madras* (Figure 14) or the moody interiors of *Palms, Chepauk, Madras* (Figure 15).

Masula Boat and Shipping.

Figure 10. *Masula Boat and Shipping.* Higginbotham & Co., Madras & Bangalore, No. 53, c. 1905. Coloured collotype, Divided back, 13.65 x 9.05 cm, 5.37 x 3.56 in.

Sent to Miss Oloe [?] "Highweek" Newton Abbot. Devon England and Postmarked 14 September 1905 Fort St. George [Madras].

[*Verso*] "1. The interest of these boats lies in the making of them, they are simply planks sewn together with opium yarn [?], hardly credible unless you seem them for yourself. They were greatly used to take passengers out to the larger vessels before [*Recto*] the pier was built. I remember it well. The boats leak awfully two [too?], men are continually employed in baling."

The capital of Madras Presidency, which included all of South India, was the centre of South Indian photography. Unusually a bookseller,[1] Higginbotham & Co. of Madras and Bangalore, became the region's dominant postcard publisher.[2] The firm's coloured collotypes featured the signature red—probably stencilled in at the firm's premises in Chennai—of *Our Dhoby, Madras* (Figure 16) or on the carpet streaming out of the picture in *Tanjore Palace* (Figure 17). In the vanished *Moore Market, Madras* (Figure 18), a daub of colour anchors the eye to the frame. Pink is more of an accent in Higginbotham's colour repertoire, used in this case for ethereal effect among the blues, yellow and white of *"A full load"* (Figure 19).

Figure 11. *Madras from the Pier.*
Wiele & Klein, Madras, c. 1905.
Collotype, Divided back,
13.95 x 8.9 cm, 5.49 x 3.50 in.

Postmarked 19 Feb [1907] and addressed to Mrs. A.L. Adams, 834 Second Ave., Cedar Rapids, Iowa, U.S.A.

[*Verso*] "Febr. 15 - 1907. Dear cousins. We are busy in India and sensibly nearer the equator. After 3 days here we go through S. [South] India with 3 stops & in a week now will be in Ceylon. All going well. With love, Ernest"

MADRAS. SENATE HOUSE.

Figure 12. *Madras. Senate House.*
Raphael Tuck & Co., London, *Madras Series I. #7065*, c. 1905. Coloured halftone, Divided back, 13.8 x 8.65 cm, 5.43 x 3.41 in.

[*Verso*] **Madras. Senate House.**
This handsome building, designed by Mr. Chisholm, was begun in 1874 and completed in 1879, at a cost of nearly three hundred thousand rupees. Near its southern entrance, and facing the Chepauk Palace, stands the Jubilee statue of Queen Victoria, a replica of Boehm's statue at Windsor. This was unveiled June 20, 1887, and was presented to the city by the Rajah of Vizagapatam."

Figure 13. *Madras. Numgumbakum Bridge.* Raphael Tuck & Co., London, *Madras Series I. #7065*, c. 1905. Embossed coloured halftone, Divided back, 13.85 x 8.9 cm, 5.45 x 3.50 in.

[*Verso*] "Numgumbakum Bridge. To the west of George Town named after King George V, Emperor of India, are the suburbs of Egmore and Nungumbakum adorned with mansions embowered in spacious parks that make Madras 'a city of magnificent distances.' Its 600,000 inhabitants are spread over an area as extensive as that occupied by 6 million Londoners. Nungumbakum is a rural hamlet with no sign of urban influence beyond the municipal lamp-posts that dot its roads."

Figure 14. *Pycroft's Road. Triplicane Madras.* Wiele & Klein, Madras, c. 1905. Coloured collotype, Divided back, 13.85 x 8.95 cm, 5.45 x 3.52 in.

Figure 15. *Palms, Chepauk, Madras.* Wiele & Klein, Madras, c. 1910. Sepia collotype, Divided back, 13.8 x 8.8 cm, 5.43 x 3.46 in.

Postmarked December 28, 1913 [Madras?]. Addressed to Miss Tillinghast, 1935 Santa Barbara St., Santa Barbara, California, U.S.A.

[*Verso*] "Madras. 27.12.13. On the run again this time Madras Bombay Karachi Lahore Calcutta Rangoon. Best of salaams [&] Greetings I remember the compliments but cannot take them! IdhuhilNabum [sp?]"

Palms, Chepauk, Madras

Our Dhoby, Madras.
Higginbotham & Co., Madras & Bangalore. No. 97A.

Figure 16. *Our Dhoby, Madras.* Higginbotham & Co., Madras & Bangalore, No. 97a, c. 1905. Coloured collotype, Divided back, 13.8 x 8.6 cm, 5.43 x 3.39 in.

Started in 1844 by a church librarian with a deep interest in literature, Higginbotham's became a printer of textbooks and in 1875 the only bookseller in India appointed to serve the visiting Prince of Wales. The business still thrives, with branches throughout South India, and occupies its original premises in Chennai and Bengaluru (Bangalore). Another Higginbotham (J. J.) wrote the primary guidebook to the city, as well as biographies of famous Indian officials and musings like *Pickings from Old Indian Books* (1872).

Figure 17. *Tanjore Palace.* Higginbotham & Co., Madras & Bangalore, No. 158a, c. 1905. Coloured collotype, Divided back, 13.8 x 8.6 cm, 5.43 x 3.39 in.

Moore Market, Madras.

93168 Higginbotham & Co., Madras & Bangalore. No. 4.

Figure 18. *Moore Market, Madras.* Higginbotham & Co., Madras & Bangalore, No. 4, 93618, c. 1905. Coloured collotype, Divided back, 13.8 x 9 cm, 5.43 x 3.54 in.

Figure 19. *A full load.* Higginbotham & Co., Madras & Bangalore, No. 112, c. 1905. Coloured collotype, Undivided back, 13.8 x 8.9 cm, 5.43 x 3.50 in.

Postmarked November 2, 1905, Fort Saint George, Madras and addressed to Mrs. F. Martin, 12 Kings Street, Queenstown, County Cork, Ireland.

[*Recto*] "Card is very familiar to me. There has been a big row over at Torquay? Your mother. [*Verso, continued*] 201 D. P & F? – Your cards came very welcome indeed. I had written over & over again for your address. I know these parts very well indeed. I was in Ireland for 3 years & only last year our ship went to Queenstown to take up Drafts, so the long."[8]

"A full load."

97f6 Higginbotham & Co., Madras & Bangalore. No. 112.

Goods and raw materials flowed from the South Indian peninsula to the port of
Madras. One hundred sixty miles west was the *Kolar Gold Field—Champion Reef Mine*
(Figure 20). Gold had long been known in the area, but it was only after the application
of new engineering methods that sizeable finds in the 1880s justified larger investments.
By 1904 the Kolar fields produced nearly all the gold in India, valued at over 20 million
pounds sterling annually (the mines were only shut down recently). Some sense of the
novelty of the enterprise is expressed in Wiele's court-sized *Hajee Ismail Seths New
Saw Mill, Kolar Gold Fields* (Figure 21). The mill was already powered by electricity in
1902. Another postcard by the firm, *Extracting Gold, Cyanide Works, Kolar Gold Fields*
(Figure 22) shows how other, less technical means were still part of the process, in this
case one which must have accrued enormous costs to the workers involved.

Kolar Gold Field---Champion Reef Mine.   Higginbotham & Co., Madras & Bangalore.   No. 138a.

Figure 20. *Kolar Gold Field – Champion Reef Mine.* Higginbotham & Co., Madras & Bangalore, No. 138a, 97572, c. 1905. Coloured collotype, Divided back, 13.75 x 8.75 cm, 5.41 x 3.44 in.

The mine employed tens of thousands of workers a year, including a Higginbotham as an engineer.[9]

Hajee Ismail Saits New Sawmill, Kolar Gold Fields

Printed in Saxony

Extracting Gold, Cyanide Works, Kolar Gold Fields

Printed in Saxony

Figure 21. *Hajee Ismail Seths New Saw Mill, Kolar Gold Fields.* Wiele & Klein, Madras, c. 1901. Coloured collotype, Undivided back, 12.4 x 9.15 cm, 4.88 x 3.60 in.

Figure 22. *Extracting Gold, Cyanide Works, Kolar Gold Fields.* Wiele & Klein #508, Madras, c. 1901. Collotype, Undivided back, 12.9 x 8.9 cm, 5.08 x 3.50 in.

A figure specific to the South is found in *A Toddy Drawer* (Figure 23). Palm wine was made from sap collected from trees in little pouches. Fermentation from yeast was so fast in the humid air that a mildly alcoholic drink could be had in a few hours. Huts like in *A Toddy Shop* (Figure 24) featured sleepy men waiting for the next customer. Toddy, or something similar, was present in Higginbotham's *The Coolest Place in the House* (Figure 25), a postcard that summed up the fantasy of colonial life for Europeans.

A Toddy Drawer, Madras.
Higginbotham & Co., Madras & Bangalore.   No. 48A.

RIGHT
Figure 23. *A Toddy Drawer.*
Higginbotham & Co., Madras & Bangalore, No. 48A, c. 1905.
Coloured collotype, Divided back, 13.85 x 8.7 cm, 5.45 x 3.43 in.

BELOW
Figure 24. *A Toddy Shop.* Spencer & Co., Madras, c. 1902.
Coloured halftone, Undivided back, 13.75 x 8.75 cm, 5.41 x 3.44 in.

Sometimes a postcard uncovers an unexpected slice of history.[3] Kolam is the Tamil tradition of painting geometrical designs with rice flour each morning. Each unique design of the kind in *Chalking the Doorstep, Madras* (Figure 26) was of great complexity and passed from mother to daughter over the centuries; yet another Indus artefact in open view?

Figure 25. *The Coolest Place in the House.* Higginbotham & Co., Madras & Bangalore, No. 130a, c. 1905. Coloured collotype, Divided back, 13.8 x 8.7 cm, 5.43 x 3.43 in.

The dog resting by the tub is to Indians most unhygienic, while to Europeans, the ultimate Raj bathroom accessory.

BELOW
Figure 26. *Chalking the Doorstep, Madras.* Higginbotham & Co., Madras & Bangalore, Nos. 123, 97571, c. 1905. Collotype, Divided back, 13.75 x 8.9 cm, 5.41 x 3.50 in.

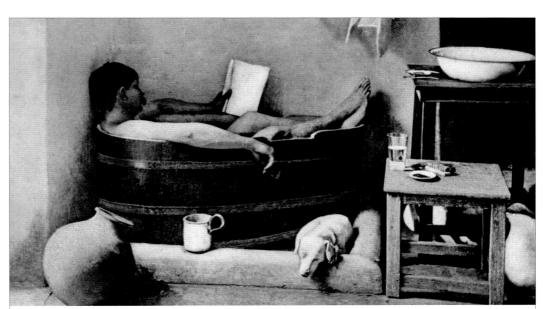

The Coolest Place in the House.   Higginbotham & Co, Madras & Bangalore.   No. 130a.

Chalking the Doorstep, Madras.

The great surprise to me in Chennai, as to many visitors, is *Madras San Thome Cathedral* (Figure 27), built to commemorate the Apostle St. Thomas who came here in 60 CE to spread Christianity in South India. This was probably long before the temples (Figures 3-5) were built. Indeed, the vividness of the scenes in *San Thome Cathedral Mylapore Stained Glass Window above High-Altar* (Figure 28) must have seemed familiar to those who worshipped at the Vishnu and Shiva Temples in Mylapore.

Figure 27. *Madras. San Thome Cathedral.* Raphael Tuck & Co., London, *Madras #8988*, c. 1905. Embossed coloured halftone, Divided back, 13.85 x 8.9 cm, 5.45 x 3.50 in.

[*Verso*] "**San Thome Cathedral**. The town of S. Thome, now part of Madras City, was named after the Portuguese pioneers, after St. Thomas the Apostle, who is said to have evangelized the country. A series of memorials of these pioneers will be found in the Cathedral that stands over the tomb of the Apostle, martyred here on the 21st of December, A.D. 68."

San Thomé Cathedral Mylapore,
Stained Glass Window above High-Altar

Figure 28. *San Thome Cathedral Mylapore Stained Glass Window above High-Altar.* Unknown Publisher, c. 1920. Coloured halftone, Divided back, 14.15 x 8.9 cm, 5.57 x 3.50 in.

A favourite place in the city for me is the quiet Madras Club, formerly and still identical to *Government House, Madras* (Figure 29), although the pond that would have been in the foreground of this postcard is now a walking oval for the privileged few.

Other transplanted history is not so well respected. There was *The Banqueting Hall, Madras* (Figure 30), whose plaster walls I was fortunate enough to visit and photograph one afternoon some years ago. It was deteriorating, slowly and deliciously, exposing rich Hapsburg yellows until one day, about 10 years later, it was bulldozed in the middle of the night to facilitate a land sale (the history of the Raj crumbles somewhere every day).

Figure 29. *The Madras Government House.* Raphael Tuck & Co., London, Bangalore #8986, c. 1905. Coloured halftone, Divided back, 13.95 x 8.9 cm, 5.49 x 3.50 in.

[*Verso*] Madras. Government House. "The Madras Government House looks out upon the Cooum river at the back, and its front gives upon Mount Road, the principal street in Madras. It has a noble banqueting hall constructed during Lord Clive's Government to commemorate the fall of Seringapatam, and possesses some very fine portraits of royalties and vice-royalties."

Figure 30. *The Banqueting Hall, Madras.* Higginbotham & Co., Madras & Bangalore No. 111, c. 1905. Collotype, Divided back, 14.15 x 8.9 cm, 5.57 x 3.50 in.

BANGALORE
[Bengaluru]

Bengaluru, as *In the Market, Bangalore* (Figure 31), is today the capital of Karnataka and the third most populous city in India. It used to be the capital of the former princely state of Mysore and a sparsely populated cantonment of less than 300,000 people; today there are endless traffic jams in this semi-hill station 3,000 feet above sea level. *Royal Palace, Bangalore* (Figure 32), with the postmark fluttering like a flag, was actually built by a British educationist before being purchased and occupied by the ruling Wodeyar family in 1881.

Figure 31. *In the Market, Bangalore.* Higginbotham & Co., Madras & Bangalore, #2542, Madras, c. 1903. Coloured collotype, Divided back, 13.8 x 8.75 cm, 5.43 x 3.44 in.

ROYAL PALACE, BANGALORE. INDIA

I do not wish to exchange any more post cards with you. F. Jerry

Figure 32. *Royal Palace, Bangalore.* Unknown Firm, c. 1905. Lithograph, Undivided back, 14 x 9.1 cm, 5.51 x 3.58 in.

Postmarked Kolkata, 1907 and received in Halifax, Nova Scotia, Canada on April 9, 1907 and sent to Miss Florence Irwin, 256 Gottingen Street, Halifax Nova Scotia, Canada.

[*Recto*] "I do not wish to exchange any more postcards with you. F. Jerry."

Tuck's offered some excellent views, including *Bangalore, Parade* (Figure 33) and *Bangalore. Commercial Street* (Figure 34), the first Tuck's embossed postcard I found, and is still a favourite for its light purple hues and shimmering effects. The postcard shows the offices of retailer Spencer & Co., publisher of a number of postcards in this chapter (Figures 1, 2 and 22). Another standout is *Bangalore. Alsur Temple Gateway* (Figure 35), one of the oldest temples in the city. *Twilight, Ulsoor Rock. Bangalore* (Figure 36) is one of the few artist-signed Bangalore postcards.

Figure 33. *Bangalore, South Parade.* Raphael Tuck & Co., London, Bangalore #8986, c. 1905. Embossed coloured halftone, Divided back, 13.9 x 8.85 cm, 5.47 x 3.48 in.

[*Verso*] "**South Parade.** Bangalore is the capital of Mysore and the largest British cantonment in South India. It stands 3000 feet above the sea and is an important railway centre."

BELOW
Figure 34. *Bangalore. Commercial Street.* Raphael Tuck & Co., London, Bangalore #8987, c. 1905. Embossed coloured halftone, Divided back, 14 x 8.9 cm, 5.51 x 3.50 in.

[*Verso*] "**Commercial Street,** Bangalore. Busy and thriving for it is so in Mysore that the most serious and successful effort has been made to develop the mineral resources of India. Some of the richest mines in the world are being worked in the Kolar gold-field."

Figure 35. *Alsur Temple Gateway.* Raphael Tuck & Co., London, Bangalore #8986, c. 1905. Coloured halftone, Divided back, 13.95 x 8.85 cm, 5.49 x 3.48 in.

[*Verso*] "**Alsur Temple Gateway.** It is impossible to express in a few lines the wonder and beauty of the Temples of India, of which some fine examples are to be found in Mysore. Their solidity, their elaborate decorative sculpture, are full of interest to the traveller, the student of Art or Architecture and to those who seek to unravel the tangled history of the people of bygone days who built them."

Figure 36. *Twilight, Ulsoor Rock, Bangalore.* J.B. MacGregor 1919 [signed], The Calcutta Phototype Co., c. 1920. Coloured halftone, Divided back, 13.95 x 9 cm, 5.49 x 3.54 in.

OOTY

[Udagamandalam]

Ootacamund is still Ooty to the residents of Chennai who spend summers in the "blue mountains" of the Nilgiri Hills, visiting sights like *The Pyarka Falls, Nilgiris* (Figure 37). Ooty lies above 7,000 feet. Most big Chennai studios and retailers had branches here, like Wiele and Klein, purveyor of the court-sized *View of Ootacamund* (Figure 38). The face of a Toda girl anchors the three vignettes, the largest showing the artificial lake at the centre of the hill station, set off by a deep black ink forest.

The Pykara Falls, Nilgiris.
Higginbotham & Co., Madras & Bangalore. No. 190A.

Figure 37. *The Pykara Falls, Nilgiris.* Higginbotham & Co., Madras & Bangalore, #190A, Madras, c. 1903. Coloured collotype, Divided back, 13.9 x 8.8 cm, 5.47 x 3.46 in.

The falls were first used for electric power in 1929.

Figure 38. *View of Ootacamund. A Toda Girl. Enroute to the Hills.* Wiele & Klein, Madras, No. 124, 97572, c. 1900. Collotype, Undivided back, 12.6 x 9.2 cm, 4.96 x 3.62 in.

Figure 39. *A Toda Hut and Family.* Wiele & Klein, Madras, No. 219, c. 1905. Collotype, Undivided back, 14 x 9 cm, 5.51 x 3.54 in.

Postmarked Ootacamund, May 23, 1906 and addressed to Miss XXXXXX [deliberately rendered illegible] XXXXXX Gardens, Folkestone, Kent, England.

[*Recto*] "Ootacamund Neilgherry Hills with love from the 2 Wanderes 22.III.06."

The Todas were the largest of a handful of tribal groups in the area for a thousand years or more. Toda's postcards were much favoured by postcard publishers for their unusual appearance, traditions and round homes. *A Toda Hut and Family* (Figure 39), *A Toda House, Its Master and Mistress* (Figure 40) and *Types of India A Pair of Toda Beauties* (Figure 41) are a few of many such cards. Todas still live in homes atop the Botanical Gardens, where one can visit them, their lives from the arrival of the British until now on constant display in a real life theatre. To be sure, high above these beautiful gardens, I too found myself fascinated, and wondered if the cattle rustling culture that their world was based on has anything to do with the cattle rustling around Harappa today, and where their ancestors might have lived in an ancient Indus atlas.

Figure 40. *A Toda House, Its Master and Mistress.* Raphael Tuck & Co., London, Bangalore #8971, c. 1905. Coloured halftone, Divided back, 14 x 8.7 cm, 5.51 x 3.43 in.

[*Verso*] "A Toda House, Its Master and Mistress. – A native residence of the roughest kind of architecture, thatched or wattled roof, unglazed holes for windows and a general air of crampy discomfort, but the hot season begins early in the year and life in the open air makes many things endurable."

Figure 41. *Types of India. A Pair of Toda Beauties.* Raphael Tuck & Co., London, *Historic India Series III #8973*, c. 1905. Coloured halftone, Divided back, 14 x 8.7 cm, 5.51 x 3.43 in.

[*Verso*] "A Pair of Toda Beauties. – Faces burned by the Indian sun to a rich brown, streaming locks that frame faces symmetrical and not unpleasing, these ladies are seen squatting on their heels after the native mode. Little enough here of the brightness of city costumes; shawls only of a somewhat blankety appearance."

MALABAR

The western Malabar coast in today's Kerala state is lightly-documented in early photographs and postcards, with exceptions like *Sailboat on the Coast of Malabar* (Figure 42) from a German series on the ships of the world. This visual under-representation is despite the fact that it was along this coast that the Portuguese explorer Vasco da Gama first established European factories in India. *Anniversary of Vasco da Gama's Voyage to India 1498–1898* (Figure 43), celebrating the 400th anniversary of his first voyage to Malabar is notable for the immense time span commemorated by a single postcard.

Nonetheless there are gems, like these two from Nicolas & Company, *Moplah Women, Malabar* (Figure 44) and *Moplahs, Malabar* (Figure 45). Moplahs are the Muslim descendants of Arab traders who married local women and settled on the coast over the centuries. *A Nair Lady* (Figure 46) shows someone from the dominant landholding caste with whom the Moplahs remained in sporadic conflict.

There is more nudity on postcards from South India than elsewhere in the subcontinent, like Wiele's *A Malabar Girl* (Figure 47). As Keralite women did not wear blouses as a matter of course, the subject was within limits for a reputable publisher.[4]

Figure 42. *Segelschiff an der Kueste von Malabar [Sailing Ship on the Cost of Malabar].* Marine Gallerie [Germany] *Ausgabe von 300 verschiedenen Karten [One of 300 different cards]* #204. Coloured halftone, Divided back, 13.9 x 8.95 cm, 8.00 x 3.52 in.

Figure 43. *Centario da India Vasco da Gama 1498-1898 [Anniversary of Vasco da Gama's Voyage to India 1498-1898].* Unknown Publisher, Portugal, No. 124, 97572, 1898. Collotype, Undivided back, 12.5 x 9.15 cm, 4.92 x 3.60 in.

Figure 44. *Moplah Women, Malabar.* Nicolas Brothers, Calicut, c. 1905. Collotype, Divided back, 13.9 x 8.8 cm, 5.47 x 3.46 in.

John P. Nicholas' presence in Chennai dates back to 1858,[10] where he became known for high quality photography. The firm also had a studio in Calicut. Nicholas died in 1895.[11]

Figure 45. *Moplahs, Malabar.* Nicolas Brothers, Calicut, c. 1905. Collotype, Divided back, 13.9 x 8.7 cm, 5.47 x 3.43 in.

A Nair Lady, Malabar.

Figure 47. *A Malabar.* Wiele & Klein, Madras, c. 1908. Sepia collotype, Divided back, 13.8 x 8.9 cm, 5.43 x 3.50 in.

Figure 46. *A Nair Lady.* Nicolas Brothers, Calicut c. 1905. Collotype, Divided back, 13.8 x 8.9 cm, 5.43 x 3.50 in.

Notes

1. Other booksellers who became postcard publishers include Combridge & Co. of Mumbai, Anand & Sons of Peshawar, and of course D.B. Taraporevala & Sons in Mumbai.

2. Higginbotham's postcards may pre-date Weile's court-sized efforts, although I have found few undivided back *(Girls at Well, Madras)* or court-sized cards among their offerings. A less-than-court-sized *A Tamil Lady*, where the image occupies about a third of the front, was sent on an illegible date likely before 1900.

3. Dr. Vijaya Natarajan at the University of San Francisco and author of *Feeding a Thousand Souls: Women, Ritual and Art in southern India—The Kolam* (forthcoming, Oxford University Press, 2018).

4. Dhurandhar's Kerala woman in the book *Women of India* was the only topless one (see *Kashmir*).

5. C.W. Faulkner & Co.'s Historical Series No 540, circa 1905. Faulkner is described "as well established artistic colour printers the firm was admirably suited to join the ranks of the pioneer postcard publishers, producing a wide range of issues from about 1899, with many of the early cards very hard to find today." Anthony Byatt, *Picture Postcards and Their Publishers* (Malvern: Golden Age Postcard Books, 1978), p. 94.

6. See Joachim Bautze, "Wiele and Klein, Chennai" in the *Indo-Asiaticsche Zeitschrift*, 12-2, pp. 91-92.

7. "It cannot be pretended that the photo printing blocks produced in India are in all respects up to the standard of the British and American productions, but some of the work turned out by this firm has fallen very little short of that high standard..." In Higginbotham's *Guide to the City of Madras*, 1903, p. 101.

8. A later divided back version of the same postcard, although following a somewhat similar colour-scheme has much less detail, showing how quality could decline as postcards were mass-produced.

9. Record from FIBIS, *The Families in British India Society*, http://search.fibis.org/frontis/bin/aps_detail.php?id=1077401, shows a Herbert Penn Higginbotham, an engineer at the Kolar Mines, married in Chennai on April 13, 1898.

10. *Luminous Lint* accessed September 19, 2015, http://www.luminous-lint.com/app/photographer/John_P__Nicholas/A/.

11. Christopher Penn, *The Nicholas Brothers & A.T.W. Penn: Photographers of South India 1855-1885* (London: Bernard Quaritch, 2014), p. 84.

Printed in Ceylon

Ceylon

[Sri Lanka]

The story of postcards in the subcontinent is not complete without including the island of Sri Lanka, once called Ceylon. I find Sri Lankan postcards have the highest ratio of beautiful cards divided by square miles. They also show that once again, the right combination of firm or artist, technology, subject and place could lead to a whole new vista of exceptional cards. For me, collecting Sri Lankan cards is a guilty pleasure, something done entirely for its own sake.

The British started taking over the "cinnamon and spice island" from the Dutch in the 1790s. By 1815 they had made the central highland kingdom of Kandy capitulate. They took over the rest of the island in *Map of Ceylon showing her Tea industry* (Figure 1), and by 1882 the port in *Colombo Harbour and Shipping* (Figure 2) became the port of call for mail steamers on their way to Kolkata and to the rest of Asia. Ceylon used its location to pioneer some of the lowest postal rates in the world.[1] All this contributed to making this an outsize postcard market relative to population. Visual standards were also high: the early art photographer Julia Margaret Cameron worked here, as did Charles Scowen, whose 1870s works rival the best of albumen Raj photographers. A classic Scowen image like *Four Kandyan Girls, Ceylon* (Figure 3) or *The Satmahalparasade* (Figure 4) were made into postcards by The Colombo Apothecaries Co., which bought Scowen's stock out in 1896.[2]

The firm that dominated postcard publishing in Ceylon was A.W. Plate & Co. Although I know of no court-sized Plate cards and the postmark on a regular undivided back postcard goes back no further than April 1899, after that date Plate published hundreds of postcards in "In Great Variety."[3] The firm sold half a million postcards in 1907 alone,[4] one of the few documented volumes we have that shows how large the postcard trade could be for a single publisher. "When picture postcards came

Figure 1. *Map of Ceylon showing her Tea industry.* Ceylon Tea Propaganda Board, MacDonald Gill [artist], H & C Press [Printer], Colombo, c. 1934. Lithograph, Divided back, 13.85 x 9.2 cm, 5.45 x 3.62 in.

[*Verso, not postmarked*] "Dearest Dulcie , Just a Souvenir of Colombo which I am sending as well as the letter. The Harbour is artificial, & it is partly enclosed by a sea wall. The water is shallow and very dirty & the ship did not tie up at the wharf, but anchored in the channel. Colombo has a smell of its own, & anything but pleasant, but the East is famous for that Your loving husband, Les. XXXXXXX"

Colombo Harbour and Shipping.

No. 65 - *Four Kandyan Girls, Ceylon.*

Figure 2. *Colombo Harbour and Shipping.* Plate & Co. #98, Colombo, c. 1910. Coloured collotype, Divided back, 13.7 x 8.75 cm, 5.39 x 3.44 in.

A guidebook was "Dedicated to that Never-Failing Stream of Travellers which flows through Lanka's Isle (For Lanka's good) en route to other climes."[13]

Figure 3. *Four Kandyan Girls, Ceylon.* The Colombo Apothecaries Co. #65, Colombo, c. 1905 (from a Charles Scowen photograph, c. 1880). Coloured halftone, Divided back, 13.9 x 9 cm, 5.47 x 3.54 in.

so universally into vogue, the firm again extended its trade to embrace this new line of business, becoming the first in the island to supply the demand of this novelty" wrote an editor that year.[5] Together with Skeen & Co., the photo-historian Ismeth Raheem considers Plate to be the most successful photographic studio in Colombo.[6] It still exists.

60. - *The Satmahalparasade.*

Figure 4. *The Satmahalparasade.* The Colombo Apothecaries Co. #60, Colombo, c. 1905 (from a Charles Scowen photograph, c. 1880). Coloured halftone, Divided back, 13.85 x 8.85 cm, 5.45 x 3.48 in.

Among the firm's first advertising cards is the *Galle Face Hotel, Ceylon* (Figure 5), which had its own small port; Plate had a branch office here. Hotel postcards were the apotheosis of the "Gruss Aus" [Greetings from] postcard (see the *Preface)*, invitations to a specific place. Palm trees streak across the surface to frame a billboard view of the Galle Face Hotel, a *grande dame* of international hotels, built in 1864 with a "permanent European hotel orchestra."[7] A man in the driveway waits for the next guest. Could it be you?

Figure 5. *Galle Face Hotel, Ceylon.* Plate & Co., Colombo, c. 1901. Collotype, Divided back, 13.8 x 9 cm, 5.43 x 3.54 in.

Plate spent the first three years of his career with The Colombo Apothecaries, a retailer founded in 1883,[14] and started his own business in 1890. In 1903 Plate employed 10 European and 60 Ceylonese assistants in Colombo, Kandy, and the hillstation Nuwara Aliya.[15] The firm printed books and catalogues too, including works on Ceylonese culture featuring Plate's photographs, and had "Competent European Artists in Attendance" who could converse with travellers in French and German.[16] It published postcards of India and sold them there as well.[17] Plate also ran a studio and bookstore in the Queen's Hotel, Kandy.

Figure 6. *Kandy.* Plate & Co., Colombo, c. 1900. Collotype, Undivided back, 13.9 x 9.05 cm, 5.47 x 3.56 in.

Postmarked Feb. 5, 1905 and addressed to Mrs. Farmstone, 41 Clapton Road in Nottingham, England.

[*Verso*] "Jan. 15, 1905 India. Dear friend I write to you hoping to find you in the best of health as it leaves me at present your faithful Friend Mr. H. Parker, 24 Ives, H.I. S. Hyacinth [sp?] India."

Kandy (Figure 6) exemplifies Plate's success with the early vignette postcard. A light colour pigment brings the central cone of this Stengel-printed card to life, unfurling three scenes from the lake capital. On the bottom left is Kandy's magnet for visitors from all over the world, the *Temple of the Holy Tooth Kandy* (Figure 7), watched over by men like *A Buddhist Priest, Ceylon* (Figure 8). So integral did this Buddhist temple become to Ceylon's identity that Tuck's chief postcard artist Charles E. Flowers was employed to reproduce it in *The Ceylon Pavilion* (Figure 9) at The British Empire Exhibition in 1924.

Figure 7. *Temple of the Holy Tooth Kandy. (Temple of the Buddhists in Ceylon and contains a tooth of Buddha).* Plate & Co. "Art" Postcard #18, Colombo, c. 1908. Coloured halftone, Divided back, 13.85 x 8.8 cm, 5.45 x 3.46 in.

Figure 8. *A Buddhist Priest, Ceylon.* Plate & Co. "Art" Postcard #53, Colombo, c. 1908. Coloured halftone, Divided back, 13.9 x 8.9 cm, 5.43 x 3.50 in.

Figure 9. *The Ceylon Pavilion.* Charles E. Flowers [signed], Raphael Tuck & Sons "OIL FACSIM", #7023, London, 1924. Embossed coloured halftone, Divided back, 13.8 x 8.9 cm, 5.47 x 3.50 in.

[*Verso*] "THE CEYLON PAVILION with its four entrance lamps at Kandy is a faithful copy of the old Kandyan style of architecture, the panels and circular moonstones of the doorway having been brought from Ceylon. Here are on exhibit rubber and some of the articles made there from, and other products of the island, together with its arts and crafts, and here can be obtained a cup of Ceylon tea 'served as it should be served.'"

For the past 2,000 years at least, during the Kandy Perahera, a stand-in for *The tooth Relic of the Lord Buddha, Ceylon* (Figure 10) is paraded under a golden canopy through the centre of town. The eight-day festival was a favourite of Plate's later halftone-coloured "Art Postcard" series. The "Art" refers to halftone imagery touched with thick reds, browns, whites, blues and greens as in *The Procession of the Holy Relic of the Tooth, Ceylon, (The Kandy Perahera)* (Figure 11) and *The Kandy Perahera, Ceylon* (Figure 12). At its best, an Art Postcard like *Lakeside Scene, Kandy, Ceylon* (Figure 13) could evoke an impressionist painter like Claude Monet.

Figure 10. *The tooth Relic of the Lord Buddha, Ceylon.* Plate & Co., Colombo, c. 1905. Coloured collotype, Divided back, 13.9 x 8.8 cm, 5.47 x 3.46 in.

Figure 11. *The Procession of the Holy Relic of the Tooth, Ceylon, (The Kandy Perahera).* Plate & Co. "Art Postcard" #20, Colombo, c. 1908. Coloured halftone, Divided back, 13.9 x 8.8 cm, 5.47 x 3.46 in.

Figure 12. *The Kandy Perahera, Ceylon.* Plate & Co. "Art Postcard" #19, Colombo, c. 1908. Coloured halftone, Divided back, 13.85 x 8.9 cm, 5.45 x 3.50 in.

Figure 13. *Lakeside Scene, Kandy, Ceylon.* Plate & Co. "Art Postcard" #33, Colombo, c. 1908. Coloured halftone, Divided back, 13.65 x 8.75 cm, 5.37 x 3.44 in.

The main driver of Sri Lanka's economic growth during the colonial period was the tea industry. Developed by a number of enterprising European investors who came to the island seeking a fortune, there was once again a German connection. *Gruss von* [*Greetings from*] *John Hagenbeck & Co. Ceylon Thee Import* (Figure 14), sent in May 1899, was published by the younger half-brother of Carl Hagenbeck, the famous German animal promoter and founder of the Hamburg Zoo in 1907. Together, the brothers published postcards of exotic people and scenes at European exhibitions while the younger Hagenbeck became a tea planter.

Figure 14. *Gruss von John Hagenbeck & Co. Ceylon Thee Import.* John Hagenbeck & Co., Colombo, c. 1899. Lithograph, Undivided back, 14.1 x 9.35 cm, 5.55 x 3.68 in.

John Hagenbeck (1866–1940) set up plantations in Ceylon at the age of twenty. His firm is also described in a Colombo merchant directory from 1906 as a "ship chandler"—one who supplies services to ships at port—and as an "exporter of wild animals."[18]

The Sri Lankan tea industry grew from 250 acres under cultivation in 1876 to almost 400,000 acres in 1900.[8] Some 150 million tonnes of tea were produced in 1900 worth 50 million rupees, half of Ceylon's total exports. Growth was stimulated by marketing postcards like this one from Lipton's, today the most recognizable tea brand around the world and certainly in the subcontinent. It advertised its new offerings at the San Francisco Exposition with *Thos. J. Lipton, Tea, Coffee and Cocoa Planter, Ceylon* (Figure 15).

The herb to harbour journey began with *Carting Tea from Factory, Ceylon* (Figure 16). A later, popular Lipton series highlighted the *Tea-in-Transit to Wharf, Ceylon* (Figure 17). It arrives at the docks in *Shipping Tea, Ceylon* (Figure 18), where the carts are lined up in front of a large hut much like the one shown in the left foreground of *Colombo Harbour and Shipping* (Figure 1). From 1905 through 1908, millions of rupees were spent on new docks, dredging and breakwaters to allow larger tea-laden ships to come and go.

Figure 15. *Thos. J. Lipton, Tea, Coffee and Cocoa Planter, Ceylon.* Thomas J. Lipton, Ceylon, 1915. Coloured halftone, Divided back, 13.85 x 8.7 cm, 5.45 x 3.43 in.

Figure 16. *Carting Tea from Factory, Ceylon.* Plate & Co. #30, Colombo, c. 1905. Coloured collotype, Divided back, 13.85 x 8.75 cm, 5.45 x 3.44 in.

Figure 17. *Tea-in-Transit to Wharf, Ceylon.* The Photochrom Co., London and Detroit, c. 1910. Coloured halftone, Divided back, 13.9 x 8.85 cm, 5.47 x 3.48 in.

Figure 18. *Shipping Tea, Ceylon.* The Colombo Apothecaries Co. #46, Colombo, c. 1905. Coloured halftone, Divided back, 13.85 x 8.8 cm, 5.45 x 3.46 in.

Colombo became a multi-national port of about 50,000 Singhalese, Tamil, European, Chinese, Arab, Malay, Parsee and original colonial Dutch "Burghers."[9] *"A Street Arab", Ceylon* (Figure 19) seems to have been Colombo's signature postcard character, shown also in a version adapted for a new consumer habit, *"Cigarette" Greetings From Ceylon* (Figure 20).

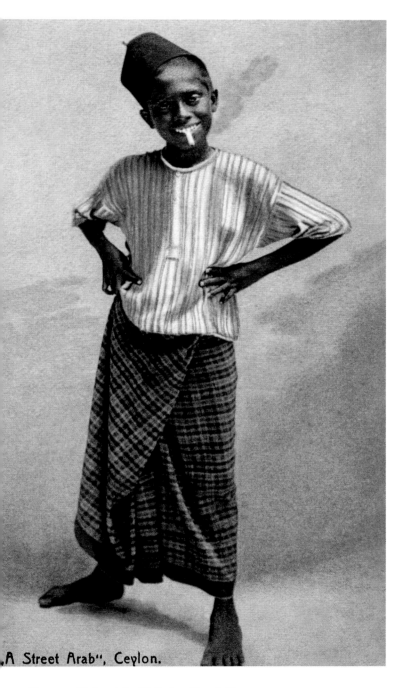

Figure 19. *"A Street Arab", Ceylon.* Plate & Co., Colombo, c. 1905. Coloured collotype, Divided back, 13.75 x 8.75 cm, 5.41 x 3.44 in.

Figure 20. *"Cigarette" Greetings From Ceylon.* Plate & Co., Colombo, c. 1905. Coloured collotype, Divided back, 13.75 x 8.8 cm, 5.41 x 3.46 in.

There is a note of celebration in Plate's Colombo street cards like *Betel Leaf Seller, Colombo* (Figure 21), even if it probably was shot in a studio. Then there is *Madras Merchant, Colombo* (Figure 22), the rich black ink bringing out the white of the merchant's shirt and turban. The island had a close relationship with South India. Tamil rule in the northern part of Ceylon went back to the 12th century. The needs of the growing tea plantations led to the wholesale importation of Tamil "coolies" into Ceylon by the British during the late 19th and 20th centuries. There were so many workers they supported outfits like *Tamil Theatrical Company, Ceylon* (Figure 23). One of Plate's most reprinted portraits was *Head of a Tamil Girl* (Figure 24). The sitter's startled expression is, for me, one of the more memorable among antique postcards.

Betel Leaf Seller, Colombo.

Madras Merchant, Colombo.

Figure 21. *Betel Leaf Seller, Colombo.* Plate & Co. #305, Colombo, c. 1905. Collotype, Divided back, 13.7 x 8.45 cm, 5.39 x 3.33 in.

Figure 22. *Madras Merchant, Colombo.* Plate & Co., Colombo, c. 1905. Coloured collotype, Divided back, 13.85 x 8.8 cm, 5.45 x 3.46 in.

Figure 23. *Tamil Theatrical Company,*
Ceylon. Plate & Co. #65, Colombo, c.
1905. Collotype, Divided back,
13.9 x 8.9 cm, 5.47 x 3.50 in.

Head of Tamil Girl

Figure 24. *Head of a Tamil Girl.* Plate &
Co. #65, Colombo, c. 1905.
Coloured collotype, Divided back,
13.85 x 8.7 cm, 5.45 x 3.43 in.

Singhalese ayah (Nurse Maid).

Figure 25. *Singhalese ayah (Nurse Maid).*
Plate & Co. #57, Colombo, c. 1905.
Coloured collotype, Divided back,
13.8 x 8.65 cm, 5.43 x 3.41 in.

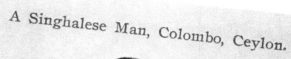

A Singhalese Man, Colombo, Ceylon.

Figure 26. *A Singhalese Man.* Plate & Co. #33,
Colombo, c. 1905. Collotype, Divided back, 13.7 x 8.7 cm,
5.39 x 3.43 in.

Figure 27. *Mendicant.* Plate & Co. "Art" Postcard #69, Colombo, c. 1905. Coloured halftone, Divided back, 13.90 x 8.9 cm, 5.47 x 3.50 in.

The Sinhalese majority (nearly three-fourths of the island's residents) came from India in the fifth century BCE. They were generally Buddhist, and were subjects of Plate's camera in *Singhalese ayah (Nurse Maid)* (Figure 25). Note the wonderful, multi-cultural, multi-epoch clothing of *A Singhalese Man* (Figure 26). The *Mendicant* (Figure 27) is one of the more individualized of fakir postcards. "The portrait work of this firm has gained a wide reputation,"[10] wrote a contemporary chronicler.

On the other hand, there is the striking but absurd "ethnic" postcard, *Cingalais* ["Sinhala"] (Figure 28), which advertised a potion to fight "constipation and its consequences," available in pharmacies across France around 1900.

The original inhabitants of the Ceylonese island, as far as we know, were actually the Veddas, seen in *Veddahs. Aborigines of Ceylon* (Figure 29). They are shown in a high-quality photo-postcard format increasingly offered by Plate after 1910, or in a colourized version from a famous Scowen photograph, *Veddahs. Wild Men of Ceylon.* (Figure 30). Their presence on the island goes back tens of thousands

Figure 28. *Cingalais.* Herold & Co., Paris, c. 1900. Lithograph, Undivided back, 14.3 x 9 cm, 5.63 x 3.54 in.

"[For] Constipation and its consequences. Spirits beneficial to health from Doctor Franck."

Constipation et ses Conséquences
VÉRITABLES
GRAINS DE SANTÉ
DU
Docteur FRANCK

CINGALAIS

Collection Delaporte.s

VEDDAHS. ABORIGINES OF CEYLON.

44 Veddahs. Wild men of Ceylon.

FACING PAGE, ABOVE
Figure 29. *Veddahs. Aborigines of Ceylon.* Plate & Co. #57, Colombo, c. 1915. Real photo postcard, Divided back, 13.75 x 8.65 cm, 5.41 x 3.41 in.

FACING PAGE, BELOW
Figure 30. *Veddahs. Aborigines of Ceylon.* Plate & Co. #44, Colombo, Jaipur, c. 1905. Coloured halftone, Divided back, 13.9 x 8.85 cm, 5.47 x 3.48 in.

Figure 31. *Rodiya Woman Carrying Water, Ceylon.* #77, Plate & Co., Colombo, c. 1910. Real photo postcard, Divided back, 13.8 x 8.75 cm, 5.43 x 3.44 in.

It was sent from Dutch Indonesia ('Batavia') to Madagascar around 1910. In the words of a contemporary stereo-typist "one can hardly view a race so fine in a physical point of view, so degraded in a moral aspect...."[19]

A RODIYA WOMAN CARRYING WATER, CEYLON.

Figure 32. *Kandian Chief and Family.* The Colombo Apothecaries Co., Colombo, c. 1905. Collotype, Divided back, 13.9 x 8.8 cm, 5.47 x 3.46 in.

Kandian Chief and Family.

of years, with many living in a forest belt that separated the northern Tamil and Sinhalese populations. The Veddas were said to have once ruled great cities and cooked with golden pots until their dominance was undercut by the Sinhalese arrival.

Plate & Co., like many Ceylon-based firms,[11] also published semi-nude postcards of women, more common here than even in South India. *A Rodiya Woman Carrying Water, Ceylon* (Figure 27) has a nicely placed purple stamp. Rodiyas, a "hunting" caste, are said to have dishonoured an early ruler of the island, and thus have been condemned to live as "untouchables". The most common nude or semi-nude women shown in these cards are drawn from this caste group. Their loosely regulated interactions with the ruling clans—shown in another Scowen image, *Kandian Chief and Family* (Figure 32)—were said to explain their unusually good looks: nobles who ran afoul of rulers could find their wives and daughters banished into the Rodiya caste.[12]

Notes

1. It cost five cents to send a postcard abroad, less than the penny most of the world charged (within the subcontinent postage was only two cents).

2. Scowen tried to become a tea plantation manager, and thereafter disappears from the record.

3. In George J.A. Skeen, *A Guide to Colombo* (Colombo: A.M. and J. Ferguson, 1906), Madame Del Tufo's, Colombo Apothecaries, and Skeen & Co. do not mention postcards in their studio advertisements.

4. Arnold Wright, *Twentieth Century Impressions of Ceylon*, 1907, p. 470 quoted in John Falconer and Ismeth Raheem, *Regeneration: A Reappraisal of British Photography in Ceylon, 1850-1900* (London: British Council, 2000), p. 25.

5. Ibid., p. 470.

6. Ibid., p. 95. The earliest Wiele & Klein postcard that I have *A Greeting from South India* was sent from Madras on Nov. 29, 1898.

7. Ismeth Raheem and Percy Colin-Thomé, *Images of British Ceylon: 19th-century photography of Sri Lanka* (Singapore: Times Editions, 2000), p. 146. Ad copy on the back of the postcard *Swimming Pool Galle Face Hotel Colombo* in the Author's Collection.

8. G.C. Mendis, *Ceylon Under the British*, The Colombo Apothecaries Ltd., 1948, p. 104.

9. T. Vimalananda, *The Ceylon Gazetteer*, University of Ceylon, M. Gunasera & Co., 1972, p. 77.

10. Wright, op. cit., p. 470.

11. For example Andre & Co.

12. http://www.lankalibrary.com/cul/rodi.htm, seen September 27, 2015.

13. George J.A. Skeen, *A Guide to Colombo* (Colombo: A.M. and J. Ferguson, 1906), frontispiece.

14. Wright, op. cit., p. 450.

15. *Images of British Ceylon*, op. cit., p. 146.

16. George J.A. Skeen, op. cit.

17. The author has a number of India cards mailed from India by A.W. Plate & Co.

18. George J.A. Skeen, op. cit., p. 27.

19. Wright, op. cit., p. 339.

Types.-North-West Frontier
India

Afridi

Afghan

Waziri

Waziri

Khyberi

Mahsud

Swatis

Tochi

North-West Frontier Province

[Khyber Pakhtunkhwa]

Frontier postcards are distinctive for their emphasis on conflict and uniquely disturbing subject matter. Pakhtuns (Pathans) were the majority inhabitants of the British India's North West Frontier Province (NWFP), recently renamed Khyber Pakhtunkhwa (KPK) or "homeland of the Pakhtuns." This region has been a part of Pakistan since 1947. NWFP bordered on, and included, large chunks of Afghanistan taken by the British during the 19th century. *Types Northwest Frontier India* (Figure 1) represents the many tribes officially constituted into a "Frontier" province by Lord Curzon in 1901—Afridis, Afghans, Waziris (North and South), Mahsuds, Khyberis, Swatis and Tochis. There was even a name for those who floated between NWFP and Afghanistan: *"Watchers" Trans-Border Type* (Figure 2). Both portraits were published by Holmes, a father and son studio that served as the elite photographers of Peshawar for over half a century. I particularly like the *Trans-Border* postcard: my father's family were once of this type, from a tribe that made their way from Jalalabad, Afghanistan to the village of Jalalabad in east Punjab in the 1790s. We still have a piece of paper listing the animals they brought with them.

General View, showing Clock Tower, Peshawar City (Figure 3) and the main *Sudder Bazaar, Peshawar* (Figure 4) show the palace of tribes that assembled here from the province's five tribal and five "settled" districts. In tribal districts, the laws of British India did not hold except on major roads and a few feet to either side (a policy that has continued to this day). Hardly a hundred thousand people lived in Peshawar city then, but a healthy commerce with Kabul in Afghanistan and Bokhara in Central Asia

Figure 1. *Types Northwest Frontier India.* Holmes Brothers, Peshawar, c. 1924. Sepia halftone, Divided back, 14.05 x 9.15 cm, 5.53 x 3.60 in.

A British officer in Peshawar wrote of the Pathan's "innate love of their own freedom and independence. It mattered nothing to them that this freedom was largely anarchy, or that the constant threat of death in the pursuance of blood feuds prevailed in place of law and order. To them life and freedom were inseparable, however precarious life might be."[18] Holmes was founded by William Dacia Holmes in 1889-1890, who ran it until he died in 1923, when his son Randolph took over. Randolph accompanied British troops into the 3rd Afghan War in 1919 as a photographer, while Melvin of Holmes Brothers in the electrotype, served with British troops.

flowed through the *Caravanserai, Peshawar City* (Figure 5). Many similar postcards would support the claim that the value of this trade was enormous, with the most valuable commodity being gold on its way to Mumbai.[1]

In Peshawar City (Figure 6) shows how the Holmes studio, like the best publishers, developed its own postcard style.[2] Both sides of the streets and the sky have line drawings in pencil or crayon, which must have been added by hand to photographs sent to England for printing. Together with the distinct sepia tone[3] of Holmes's postcards it would seem to place them somewhere between albumen photographs and paintings.

General View, showing Clock Tower, Peshawar City.

ABOVE
Figure 2. *"Watchers" Trans-Border Type.* Holmes, Peshawar, c. 1915. Sepia halftone, Divided back, 13.95 x 8.8 cm, 5.49 x 3.46 in.

Many Pakhtun postcard images come from W.D. Holmes album of the Tirah Campaigns in 1897-98.[19]

[*Verso, handwritten, not postmarked*] "These are what wear the Swati blankets. Dick says that really these particular ones come from the wrong place to live [?] I saw some who evoked like this exactly wearing them. Gives you an idea anyway."

BELOW
Figure 3. *General View, showing Clock Tower, Peshawar City.* D.C. Mehra, Peshawar and Cherat, c. 1915. Coloured halftone, Divided back, 14 x 8.9 cm, 5.51 x 3.50 in.

Figure 4. *Sudder Bazaar, Peshawar.*
H.A. Mirza & Sons, Delhi, c. 1910.
Coloured collotype, Divided back,
14 x 9 cm, 5.51 x 3.54 in.

Figure 5. *Caravanserai, Peshawar City.*
R.B. Holmes, Peshawar, c. 1925. Sepia
halftone, Divided back, 13.9 x 8.85 cm,
5.47 x 3.48 in.

Sent to Mr. William Dorman, Piqua, Ohio,
U.S.A. (Walnut Hills), [*Verso*] "Yours truly
Uncle Geo[rge] in India 3/3/26."

Figure 6. *In Peshawar City.* R.B. Holmes, Peshawar, c. 1920. Sepia halftone, Divided back, 13.9 x 8.65 cm, 5.47 x 3.41 in.

Randolph Holmes wrote in a booklet he produced in 1963: "Then each kind of bazaar thronged with a noisy, virile humanity–the outstanding features of which seems a medley of large turbans and baggy Pathan breeches, with here per chance a bearded trans-border tribesman, fully armed, swaggering through a shoal of less fry and there a woman veiled from head to foot in white, picks her way through the crowd in her little red shoes peeping beneath the voluminuous folds of her burkah, the one dash of colour about her. These shrouded ghost-like figures ever were intriguing, and add the necessary flavour for all Pathan vendettas which go on family-wise till "blood" pays the price of blood or fancied insult to honor."[20]

Figure 7. *Edwardes Gate, Peshawar City.* Holmes, Peshawar, c. 1920. Sepia halftone, Undivided back, 13.9 x 8.75 cm, 5.47 x 3.44 in.

Figure 8. *Kabli [Kabul] Gate, Peshawar City (Decorations in Honour of Sir George Roos-Keppel's Visit).* D. Baljee & Co., Peshawar, c. 1912. Coloured collotype, Divided back, 14 x 9 cm, 5.51 x 3.54 in.

The Coppersmith's Bazaar (*Figure 6*) was one of the firm's most popular postcards. Another was *Edwardes Gate, Peshawar City* (Figure 7). Herbert Edwardes was an early evangelical Christian Commissioner of Peshawar. Coincidentally or not, a cross is visible just beneath the central arch of the gateway.[4] A view from inside the gateway by the Indian photographer Baljee (see *Lahore*), with its nicely hand-coloured tribal textiles, uses the vernacular name of the city this landmark faces, *Kabli Gate, Peshawar City Decorations in Honor of Sir George Roos-Keppel's Visit* (Figure 8). It depicts the 1911 visit by the Chief Commissioner of NWFP from 1908-1919 and primordial Frontier colonial administrator. Roos-Keppel helped establish *Islamia College, in the way of Jamrud* (Figure 9), shown on a postcard taken on inauguration day October 1, 1913, the principal seat of learning in the province for over a century. The foundation stone of the College was laid by Roos-Keppel in 1911, an event attended even by a tribal rebel leader, the Haji of Turangzai, who was given special dispensation to attend without being arrested—everyone then, unlike today, appreciated the value of education. Roos-Keppel was an author of dictionaries and translations, and delivered his inaugural address in fluent Pushto, using appropriate local idioms, to the amazement of Pukthuns in the audience.[5] Nonetheless, he opposed the slightest of democratic reforms in the Frontier when they became available to the rest of British India in 1919.[6]

Copyright
80

Islamia College, in the way of Jamrud.

Mela Ram & Sons
Peshawar

Figure 9. *Islamia College, in the way of Jamrud.* Mela Ram & Sons No. 80, c. 1920. Real photo postcard, Divided back, 14.1 x 8.8 cm, 5.55 x 3.46 in.

The eye of the needle in the Frontier was the Khyber Pass. It was protected at the half-way mark from Peshawar with *Jumrood Fort. 10 Miles out of Peshawar.* (Figure 10). The rare panorama card by Holmes, *Landi Khana and the Afghan Frontier* (Figure 11) gives a good sense of the western side of the Khyber Pass as it descends towards the Afghan border after rising from Jamrud. There was something transgressive in these images—as late as 1913, regular visitors who had permits to visit the border were not allowed to take photographs.[7] "Tribal unrest may lead to the closing of the Pass at any time" said a guidebook.[8] In some of the border areas, no clear lines were demarcated until well into the 20th century. *Indo-Afghan Border* (Figure 12) and *At the Frontier, Landi Khana* (Figure 13) include the much-photographed frontier signs (only a few words were changed after Independence). The British were occupied with military campaigns virtually every decade somewhere in NWFP, and between campaigns, they fought three wars with Afghanistan.

Figure 10. *Jumrood Fort. 10 Miles out of Peshawar.* Moorli Dhur & Sons, Ambala, c. 1915. Coloured collotype, Divided back, 13.8 x 8.75 cm, 5.43 x 3.44 in.

LANDI KHANA and the AFGHAN FRONTIER

by Holmes, Peshawar.

Figure 11. *Landi Khana and the Afghan Frontier. 10 Miles out of Peshawar.* Holmes, Peshawar, c. 1915. Halftone, 27.8 x 8.9 cm, 10.94 x 3.50 in.

Holmes writes (1961): "This historic pass is the main ancient northern highway to Afghanistan through the frontier hills. There are other routes, but this one stands out with the romance of British occupation. ... Standing by the block house of Michni Kandao, we get a view of the most historical and picturesque hill-scenery of this globe; for here have passed the conquerors who invested India from time immemorial with their armed forces, representing every epoch from bows and arrows to the last war [World War II], when tank traps were laid across the highway down to the small plains of Landi Khana and every modern device of cement in look-out posts enfiladed the approaches. This however is not our interest; but the Durand border [the dotted line] holds us enthralled. For running on top of the Khargali ridge clearly stands out an ancient wall more than two thousand years old; and besides the block house of Bagh there is a wonderful stupa which had subterranean passages running to the perennial spring nearby and maybe to the ancient road down in the valley below. Perchance Alexander's satraps lived there before the Kushans took it over: but today Afghan emplacements look down from the Durand border which runs along the higher ridge and down the escarpment to Torkham. There lies the check and Customs Post for travellers to Afghanistan, and Pakistan's roadway ends."[21]

Figure 12. *Indo-Afghan Border.* Holmes Bros., Peshawar, c. 1925. Sepia halftone, Divided back, 14.05 x 8.9 cm, 5.53 x 3.50 in.

The border signboard reads "FRONTIER OF INDIA TRAVELLERS ARE NOT PERMITTED TO PASS THIS NOTICE BOARD UNLESS THEY HAVE COMPLIED WITH THE PASSPORT NEGOTIATIONS."

Figure 13. *Untitled.* Unknown Publisher, c. 1930. Real Photo postcard, 13.5 x 8.2 cm, 5.51 x 3.44 in.

The border signboard reads "IT IS ABSOLUTELY FORBIDDEN TO CROSS THIS BORDER INTO AFGHAN TERRITORY."

TIRAH FIELD FORCE.

Figure 14. *Tirah Field Force.* Mela Ram, Photographer, Peshawar, c. 1905. Collotype, Divided back, 13.8 x 8.9 cm, 5.43 x 3.50 in.

Postmarked Lahore Dec. 19, 1907 and sent to Monsiuer Ajui [sp?], Charing Cross Hotel, Lahore. This postcard is also found in the royal postcard album (see *Bombay*), and was sold by other publishers too.[22] Mela Ram & Sons, a firm dating to the 1890s, still survives in the hill station of Dehra Dun, India, where they are official photographers of the elite Doon School. Mela Ram's studios in Peshawar and Cherat produced at least as many surviving CDVs of British army personnel as did Holmes. Mela Ram would have known Holmes' work well, and in 1907 for example, there was a "Mela Ram & Holmes" studio in Patna, Bihar;[23] they may have briefly joined forces in Peshawar under the same name as well.[24]

Returning Caravans Khyber Pass

Holmes

Figure 15. *Tribal Towers Khyber Pass.* R. B. Holmes, Peshawar, c. 1925. Sepia halftone, Divided back, 13.8 x 8.8 cm, 5.43 x 3.46 in.

Indian photographers who accompanied military expeditions generally opted for real photo black and white postcards in contrast to Holmes' softer idealized sepia products. Mela Ram & Sons, another leading Peshawar-based military photographer, published *Tirah Field Force* (Figure 14) showing General Lockhardt on June 4th, 1897, in the Arhanga Pass above Swat Valley. It commemorated a British victory in the largest Frontier campaign since the Second Afghan War in 1878-1880. For the first time in 1897, a British Indian force even occupied the Afridi homeland in Tirah in the Khyber Pass for a few weeks. Mela Ram accompanied twenty thousand British Indian troops whose avowed purpose was to destroy as many *Tribal Towers Khyber Pass* (Figure 15) as possible. "Every home here is a fort," went the British adage, "…for a village to be allowed to have a tower was a mark of trust and on the understanding that men of that village would actively resist gangs of outlaws."[9] When they did not, weapons[10] like those in *A Battery in Action at Landikhana, N.W.F.P.* (Figure 16) were turned on them.

A BATTERY IN ACTION, AT LANDIKHANA, N.W.F.P   79.

K C. MEHRA & SONS
PESHAWAR. INDIA

Figure 16. *A Battery in Action at Landikhana, N.W.F.P.* K.C. Mehra & Sons, Peshawar, c. 1915. Real photo postcard, Divided back, 14.05 x 9 cm, 5.53 x 3.54 in.

Figure 17. *Site of Action of 24-04-08 against Mohmands.* Baljee, Peshawar/ Murree, c. 1908. Collotype, Divided back, 13.8 x 8.9 cm, 5.43 x 3.50 in.

Figure 18. *Shabkadar Fort (Mohmand Field Force), [handtitle inscribed on negative:] General Willock's Residence at Shabkadr.* Baljee, Peshawar/Murree, c. 1908. Coloured collotype, Divided back, 14.05 x 8.95 cm, 5.53 x 3.52 in.

Figure 19. *Seaforths & their trenches at Shabkadar (Mohmad Expedition).* D. Baljee & Co., Peshawar/Murree, c. 1908. Coloured collotype, Divided back, 14.05 x 9.1 cm, 5.53 x 3.58 in.

Baljee, also originally a military photographer on the Frontier, offered *Site of Action of 24-04-08 against Mohmands* (Figure 17). This conflict was with the so-called "Hindustani Fanatics" who found sanctuary from the Sikhs in the mountains north of Swat in the 1840s (they survive to this day). On April 24th, 1908 they inspired thousands of Mohmand tribesmen to launch an attack into Peshawar district. The Mohmands lived on very arid land adjacent to the Khyber Pass, and often had no recourse but to raid settled areas. They were repulsed by British Indian troops; the press referred to the fighting as a "weekend war"[11] even when, unusually, fighting extended into the summer months. Thousands of troops passed, eighteen miles outside of Peshawar, through *Shabkadar Fort (Mohmand Field Force)* (Figure 18) and *Seaforths & their trenches at Shabkadar (Mohmand expedition)* (Figure 19). Sometimes things went wrong, as captured by this evocative Baljee postcard of British graves dug that summer, *at Mutta, Mohmand Field Force* (Figure 20).

Figure 20. *at Mutta, Mohmand Field Force. [handtitle inscribed on negative:] In Loving Memory of (1) Lt. G.D. Martins, Warwicks (2) Pvt. W. Adam, R.W.R. (3) Pvt. Morris N.E. (4) Pvt. Rose 5*[th] *Fusiliers Buried in the Field.* Baljee, Peshawar/Murree, c. 1908. Collotype, Divided back, 13.85 x 8.95 cm, 5.45 x 3.52 in.

Who were the *mullahs* or religious leaders who could draw the many followers it took to stage these uprisings? There was *A Mad Mullah (Religious Fanatic) with his Followers, N.W. Frontier* (Figure 21). Mela Ram also published the stunning portrait *A Mhamadan [Mohammedan] Mullah N.W.F.P.* (Figure 22), a man only momentarily cornered by the camera. In one British soldier's album, I found this postcard placed next to smaller photographs of Pakhtun corpses.[12] In fact, bullet-ridden bodies and hangings are found, exceptionally, among Frontier postcards. Bodies are shown dismembered in *A Frontier Loosewala or Raider N.W.F.P.* (Figure 23), or in the gory *A Frontier Raider Shot Near Nowshera N.W.F.P.* (Figure 24). "Raiders" or "loosewallahs" were a concern in cantonments with homes isolated by the large gardens on *The lower Mall, showing Residency and Sentry on Guard, Peshawar N.W.F.P.* (Figure 25). Not all raiders were motivated by religion; often it was just the pursuit of property that drove them, but the fact that such postcards were available reflects the fear they engendered.

A MAD MULLA (RELIGIOUS FANATIC) WITH HIS FOLLOWERS, N. W. FRONTIER.   SPECIAL SERIES 26

Figure 21. *A Mad Mullah (Religious Fanatic) with his Followers, N.W. Frontier.* K.C. Mehra & Sons Special Series No. 26, c. 1920. Real photo postcard, Divided back, 13.75 x 8.7 cm, 5.41 x 3.43 in.

A Mhamadan Mullan, N.W.F.P.

Copyright 33

Mela Ram & Sons Peshawar

Figure 22. *A Mhamadan [Mohammedan] Mullah N.W.F.P.* Mela Ram & Sons No. 33, c. 1920. Real photo postcard, Divided back, 14 x 9 cm, 5.51 x 3.54 in.

[*Verso, handwritten*] "Dearest Spens [sp?], How art? I'm having a rare time with your nephew! He's a divil [devil] but such a pet—you'd be so amused at him I think he is heading for an actor. When you pick him up he throws up both arms and look dreadfully alarmed, as if to say 'boo, chap! Now we're for it' It nearly send me into hysterics, and he has a most adorable way of stretching himself like an old man.

It's darned hot here now and we are off on Sunday week – a month in Kashmir think then Murree. I'm wondering how Geoffrey will like the long journey in the car. Cheerio, lots of love. Kathleen"

SPECIAL SERIES NO. 218   A FRONTIER LOOSEWALA OR RAIDER N W F P

A FRONTIER RAIDER SHOT NEAR NOWSHERA· N.W.F·P.   KCM.39.

Occasionally postcards may help uncover the real story. On April 30th 1930, for example, the Pakhtun pacifist leader Khan Abdul Ghaffar Khan ("Bacha Khan," also known as the "Frontier Gandhi") led a peaceful march on Peshawar. The subsequent Kissa Khani [Storyteller's] Bazaar massacre on May 4th became an all-India scandal and helped launch Gandhi's Second Non-Cooperation Movement (a serious challenge, it led to long jail sentences for both Gandhi and Bacha Khan). A controversy since then has been whether or not retaliatory hangings were carried out by the British

The lower Mall, showing Residency and Sentry on Guard, Peshawar N.W.F.P

FACING PAGE, ABOVE

Figure 23. *A Frontier Loosewala or Raider N.W.F.P.* K.C. Mehra & Sons No. 219, c. 1921. Real photo postcard, Divided back, 14 x 8.85 cm, 5.51 x 3.48 in.

FACING PAGE, BELOW

Figure 24. *A Frontier Raider Shot Near Nowshera. N.W.F.P.* K.C. Mehra & Sons No. 39, c. 1921. Real photo postcard, Divided back, 14.15 x 8.95 cm, 5.57 x 3.52 in.

Figure 25. *The lower Mall, showing Residency and Sentry on Guard, Peshawar N.W.F.P.* Colored halftone, K.C. Mehra & Sons, Peshawar, c. 1910. Divided back, 13.9 x 8.9 cm, 5.47 x 3.50 in.

following the killing of a motorcycle dispatch rider that sparked the riots.[13] The rare mini (half-size) real photo postcard *"Hanging of Rioters. Peshawar"* (Figure 26) by P. D. Kapoor & Sons of Peshawar could settle the case. At least five men dangle from the ropes. There is also *The Gallows at Peshawar where Ghazis are hung* (Figure 27) which suggests that executions were not infrequent in *Peshawar Fort* (Figure 28), even today a forbidding presence in the city ("Ghazis" are the term for religious martyrs).

7290.   The Gallows at Peshawar where Ghazis are hung.

ABOVE

Figure 26. *"Hanging of Rioters. Peshawar."* P.D. Kapoor & Sons, Peshawar, c. 1930. Real photo mini-postcard, 8.7 x 6.2 cm, 3.43 x 2.44 in.

This image was printed on real photo postcard paper and then cut in half, the publisher identified from the other half among a collection of 20 half-sized cards.

Figure 27. *The Gallows at Peshawar where Ghazis are hung.* Johnston & Hoffmann, Kolkata [?] No. 7290, c. 1905. Collotype, Divided back, 13.7 x 8.7 cm, 5.39 x 3.43 in.

Equally disturbing postcards came from across the border. *Bachha Sakoo the Bandit King of Afghanistan and his Comrades Stoned to Death at Kabul* (Figure 29) shows Habibullah Kalkani—"Bachha Sakoo," the "son of a water-carrier"—who led a successful revolt against *H.I.M. [His Imperial Majesty] The Amir Amanullah Khan of Afghanistan* (Figure 30) in January 1929. The British, who liked neither Amanullah nor Kalkani, helped Amanullah's former commander Nadir Shah defeat Kalkani and exile Amanullah in one fell swoop (this led to the Barakzai dynasty which ruled Afghanistan until 1973). How exactly was Kalkani killed? Another K.C. Mehra postcard is *The End of Bachha Sakoo and his Accomplices by the Ropes in their Necks* (Figure 31). Which one was it? They don't even seem to be the same people in both postcards, but that Kalkani's end was violent there is little doubt.

Figure 28. *The Fort Peshawar.*
Holmes, Peshawar, c. 1908. Sepia
halftone, Divided back, 13.85 x 8.85 cm,
5.45 x 3.48 in.

My favourite find among Frontier postcards is Mela Ram's *Mahajrins going to Kabul* (Figure 32). It offers a glimpse into an event from which almost no other visual remnants exist. In 1919 the Khilafat Movement, led by the Ali Brothers (see *Independence*, Figure 12), demanded immediate freedom in response to British action against the Muslim Ottoman Empire at the end of World War I. In solidarity with the Khilafat call, countless Pakhtuns decided that they could no longer live under colonial rule and were determined to re-unite with their brothers in Afghanistan. Pakhtun leaders like Bacha Khan and the Haji of Turangzai supported a mass exodus to Afghanistan. Many thousands left. As it turned out, the refugees would put tremendous strain on the infrastructure and hospitality of the Afghans, and most would soon return in disappointment.

165. BACHHA SAKOO THE BANDIT KING OF AFGHANISTAN AND HIS
COMRADES STONED TO DEATH AT KABUL.

Figure 29. *Bachha Sakoo the Bandit King of Afghanistan and his Comrades Stoned to Death at Kabul.* K.C. Mehra & Sons No. 165, Peshawar, c. 1929. Real photo postcard, Divided back, 13.85 x 8.75 cm, 5.45 x 3.44 in.

Contemporary accounts of how Kalkani died are unclear. Nadir Khan is said to have chased him to his village in October 1929 where he was stoned to death by residents, which this postcard may show. Other witnesses have him executed by firing squad in Kabul.

अमीर अमानुलाह खान (काबुल).

H. I. M. The Amir Amanullah Khan of Afghanstan.

[544] Joshi Bros. Bazargate Street Fort Bombay.   B.A.P.W.

Figure 30. *H.I.M. [His Imperial Majesty] The Amir Amanullah Khan of Afghanistan. [Urdu] Amir Amanullah Khan King of Kabul.* Joshi Brothers, Mumbai, c. 1925. Halftone, Plain back, 14.35 x 9.15 cm, 5.65 x 3.60 in.

Many years later I got to know Khan Abdul Ghani Khan, Bacha Khan's son and the leading Pakhtun poet in the 20th century. He lived on a farm in Charsadda outside Peshawar. I spent hours talking to him, discussing the violence of the British, and yet how, many years later, when he visited Britain, he stayed with the retired Sir Olaf Caroe, a Governor of the province known for his brutality and hounding of Ghani's father.[14] Ghani always lamented the lack of visual materials from those times, and encouraged me to find anything I could and bring it back to him. He died before I could show him this postcard, but I am sure he would have laughed had I told him that in 1934 a British boys' publication used the same image and called it *The Peshawar Bazaar. Tribesmen gather together in search of bargains.*[15]

THE END OF BACHHA SAKOO AND HIS ACCOMPLICES
BY THE ROPES IN THEIR NECKS.

Figure 31. *The End of Bachha Sakoo and his Accomplices by the Ropes in their Necks.* K.C. Mehra & Sons No. 166, Peshawar, c. 1929. Real photo postcard, Divided back, 12.7 x 8.8 cm, 5.00 x 3.46 in.

Mahajrins going to Kabul.

Figure 32. *Mahajrins going to Kabul.* Mela Ram & Sons No. 42, c. 1920. Real photo postcard, Divided back, 14.15 x 8.75 cm, 5.57 x 3.44 in.

Things could be complicated on the British side too. In 1990 I visited Holmes's crumbling bungalow at 42, The Mall (much like Figure 25). The family had left fifty years earlier. In the studio, cracked glass photos of the visit of the Prince of Wales to Peshawar in 1905 still served as windows.[16] Above the living room mantelpiece hung a hand-colored photograph of a mountain valley in Kashmir. An old *chaukidar* told me of a Holmes relative breaking down in tears when visiting the place after Independence. Digging through family papers at the British Library one afternoon, I found that Randolph penned an unpublished treatise before he died in 1973. He closed the typescript with: "The tonga drives me away from the Cantonment I have loved, and from the line of barren Khyber Hills [Figure 33] – where my heart is left."[17]

Figure 33. *Incoming Caravans Khyber Pass.* Holmes, Peshawar, c. 1908. Sepia halftone, Plain back, 14 x 9.1 cm, 5.51 x 3.58 in.

Notes

1. The *Peshawar District Gazetteer 1897-98, Punjab Government* (Lahore: Sang-e-meel Publications, 1989), p. 236, put the value of this trade at Rs. 12,00,000 per year, "all of which flowed to Bombay."

2. One reason for this style besides aesthetic considerations may have been to protect copyright. Randolph Holmes pursued a number of cases against infringers in the Peshawar courts, for example one against T.C. Dewan in 1920. Postcards seem to have been an important part of the firm's business at different points, with the *Dak* (mail) book from the mid-1920s recording numerous postcard and Christmas card orders. *Dak Book*, 18-12-1937 31-12-1937, University of Canterbury Library, Christchurch, New Zealand.

3. The Standard Bookstall, a missionary and commercial publisher in Lahore, also printed their Lahore postcards in a sepia tone so similar to Holmes, the same British printer was probably involved.

4. The Holmes family was itself deeply religious, having given over properties in Murree to Christian missionaries (see for example Murree Municipal Land Records, 1930s).

5. Recollection of Dr. M. Zarif of Nishtarabad, present in the audiences, as narrated by his grandson Dr. Ali Jan in http://www.britishempire.co.uk/article/pashto.htm.

6. Olaf Caroe, *The Pathans 550 B.C. – A.D. 1957*, Karachi: Oxford University Press, 1984 (1958), pp.424-425.

7. The Holmes collection at the University of Canterbury Library, Christchurch has a copy of a permit with these instructions. Even Holmes had to receive permission to photograph and submit his images to censorship. For example, *National Army Museum*, London, NAM 1993-08-105-1.

8. *A Handbook for Travellers in India, Burma & Ceylon*, (London: John Murray, 1938), p. 378.

9. Norval Mitchell, *Sir George Cunningham: A Memoir* (Edinburgh: William Blackwood, 1968), p. 92.

10. Ibid.

11. V. G. Kiernan, *Colonial Empires and Armies, 1815–1900*, Gernsey, Sutton Publishing, 1998, p.70.

12. Unknown personal album from the late 1930s with Royal Horse Artillery in Sialkot in Author's Collection. It is towards the end and includes this shot and three of dead bodies, one mutilated, two on *charpais*.

13. Author's Interview with Hussain Baksh Kausar, Peshawar, June 1, 1990. I interviewed this eye-witness on his deathbed, a legendary Khudai Khitmatgar (the British called them Redshirts for their dyed *khadi* clothes), who confessed to having pulled the rider off his motorcycle (and instigated the violence as the British claimed), and who then also witnessed the hangings that followed.

14. Sir Olaf Caroe (1892-1981), like Roos-Keppel, was a fluent Pushto speaker and wrote the classic *The Pathans* (1958).

15. *Chums Annual* 1934-35, Amalgamated Press, London, 1935.

16. *Visit of King George V (then Prince of Wales) and Queen Mary in 1905 to Peshawar. Arrival at Railway Station with the Chief Commissioner and Civil Officers in waiting.* The image featured in Randolph B. Holmes' *Between the Indus and Ganges Rivers, Souvenir for the Royal Visit to India and Pakistan*, Chippenham, UK, 1961, p. 6.

17. British Library, BL F265/16. Holmes also noted in his type-script which probably dates from the late 1960s: "What has happened in India and Palestine today will burst into conflagration in Europe tomorrow. The liberal-minded West like India will yet be shattered on the rock of intolerance."

18. Norval Mitchell, op.cit., p. 60.

19. *Alkazi Collection*, 97.27.0029-00.33. Pathan types already appear in a Tirah album from 1897 with names like *The Sniper, Rags and Tattters*.

20. Randolph B. Holmes, *Between the Indus and Ganges rivers: Souvenir for the Royal Visit to India and Pakistan* (England: Chippenham, 1961), p. 4.

21. Ibid., p. 5.

22. D.C. Anand & Sons, divided back for example (Author's collection).

23. *Thacker's Indian Directory, 1897*.

24. A Mela Ram real photo postcard was apparently even used by Holmes in a postcard pasted into a Christmas card from 1911 (Author's Collection).

THE GROWTH OF
"OUR EMPIRE BEYOND THE SEAS"

THE BIRTH OF OUR INDIAN EMPIRE.
THE ORIGIN OF THE EAST INDIA COMPANY.
THE GREAT MOGUL RECEIVING SIR J. MILDENHALL
QUEEN ELIZABETH'S AMBASSADOR 1599

Independence

The Birth of Our Indian Empire (Figure 1) is a diplomatic reading of the British invasion of India, which was more a matter of one battle after another, culminating in *The British Army, 1857 52nd Light Infantry at Delhi* (Figure 2). These redcoat postcards were made for British domestic consumption.[1] A very rare German variant—it took 20 years to find this one—shows another version: *Suppression of the Indian Uprising by the English* (Figure 3) was based on a painting made by an anti-colonial Russian painter.[2] The widespread uprisings against colonial rule in 1857–58 have since become known as the First War of Independence; the Second "War", more a movement than a war, took almost a century to unfold, much more deliberately and in league with the more Anglicized elements of society. Much of this struggle was peaceful, led by lawyers like *Hon'Ble Mr. P. Ananda Charlu, President, 7th Congress, Calcutta, 1891. (Figure 4)*. A Brahmin from near Hyderabad, he settled in Chennai where he strove for Hindu–Muslim cooperation, characteristic of the early days of the struggle.

Mr. Dadabhai Naoroji. President, 2nd Congress Calcutta, 1886 and 9th Congress, Lahore, 1893 (Figure 5) shows one of the first Indian professors in Elphinstone College, Bombay. He made the surprising decision to move to London in 1855 in order to promote reform in India. In 1892 he undertook a "spectacular foray into English politics"[3] and became the first Asian member elected to Parliament, representing the London working class suburb of Finsbury for the left-wing Liberal party. He also spoke, as he put it, for 250 million Indians and became known as the "Grand Old Man" of India.

Figure 1. – *The Growth of – "Our Empire Beyond the Seas" The Birth of Our Indian Empire The Origin of the East India Company The Great Mogul Receiving Sir J Mildenhall Queen Elizabeth's Ambassador 1599.* Raphael Tuck & Sons *The Rise of Our Empire Beyond the Seas Series I, #9147,* c. 1905. Coloured Halftone, Divided back, 13.85 x 8.8 cm, 5.45 x 3.46 in.

[*Verso*] "**The Indian Empire**. In 1599 the Dutch who controlled the East India trade raised the price of pepper from 3/- [shillings] to 6/- and 8/- per lb. To combat the Dutch monopoly a combination of London merchants induced Queen Elisabeth to send an ambassador to obtain privileges for trading directly with the Great Mogul, which resulted in the formation of the East India Company and gave England her first foothold in India."

The British Army, 1857   52nd LIGHT INFANTRY AT DELHI

Figure 2. *The British Army, 1857 52nd Light Infantry at Delhi.* G.R. Stewart [signed], Valentine's Artotype Series, London, c. 1905. Coloured halftone, Divided back, 13.9 x 8.5 cm, 5.47 x 3.35 in.

FACING PAGE ABOVE

Figure 3. *Underdruckung des indischen Aufstandes durch die Englander [Suppression of the Indian Uprising by the English].* Moderne Galerie, Dresden c. 1903. Collotype, Undivided back, 14.15 x 9.3 cm, 5.57 x 3.66 in.

FACING PAGE BELOW LEFT

Figure 4. *Hon' ble Mr. P. Ananda Charlu. President, 7th Congress Calcutta, 1891 and 9th Congress, Calcutta, 1893.* Unknown Publisher, c. 1905. Collotype, Undivided back, 13.9 x 8.8 cm, 5.47 x 3.46 in.

FACING PAGE BELOW RIGHT

Figure 5. *Mr. Dadabhai Naoroji. President, 2nd Congress Calcutta, 1886 and 9th Congress, Lahore, 1893.* Unknown Publisher, c. 1905. Collotype, Undivided back, 13.9 x 9 cm, 5.47 x 3.54 in.

B 391. PAUL BAYER DRESDEN.

Unterdrückung des indischen Aufstandes durch die Engländer.

W. Wereschagin.

HON' BLE MR. P. ANANDA CHARLU.

PRESIDENT, 7 TH CONGRESS, CALCUTTA, 1891.

MR. DADABHAI NAOROJI.

PRESIDENT, 2 ND CONGRESS, CALCUTTA, 1886 AND 9 TH CONGRESS, LAHORE, 1893.

Having read about and studied some of these figures while pursuing an as yet unfinished documentary on Independence, these postcards are jewels falling into my lap. While working on that project, and interviewing hundreds of people on both sides of the border, I found that there was a wealth of memory with too little visual residue. I interviewed veterans of the world wars in Europe from Punjabi villages, and was able to connect them to a whole other kind of postcard that once existed in abundance— propaganda postcards for the million Indian troops who served in World War I alone. Cards like *Comrades* (Figure 6) had the British Prime Minister Lord Asquith asking Indians to join the British army, as did *King Emperor's Message to the British Troops from India* (Figure 7). There were beautiful postcards like *The [British] Flag* (Figure 8)

COMRADES

"India, with no less alacrity, has claimed her share in the common task. Every class and creed, British and Native, Princes and People, Hindoos and Mahometans, vie with one another in a noble and emulous rivalry. Two divisions of her magnificent Army are already on their way."
—From the Guildhall Speech of
THE RT. HON. H H ASQUITH,
Prime Minister of Great Britain.

Figure 6. *Comrades.* B.B. London, Series V, Photograph by "Illustrations Bureau," c. 1914. Embossed lithograph/halftone, Divided back, 13.9 x 8.85 cm, 5.47 x 3.48 in.

in a Gujarati Parsi-Bohri dialect, exhorting people to fight for the British Empire. In Europe, the French published postcards celebrating troops who liberated their towns and villages like *Indian Soldiers Starting for the Front* (Figure 9). A signed French postcard, *Paschendaele Nov. 1914 Cavaliere indienne* (Figure 10), honoured the Indian soldiers who had helped in this critical victory in northern France, where 160,000 German soldiers fell (!) in what is better known as the first Battle of Ypres. As I learned from interviewing veterans, and from what scholars have pointed out, when these men returned to their villages, they brought with them an altered view of the world, one that exposed even more the failures and frailties of colonialism.

Figure 7. *King Emperor's Message to the British Troops from India.* C.W. Faulkner & Co. Ltd., London V, c. 1915. Coloured halftone/lithograph, Divided back, 13.95 x 8.85 cm, 5.49 x 3.48 in.

Postmarked Great Yarmouth, Dec. 16, 1915, to Mrs. J. Magee, Maryland, Bolton, Lancashire: [*Verso*] "Just a PPC [Picture Post Card] Hoping to find you in the very Best of Health as it leaves me at Present. JLW."

KING EMPEROR'S MESSAGE TO THE BRITISH TROOPS FROM INDIA.

"YOU have been recalled from service in India, together with your comrades from that country, to fight for the safety and honour of my Empire.

Belgium, whose country we are pledged to defend, has been devastated and France invaded by the same powerful foe.

I have implicit confidence in you, my soldiers. Duty is your watchword, and I know your duty will be nobly done.

I shall follow your every movement with the deepest interest and mark with eager satisfaction your daily progress ; indeed, your welfare will never be absent from my thoughts. I pray God to bless you, guard you, and bring you back victorious."

બ્રીટનનો ઝુંડો.

હસ્તીના નમુના—સે છે તું માં છુટાપણું ખરા હક ને સચ્ચાઈ,
તારા પેચની નીચે ...પણા સીપાઇઓ મગરૂબીથી કરે છે લડાઈ.
તારી હસ્તી કાયમ ...ખવા દરેક સીપાધ અપે છે પોતીકો જન,
પરવર કરે છે હર એ...ને પોતાના આશીરવાદનું હેસાન.

Figure 8. *The [British] Flag* c. 1914. Coloured halftone, Divided back, 14 x 8.8 cm, 5.51 x 3.46 in.

[Recto, Translated from Gujarati-Bohri dialect] "You are our cause of existence. You symbolize and make us aware of our truthful rights. Under your banner and oath our soldier fights the battles with pride. For your sake the soldier gives his life smilingly. Upon such dear son of soils, the Lord showers his blessings."[2]

BELOW

Figure 9. *Depart de soldats hindous pour le front. – Indian Soldiers starting for the front.* Devambe Passage Panoramas #34, Paris, for [*Verso*] "Rigaud's Sultan Boquet Perfume, 16 rue de la Paix Wholesale 8, rue Vivienne Paris (France)." Coloured halftone, Divided back, 14 x 9.1 cm, 5.51 x 3.58 in.

Figure 10. *Paschendaele Nov. 1914 Cavaliere indienne [Indian Cavalry].* Em. Dupuis [signed], Paris Color/Vise Paris, No. 11. Nos Allies [Our Allies], c. 1914. Coloured halftone, Divided back, 14 x 9 cm, 5.51 x 3.54 in.

[*Recto*] "110. Reg. Gerritoual 3 Compagnie." "100 Brigade Gerritoual 3rd Company." "17 June 1915. Maurice Collon."

[*Verso*] "Mon cher Jean Je t'envoi une jolie collection qu'il faudra garder en souvenir de la guerre. Je t'embrace bien. Ton papa, JE [?]." "[My dear Jean I am sending you a pretty collectible that you have to keep as a memory of the war. I hug you. Your Papa, JE [?]]."

World War I created a stream of Independence-related postcard activity. Annie Besant, an Irish Socialist and women's right activist who became head of the Theosophical Society in Chennai, was drawn to Indian spiritual figures in her campaign for Indian Home Rule. She refused to abandon it despite the war, during which she was imprisoned with two colleagues, S.P. Wadia and G.S. Arundale, commemorated by *For Freedom's Sake. Interned June 16, 1917* (Figure 11). Besant was soon released, and became President of the 1917 Congress Party Session. She was also a close ally of the Ali brothers, Mohammed and Shaukat Ali. They saw the demise of the Ottoman Turks—guardians of Mecca—as a cause to rally Muslims around the world to fight against British policies through the Khilafat Movement. Imprisoned from 1915 to 1919, *"Mohammed and Shaukat Ali"* (Figure 12) wore signature Turkish crescents on their hats. Mohammed Ali, an Oxford graduate, was a very gifted writer who published (and, like Kipling, often wrote complete issues of) an English journal, in his case *The Comrade*. Ali wrote in 1911: "To take first the relations of the rulers and the ruled. It is our belief that the line of demarcation between them is growing fainter and fainter every day..."[4] Reading rare surviving issues of *The Comrade* at the National Archives of Pakistan in Islamabad, I was impressed by the guarded fury of his language. By 1921, it had become too much for the British, especially once the journal was asking Muslims not to serve in the Indian army. The Ali Brothers were charged with sedition in Karachi and jailed, captured by a local publisher in *Shaukat Ali entering Prison* (Figure 13).

Figure 11. *For Freedom's Sake. B.P. Wadia. Annie Besant. G.S. Arundale. Interned June 16, 1917.* Home Rule League, Madras, 1915. Halftone, Divided back, 13.95 x 8.95 cm, 5.49 x 3.52 in.

Figure 12. *Mr. Mahamad and Mr.Shaukat Ali. Homerule leaders* (title handwritten in ink). Edward Press Ahmedabad, c. 1917. Halftone, Plain back, 14.25 x 8.7 cm, 5.61 x 3.43 in.

This card, with its owners' hand-inked titles, was sent by B. Bhorey in Baroda to "Mrs. A.G. Strong Esq., Professor of Household Arts, Olaga University, Dunedin, New Zealand."

Figure 13. *Shaukat Ali entering Prison.* The Standard Bookstall, Karachi, 1922. Sepia collotype, Divided back, 13.6 x 8.65 cm, 5.35 x 3.41 in.

One of the earliest supporters of the Ali brothers was another lawyer, Mohandas K. Gandhi. Gandhi had helped set up ambulance teams for troops on the European front in 1915 on his way back to India from South Africa, but that was when he was the younger suit-wearing *Gandhi* (Figure 14). Now, Gandhi would help turn the Khilafat Movement into the nationwide first Non-Cooperation Movement, which marked his ascendancy to the leadership of the Congress Party in 1920 after Tilak died (see *Bombay*, Figure 40). Jailed for non-violent protests from 1922–24, Gandhi was transformed into the *Mahatma* [Great Soul] who personified, internationally as well, the many-pronged struggle for Indian Independence.

Figure 14. *Mahatama Ghandi [sp. Mahatma Gandhi].* Taj Mahal Trading Co., Calcutta. Sepia collotype, Divided back, 13.9 x 8.75 cm, 5.47 x 3.44 in.

I was particularly thrilled to find the postcard *Lala Lajpat Rai Lahore* (Figure 15) by Brij Basi & Sons (see *Karachi*). It shows a Punjabi lawyer whose death on November 17, 1928 enraged a large swathe of the Indian public. I knew of him from my great-uncle Sheikh Hafeez Ahmad who, like my father, adored him. Lala Lajpat Rai (1865–1928) was attacked and badly injured by the chief British constable on the scene in Lahore on September 30, 1928 while he led a non-violent protest against an all-British commission set up to investigate Indian grievances. He died three weeks later. It was left to the French to publish a postcard of *Lala Rajpat Rai* (Figure 16) which included his immortal words that were instantly on the lips of so many, and which my great-uncle could recite fifty years later as he sat in the veranda of his home in Sahiwal near Harappa: "I declare that the blows struck at me today will be the last nails in the coffin of British rule in India..."

Figure 15. *Lala Lajpatrai Ji (Sher-i-Punjab [Lion of Punjab])*. S.S. Brij Basi & Sons, Karachi, c. 1929. Coloured real photograph of painting with glitter, Divided back, 13.8 x 8.9 cm, 5.43 x 3.50 in.

Figure 16. *Lala Rajpat Rai 30 October 1928 Died 17 November 1928*. Excelsior, Paris, c. 1929. Real photo postcard from painting, Divided back, 13.9 x 9 cm, 5.47 x 3.54 in.

Lala Lajpat Rai's death pushed activists like Bhagat Singh, a student at his nationalist school in Lahore, towards violence. On December 17, 1928 he and his associate Sukhdev Thapar murdered a British policeman. A few months later, on the run, they threw leaflets and bombs at a meeting of the Central Legislative Assembly in Delhi. They were captured after a further sensational flight, and executed after bravely confessing that they saw no wrong in opposing foreign rule. This led to a burst of postcards from local publishers like *Sardar Bhagat Singh* (Figure 17), wearing the Western disguise he used in his escape from Lahore to Calcutta after the assassination. The flavour of this postcard and that of his partner *Shukhadeo [Sukhdeo]* (Figure 18) is striking—Bhagat Singh's hat is tipped like that of a movie star, which contrasts with the religious undertone of much other political imagery at the time. Images of his partner start with a similar Western tint, then turn towards martyrdom with garlands as in the version here.

Figure 17. *Sardar Bhagat Singh.* Phoenic P. [Printing] Works, Bombay, c. 1931. Coloured halftone, Plain back, 14 x 8.9 cm, 5.51 x 3.50 in.

Figure 18. *Shukhadeo [Sukhdeo].* Indian Art Press #86, Kalbadevi Road Bombay No. 3, c. 1931. Halftone, plain back, 13.9 x 8.9 cm, 5.47 x 3.50 in.

All of this coincided with the Salt Marches or second Non-Cooperation Movement led by Gandhi which began in Dandi, Gujarat in March 1930 and protested against the lucrative British salt monopoly. This is when Gandhi's iconic image, wearing homespun cloth and carrying a walking stick, started flickering across newsreels in the West. It was also captured in a hand-drawn postcard by an Indian artist from that year (*Untitled*, Figure 19).

Figure 19. *Untitled [Gandhi].* Kulkarni Brothers [signed], Bijapur, 1930. Lithograph, Divided back, 14 x 8.8 cm, 5.51 x 3.46 in.

The execution of Bhagat Singh and Sukhdev on March 23rd, 1931—"At that moment
Bhagat Singh's name was as widely known all over India and was as popular as
Gandhiji's"[5]—made the Karachi Congress party meeting held six days later a tense
affair. It was here that Congress adopted its Swaraj ("Self rule") resolution for full
political and economic freedom, the foundations of the future Indian state. The 1931
session led to an unusual series of postcards by Johnny Stores. They have hand-written
captions on the back, and show the under-construction *Entrance to the Camp*
(Figure 20), *Hotel in the Camp* (Figure 21), *Two American Congress Supporters*
(Figure 22) and *Native Café in the Camp* (Figure 23). Johnny Stores is also a good
example of how most postcard publishers worked both sides: Jankidas, the publisher
and also the local British army photographer, used the name "Johnny" only as a
familiar British variant. I was delighted to find this rare postcard set on auction
because it conveys the often ad hoc nature of such momentous events. It is also a
credit to Jankidas the photographer, for these cards were clearly made for limited
sale or personal collection. The *shamiana*s and lost little wooden chairs are so very
familiar from Karachi weddings or government events waiting in vain for audiences.
The photographer also catches little fissures in the Independence movement that
would soon prove to be momentous. Looking closely at a card like *Native Café*, for
example, one can see a banner for "Islam Hotel," with an upturned crescent and

Figure 20. *Entrance. To the Camp.* Johnny Stores, Camp,
Karachi, 1931. Real photo postcard, Divided back,
13.8 x 8.9 cm, 5.43 x 3.50 in.

Figure 21. *Hotel in the Camp.* Johnny Stores, Camp, Karachi, 1931. Real photo postcard, Divided back, 13.8 x 8.8 cm, 5.43 x 3.46 in.

Figure 22. *Two American Congress Supportors [Supporters].* Johnny Stores, Camp, Karachi, 1931. Real photo postcard, Divided back, 13.75 x 8.8 cm, 5.41 x 3.46 in.

Figure 23. *Native. Café in the Camp.* Johnny Stores, Camp, Karachi, 1931. Real photo postcard, Divided back, 13.8 x 8.85 cm, 5.43 x 3.48 in.

Figure 24. *Eid Mubarak [Eid Greetings].* Unknown Publisher, c. 1930. Coloured halftone, Plain back, 13.85 x 8.9 cm, 5.45 x 3.50 in.

Figure 25. *Eid Mubarak. [back: Eid Greeting].* Bolton Fine Art Litho, Bombay, c. 1930. Halftone lithograph, Divided back, 12.9 x 8.95 cm, 5.08 x 3.52 in.

FACING PAGE

Figure 26. *Funeral Prayers for Abdul Qayum.* I. Sequiera, Karachi, c. 1935. Real photo postcard, Divided back, 13.95 x 8.8 cm, 5.49 x 3.46 in.

Abdul Qayum killed Nathurmal Sharma for publishing an offensive booklet on Islam. His defence lawyer used Koranic injunctions to justify Qayum's actions.

star, in other words a separate area for Muslim delegates. It was in the 1930s that the hitherto staunchly Congress Muslims started breaking off in greater and greater numbers. The adoption of the Muslim star and crescent on cards like *Eid Mubarak [Eid Greetings]* (Figure 24) showing the Kaaba in Mecca grew. Another *Eid Mubarak* (Figure 25) card features the leader of the budding Muslim League, Mohammad Ali Jinnah and his sister Fatima Jinnah. Note the two nightingales in the moonlight above the minarets, the careful composition, the familiar palm trees and river flowing into the image frame.

Less symbolic postcards like *Funeral Prayers for Abdul Qayum* (Figure 26) sometimes directly captured the growing religious tension between Hindus and Muslims. Handwritten on the back of this card dated March 19, 1935 is:

Part of the crowd at the graveyard after digging up the body of Abdul Qayum the murderer who was hung at 4 a.m. They are here preparing to take the body in procession through Karachi city. The mob swelled to 20,000 by the time it reached Chakawara at which place the shooting took place. Abdul Qayum was sentenced to death for murdering a Hindu in Karachi Police Court.

Figure 27. *Dr. Keshav Baliran Hegewar,* Vagara Art Gallery, Wardha, Central Provinces, c. 1930. Real photo postcard, Divided back, 13.9 x 8.8 cm, 5.47 x 3.46 in.

Figure 28. *[Mohammed Ali Jinnah].* Unknown Publisher, c. 1950. Real photo postcard, Divided back, 13.3 x 8.6 cm, 5.39 x 3.44 in.

These cards would have been published as event memorials to current events for Indian customers. Another card shows *Dr. Keshav Baliran Hegdewar* (Figure 27), a leader at the 1920 Congress session who, disillusioned with the slow pace of the freedom struggle, moved towards a vision of a Hindu nation, and founded the militant Rashtriya Swayamsevak Sangh or RSS. The growth of Hindu and Muslim religious political parties and the alienation of communities through the limited 1935 elections (where Congress still won a number of Muslim provinces) led to a Muslim League resolution in 1940 demanding an independent Muslim state to be called Pakistan. This was the opposite of the Congress Party's vision of a united, indivisible India. It was adopted in Lahore, and the crescent and star (for minorities) was adopted as the

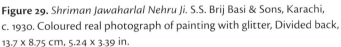

Figure 29. *Shriman Jawaharlal Nehru Ji.* S.S. Brij Basi & Sons, Karachi, c. 1930. Coloured real photograph of painting with glitter, Divided back, 13.7 x 8.75 cm, 5.24 x 3.39 in.

Figure 30. *Srimati Sarojini Naidu.* Coloured real photograph of painting, S.S. Brij Basi & Sons, Karachi, c. 1930. Divided back, 13.9 x 8.8 cm, 5.47 x 3.46 in.

symbol of the future nation. Its chief proponent and leader *Mohammed Ali Jinnah* (Figure 28) wore a "Jinnah hat" as it became called of Turkish and Afghan Islamic origins. It sat comfortably atop the head of a lawyer who spoke to his followers in English (note how the hats on the three men are similar).

A similar photo image from the period shows *Jawaharlal Nehru* (Figure 29), the Congress Party leader, wearing his own "Nehru" hat and jacket, traditional rather than Western clothing. Although schooled in Britain, and moved to enter politics partly by Annie Besant's 1917 arrest, here he is touched up like a Maharajah, in contrast to the simpler *Srimati Sarojini Naidu* (Figure 30), the poetess of the Independence movement.

નૂતન યુદ્ધ અહિંસક આદર્યું, કર્યું સ્વતન્ત્ર અભિનવ હિન્દને;
ચકિત સર્વ કર્યું જગ **મોહને** જગતવંદ્ય પથે પળજે તમે.
નૂતનવર્ષ પ્રવેશો વિજયતે ।   Rajni No. 19

અમર યૌવનના યશભાગીને, અમર કીર્તિ દિગન્ત વિષે વર્યા,
વીર, **જવાહર**ભારત હીર શા, નૂતન વર્ષ તમે બનજો હીરા.
નૂતન વર્ષાભિનંદન   Rajni No. 20

Figure 31. *Gandhi*. Rajni, c. 1948. Lithograph, Plain back, 14.05 x 8.9 cm, 5.53 x 3.50 in.

[*Verso*, Translated from Gujarati] "Mahatma Gandhi started a novel non-violence war. The mesmerized world looked in awe at Gandhi when he won the independence to a newly found (newly born) India. We should follow his sacred path of non-violence and love."

Figure 32. *Nehru*. Rajni, c. 1948. Lithograph, Plain back, 14.05 x 8.95 cm, 5.53 x 3.52 in.

[*Verso*, Translated from Gujarati] "Jawaharlal signified eternal youth. His charisma had a universal appeal. At the dawn of this New Year we send our good wishes that you become like a diamond in the glittering throne of Bharat (India)."

At the same time the Congress Party, unlike the smaller Muslim League, was large enough to bring together distinct approaches to the Independence struggle. Three cards in silver silhouettes by the publisher Rajni depict these three threads. There is *Gandhi* (Figure 31) absorbed in thought, representative of the spiritual aspect and the realities of village life. *Nehru* (Figure 32) is the more pragmatic non-violent leader whose autograph is in English. *Subhas Chandra Bose* (Figure 33) shows a third type whose espousal of violent opposition to British rule in 1939 led to a break with both Gandhi and Nehru. He was imprisoned, and then escaped from Calcutta for Berlin where he joined the Axis powers and supported the Japanese war effort as the quickest

सुघोषणाओ ' जयहिन्द ' करी, आझाद सेना रचीने गजवी;
प्रचण्ड सेना अदकी जमावी, सुभाष सिद्धि नवभारतीनी.
नृतनवर्ष प्रवेशो विजयते ।

Rajni No. 21

Figure 33. *Subhas Chanda Bose.* Rajni, c. 1948. Lithograph, Plain back, 14.2 x 8.95 cm, 5.59 x 3.52 in.

[*Verso,* Translated from Gujarati] "Mighty midget Subhash (Chandrabose) formed a mammoth battalion known as Azad Sena which filled the air with throbbing Jai Hind. He truly was a Hero of New Bharat (New India)."

Srimati Subhaschandar Bose.

S. S. Brij Basi & Sons,
Bunder Road, Karachi.

Printed in Germany

Figure 34. *Shrimati Subhaschandra Bose.* S.S. Brij Basi & Sons, Karachi, c. 1930. Sepia-coloured halftone real photograph, Divided back, 13.85 x 8.8 cm, 5.45 x 3.46 in.

means to bring Independence to India (by then the Raj had become intolerable to many, especially the young in his home province of Bengal which was suffering from a famine caused by the diversion of grain to the troops fighting Britain's war). He is shown here in Indian National Army uniform, some fifteen years after the sepia *Shri Subhaschandra Bose* (Figure 34), a much younger, saintly figure.

Among the rarest of postcards are Japanese postcards of the War, including the boastful *Burma Bombing Tinsukia Airfield, East India* (Figure 35) in Assam district in October 1942, one of the few times eastern India was attacked by Japanese aircraft.

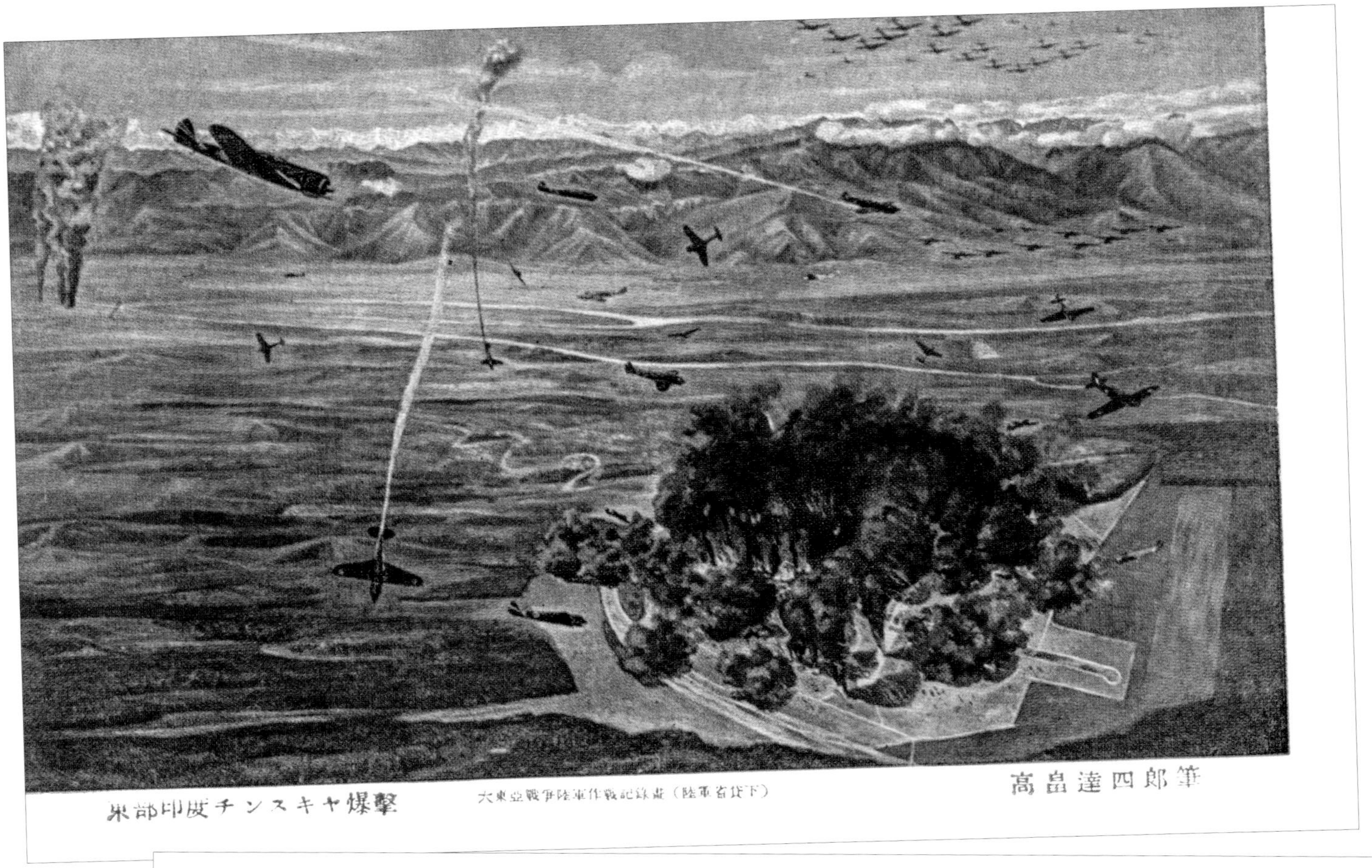

高畠達四郎筆

大東亜戦争陸軍作戦記録畫（陸軍省貸下）

東部印度チンスキヤ爆撃

ラングーンの防空とビルマ人の協力

鈴木亞夫筆

ABOVE

Figure 35. *Bombing Tinsukia Airfield, East India.* Tatsuhiro Takabatake [signed], The Greater East Asian War Imperial Army Operation Report (Loaned by Department of the Army), Tokyo, c. 1943. Coloured halftone, Divided back, 13.95 x 8.9 cm, 5.49 x 3.50 in.

BELOW

Figure 36. *Nurses in Burma.* Japan, c. 1944. Air Defense in Rangoon and Cooperation of the Burmese. Tsugio Suzuki [signed], The Greater East Asian War Imperial Army Operation Report (Loaned by Department of the Army) Coloured halftone, Divided back, 14.25 x 9.1 cm, 5.61 x 3.58 in.

A later, more honest, Japanese postcard is *Burmese Nurses in World War II* (Figure 36). The INA, composed largely of Indian troops captured at the fall of Singapore, found itself in increasingly dire circumstances after 1944. Subhas Chandra Bose apparently died in a plane crash near the end of the war in August 1945. The many INA troops who did surrender were treated as heroes by all Indian parties and considered to be freedom fighters, supported by all political parties in unified opposition to British rule. Things moved quickly thereafter, and on August 15th, 1947, some 300 million Indians realised their dreams through the Congress Party's vision of a free Mother India, while a 60-million minority was equally split into East and West Pakistan. My family ended up on the Pakistan side by choice and geographic design.

Congress Indian postcards from Independence have a hopeful edge to them, like the first day postcard issue, *Jai Hind* (Figure 37), mailed in Calcutta on August 15th, or *Stop Caste-based Discrimination* (Figure 38), which shows Gandhi's face as a black and white photograph, and the Indian flag, with a *chakra* at the centre, evoking Gandhi's spinning wheel, also the symbol favoured by Buddhist Emperor Ashoka, and one of the few icons that can probably be traced back to the ancient Indus wheel symbol.

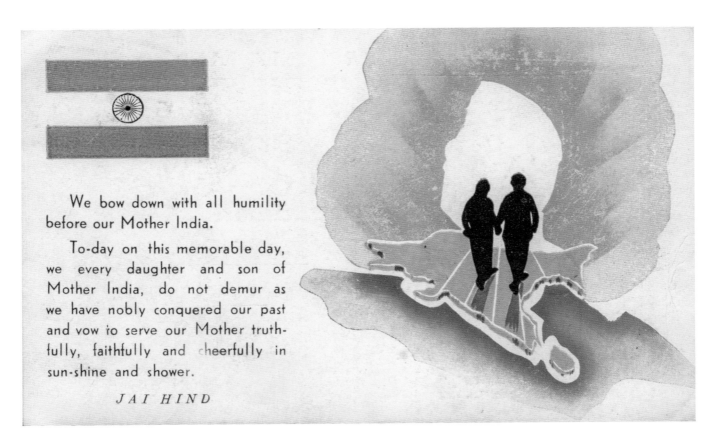

We bow down with all humility before our Mother India.

To-day on this memorable day, we every daughter and son of Mother India, do not demur as we have nobly conquered our past and vow to serve our Mother truth-fully, faithfully and cheerfully in sun-shine and shower.

JAI HIND

Figure 37. *Jai Hind.* H. G. Chakraverti, Serampore, Bengal, 1947. Coloured halftone, Divided back, 14.5 x 8.85 cm, 5.71 x 3.48 in.

[*Verso*] "15th August 1947 Bande Mataram H.G. Chakraverti 'Chatra Kutir' Serampore, Bengal".

Addressed to Mr. Rudolf Stal, Praha-77, (St. Strasnice) Na Klinku 450, Czechoslovakia.

The actual Indus cities of Mohenjo-daro and Harappa stayed in Pakistan, and large provinces like Bengal, Punjab and Kashmir were divided into halves. Families, including that of my father, found themselves suddenly cut off from contact with India and the places they had grown up in. My grandfather moved into half a mansion shared with a Hindu family that "converted" to Islam as a means of staying on successfully, but most Hindus and Sikhs left cities like Lahore, forever changing their composition.

Indeed, there is not quite the same ebullience in the few postcards from Pakistan. *Independence Day Celebrations* (Figure 39) from Johnny Stores in Karachi is somewhat prosaic. There are no banners flying and the crowd is limited in size. Some of the people with bicycles seem to have stumbled upon the scene. The promotional card *Muslim League Zindabad* (Figure 40) shows Pakistan's first Prime Minister Liaquat Ali Khan, whose electoral constituency was actually in New Delhi. It was mailed six weeks after Independence from Lahore and carries an Indian stamp overprinted "Pakistan."

Johnny Stores's postcards reflect some of the awkwardness that permeated Independence. They offered some of the few postcards to tackle the repercussions of the movements of populations between the new countries with *"Refugees on Race Course"* (Figure 41). From their clothing, they appear to be Muslim refugees from the Delhi area, even as elsewhere in Karachi, Hindu refugees gathered to make their way to India. Indeed, *The Wharf, Karachi* (Figure 42) was actually from an image elsewhere titled "Hindus Leaving Karachi."[6]

Figure 38. *Stop Caste-based Discrimination.* Lithograph, 14.5 x 8.85 cm, 5.71 x 3.48 in.

No. 212   INDEPENDENT DAY CELEBERATION   JOHNNY STORES

Figure 39. *Independence Day Celebrations.*
Johnny Stores #212, Karachi, c. 1947. Real
photo postcard, Divided back, 13.8 x 8.9 cm,
5.43 x 3.50 in.

Mr. Liaqat Ali Khan, New Delhi

Muslim League Zindabad

Figure 41. *Wharf, Karachi.* Johnny Stores, Karachi, c. 1947. Real photo
postcard, Divided back, 13.95 x 8.8 cm, 5.49 x 3.46 in.

Figure 42. *Refugees on Race Course* (handwritten in ink). Johnny Stores, Karachi,
c. 1947. Real photo postcard, Divided back, 14 x 9 cm, 5.51 x 3.54 in.

These postcards resonate, for I have spent a long time in Karachi interviewing Muslims who fled Delhi at the time, as well as Hindus who stayed on in the city. Most of the people I interviewed in Pakistan refer to Independence as "Partition," even if this was then the word used to denigrate the Muslim League's desire for a separate nation. Leaguers were, in fact, often called "vivisectionists." The millions who had to move and the million or more who died, the relentless tension between India and Pakistan seem so tragic today. At the same time, the shift of tens of millions from the lower and lower-middle classes to middle and upper classes in Pakistan and Bangladesh (formerly East Pakistan), the economic emancipation of less educated and poorer Muslim populations, including my family, probably would not have come about without Partition. If the political postcard is a triumph of image harnessed to text and message (which Independence cards did so well), it speaks to the medium's strength that it could stand witness to ambivalence as well.

Notes

1. Tuck's had a couple more.

2. Vassily Vereshchagin (1842–1904) was a preeminent Russian war painter and successful officer who later painted many vivid depictions of warfare that drew large audiences. He travelled through India in 1874–76. Although apparently criticized for the sensationalism of this image—modern rather than soldiers from 1857 were shown—similar events did unfold in barracks in the 1870s and the 1880s in Punjab, a controversy termed by newspapers as "Kukas Blown from Guns." Vereshchagin's paintings were reprinted as a postcard set in Russia during the 1960s, but this image was not included.

3. Sukanya Banerjee, *Becoming Imperial Citizens Indians in the Late Victorian Empire* (Durham and London: Duke University Press, 2010), p. 56.

4. *The Comrade*, January 14, 1911, p. 1. National Archives of Pakistan, Islamabad.

5. S.N. Sen, *History of Freedom Movement in India (1857–1947)* (New Delhi: Wiley Eastern Ltd., 1994), p. 223.

6. Postcard, Author's Collection.

7. Thanks to Ambarish for this translation.

Epilogue

Among the many postcards that fell by the wayside in the making of *Paper Jewels*—
five hundred pared from ten thousand—one I will not drop is *Meerut Post Office*
(Figure 1). I like the modernistic gloss and sharp shadow, the embossed white frame.
Post offices really were temples of communication, now open, for the first time, to a
typhoon of images. The post office is a junction box of history, out of which, if you
look at it right, truth can slip.

General Post Office, Meerutt (India).

Figure 1. *General Post Office, Meerutt (India)*. H.A. Mirza & Sons 264 [Printer no. on back], Delhi, c. 1905.
Embossed, Coloured collotype, Divided back, 14.1 x 9.2 cm, 5.55 x 3.62 in.

Aijazuddin, Faqir Syed, *Historical Images of Pakistan*, Lahore, Ferozsons, 1992.

Aijazuddin, Faqir Syed, *Lahore Illustrated Views of the 19th Century*, Ahmedabad, Mapin, 1991.

Allen, Charles and Sharada Dwivedi. *The Taj at Apollo Bunder: The Story of the Taj Mahal Palace Mumbai, Established 1903*. Mumbai: Pictor Publishing Pvt. Ltd., 2010.

Alloula, Malek. *The Colonial Harem*. Minneapolis, Texas: University of Minnesota Press, 1986.

Andrews, Barbara. *A Directory of Post cards, Artists, Publishers and Trademarks*. Irving, Texas: Little Red Caboose, 1975.

Ansichtskarten-Archiv-Philippsburg, *Die Geschichte der Ansichtskarte/ostkarte* at http://www.ansichtskarten-archiv-philippsburg.de/Geschichte_der_Ansichtskarte__/geschichte_der_ansichtskarte__.html accessed Feb. 4, 2017.

Arnold, David. *Everyday Technology Machines and the Making of India's Modernity*. Chicago and London: The University of Chicago Press, 2013.

Barr, Pat and Ray Desmond. *Simla: A Hill Station in British India.* New York: Charles Scribner & Sons, 1978.

Bauer, Oswald Georg. *Josef Hoffmann: Der Buehnenbilder der ersten Bayreuther Festspiele*. Berlin and Munich: Deutscher Kunstverlag, 2008.

Bautze, Joachim K. "Uncredited Photographs by Gobindram & Oodeyram." *Artibus Asiae* 63, no. 2, 2003.

Benson, Richard. *The Printed Picture*. New York City: Museum of Modern Art, 2008.

Beukers, Alan. *Exotic Postcards: The Lure of Distant Lands*. London: Thames & Hudson, 2007.

The Bombay Gazette. Bombay, 1899-1905.
Bourne, Samuel. *Photographic Journeys in the Himalayas 1863-66*. Edited by Hugh Rayner. Bath, UK: Pagoda Tree Press, 2009.

Bremner, Fred. *My Forty Years in India*. Banff, UK: Banffshire Journal Limited [Printer], 1940.

Buck, Edward J. *Simla Past and Present*. Calcutta: Thacker, Spink & Co., 1904.

Byatt, Anthony. *Collecting Picture Postcards – an Introduction*. Malvern, Worcestershire: Golden Age Postcard Books, 1978.

———. *Picture Postcards and their Publishers*. Malvern, Worcestershire: Golden Age Postcard Books, 1978.

Carter, John E. "The Trained Eye: Photographs and Historical Context." *The Public Historian* 15, no. 1 (Winter 1993): 55-66. New York: Cambridge University Press, 2003.

Chaudhary, Zahid R. *Afterimage of Empire: Photography in Nineteenth-Century India*. Minneapolis, London: University of Minnesota Press, 2012.

Chawla, Rupika. *Raja Ravi Varma: Painter of Colonial India*. Ahmedabad: Mapin Publishing, 2010. Distributed in North America by Antique Collectors' Club.

Cheah, Jin Seng. *Malaya: 500 Early Postcards*. Singapore: Editions Didier Millet, 2008.

———. *Singapore: 500 Early Postcards*. Singapore: Editions Didier Millet, 2006.

Coleman, F.M. *Typical Pictures of Indian Natives: Being Reproductions From Specially Prepared Hand-Coloured Photographs with Descriptive Letterpress*. 6th ed. Bombay: The Times of India and Thacker & Co., 1899.

Cortazar, Julio. *From the Observatory*. Brooklyn, New York: Archipelago Books, 2011.

Coysh, A.W. *The Dictionary of Picture Postcards in Britain, 1894-1939*. Woodbridge, Suffolk: Antique Collectors' Club, 1984.

Czeike, Felix. *Wien in alten Ansichtskarten: Innere Stadt*. Zaltbommel, Netherlands: Europäische Bibliothek, 1982.

Davis, Mike. *Late Victorian Holocausts: El Nino Famines and the Making of the Third World*. London, New York: Verso Books, 2001.

De Smet, Peter A. G. M. *Different Truths: Ethnomedicine in Early Postcards*. Amsterdam: KIT Publishers, 2010.

Dhurandhar, M.V. *Forty Years in the Temple of Art* (Gujarati). Translated by Snehaprabha Datar from a copy at the J.J. School of Art, Mumbai.

Die Illustrierte Postkarte. The Illustrated Post-Card. La Carte Postale. Official organ of the "International Association of Collectors of Illustrated Postcards", Vienna. Vienna, Austria, 1897–99.

Dutta, Krishna and Andrew Robinson. *Rabindranath Tagore: The Myriad-Minded Man*. London: Bloomsbury, 1995.

Dutta, Krishna. *Calcutta A Cultural and Literary History*. Oxford: Signal Books, 2003.

Dwiwedi, Sharada. *Premchand Roychand (1831–1906): His Life and Times*. Mumbai: Eminence Designs, 2006.

Edwards, Elizabeth. *Anthropology and Photography 1860-1900*. New Haven, Connecticut: Yale University Press; London: Royal Anthropological Institute, 1992.

Edwardes, Stephen Meredyth. *By-Ways of Bombay*. Bombay: 1912, in Project Gutenberg, Ebook #10071 2003. https://www.bookrix.com/_ebook-s-m-edwardes-by-ways-of-bombay/ accessed Feb. 10, 2017.

Evans, Eric J. and Jeffrey Richards. *A Social History of Britain in Postcards 1870-1930.* London: Longman, 1980.

Falconer, John. *India: Pioneering Photographers 1850-1900.* London: British Library and Howard and Jane Ricketts Collection, 2001.
———. *The Waterhouse Albums: Central Indian Provinces.* Ahmedabad: Mapin Publishing; New Delhi: Alkazi Collection of Photography, 2009.

Falconer, John and Ismeth Raheem. *Regeneration: A Reappraisal of British Photography in Ceylon, 1850-1900.* London: British Council, 2000.

Fanelli, Giovanni and Ezio Godoli. *Art Nouveau Postcards.* New York: Rizzoli, 1987.

Farge, Arlette. *The Allure of the Archives.* Translated by Thomas Scott-Railton. New Haven: Yale University Press, 2013.

Freeman, Larry. *"Wish You Were Here": A Centennial Guide to Postcard Collecting.* Watkins Glen, New York: Century House, 1976.

Gazetteer of the Lahore District, 1883-84. Reprint, Lahore: Sang-e-Meel Publications, 1989.

Gazetteer of the Peshawar District, 1897-98. Reprint, Lahore: Sang-e-Meel Publications, 1989.

Gazetteer of the Rawalpindi District, 1883-84. Reprint, Lahore: Sang-e-Meel Publications, 1989.

Geary, Christaud M. and Virginia Lee Webb. *Delivery Views: Distant Cultures in Early Postcards.* Washington D.C.: Smithsonian Institution Press, 1998.

Gerhard, Wietek. *Bemalte Postkarten und Briefe Deutschen KunstlerAusstellung Juni – September 1962 Altonaer Museum in Hamburg.* Hamburg: Dingwort, 1962.

Gifford, Frank. *American Holiday Postcards, 1905-1915: Imagery and Context.* Jefferson, North Carolina and London: McFarland & Company, 2013.

Gilmour, David. *Curzon Imperial Statesman.* New York: Farrar, Straus & Giroux, 1994.

Grewal, Inderpal. *Home and Harem: Nation, Gender, Empire and the Cultures of Travel.* Durham, North Carolina: Duke University Press, 1996.

Guha Thakurta, Tapati. "Women as 'Calendar Art' Icons: Emergence of a Pictorial Stereotype in Colonial India." *Economic and Political Weekly* 26, no. 43. Bombay: Sameeksha Trust, 1991.
Haks, Leo and Steven Wachlin. *Indonesia 500 Early Postcards.* Singapore: Archipelago Press, 2004.

Haroon, Hameed and Mariam Ali Baig, eds. *Visions of Empire: Karachi Under the Raj 1843-1947.* Karachi: Pakistan Herald Publications, 2004.

Higginbotham, J. J. *Men Whom India Has Known: Biographies of Eminent Indian Characters.* Madras: Higginbotham & Co., 1874.

———. *Higginbotham's Guide to the City of Madras.* Madras: Higginbotham & Co., 1903.

Holmes, Randolph B. *Between the Indus and Ganges rivers, Souvenir for the Royal Visit to India and Pakistan.* Chippenham, England, 1961.

———. *Camera Shikar in Kashmir.* 1921. Reprint, Bath, UK: Pagoda Tree Press, 2009.

Holmes, Randolph Bezzant, 1888- (B 175). Papers 1919–1948, Macmillan Brown Library, University of Canterbury, New Zealand.

India, Burma and Ceylon. Information for Travellers and Residents. London: Thomas Cook & Sons, 1923.

Jakle, John A. *Postcards of the Night Views of American Cities.* Santa Fe, New Mexico: Museum of New Mexico Press; Center for American Places, 2003.

Jhingan, Madhukar. *Post Card Catalogue of India and Native States.* New Delhi: We Philatelists, 1979.

Johnson, Robert Flynn, John Falconer, Sophie Gordon, and Omar Khan. *Reverie and Reality Nineteenth-Century Photographs of India from the Ehrenfeld Collection.* San Francisco: Fine Arts Museums of San Francisco, 2004.

Karlekar, Malavika. *Re-visioning the Past Early Photography in Bengal 1875-1915.* New Delhi: Oxford University Press, 2005.

Khan, Omar. *From Kashmir to Kabul.* Ahmedabad: Mapin Publishing; Munich: Prestel, 2002.

Kincaid, Dennis. *British Social Life in India, 1608-1937.* Port Washington, New York: Kennikat Press, 1971.

Kinnear, Michael S. *The Gramophone Company's First Indian Recordings, 1899-1908.* Bombay: Popular Prakashan, 1994.

———. *The Ceylon Handbook & Directory and Compendium of Useful Information, 1887-88.* Colombo: A. M. & J. Ferguson, 1878.

Kipling, J. L. and T. H. Thornton. *Lahore as it Was: Travelogue, 1860.* 1860. Reprint, Lahore: National College of the Arts 2002.

Klich, Lynda. "Little Women: The Female Nude in the Golden Age of Picture Postcards." Special Issue of *Visual Resources: An International Journal of Documentation* 17, no. 4 (2001): 435-448. London: Overseas Publishers Association.

Klich, Lynda and Benjamin Weiss. *The Postcard Age.* London: Thames & Hudson, 2012.

Lahiri, K.K. and Valentina Trivedi. "MELA RAM The Man, the Myth, The Legend." *The Rose Bowl* (Alumni Newsletter), pp. 3–7. 2008.

Lebeck, Robert and Gerhard Kaufmann. *Viele Grusse: Eine Kulturgeschichte der Postkarte.* Dortmund, Harenberg, 1985.

Life, Allan. "Picture Postcards by M.V. Dhurandhar: *Scenes and Types* of India–with a Difference" in *Visual Resources,* Vol. XVII No. 4, pp. 401–416 OPA 2001.

Long, Kathryn T. "'Cameras never lie': The Role of Photography in Telling the Story of American Evangelical Missions." *Church History* 72, no. 4 (2003): 820-850. New York: Cambridge University Press.

Luther, Narendra. *Raja Deen Dayal: Prince of Photographers.* Hyderabad: Creative Point, 2003.

Maclean, James MacKenzie. *Guide to Bombay: Historical Statistical Descriptive.* 31st ed. Bombay: Bombay Gazette Steam Press, 1925.

Mahadevan, Sudhir. "Traveling Showmen, Makeshift Cinemas: The *Bioscopewallah* and Early Cinema History in India." *Bioscope* I, 27-97, 2010.
Malik, M.B.K. *Hundred Years of Pakistan Railways.* Karachi: Ministry of Railways and Communications, Govt. of Pakistan, 1962.

Mathur, Saloni. *India by Design: Colonial History and Cultural Display.* Berkeley, California: University of California Press, 2007.

Mendelson, Jordana. "Introduction: Postcards from Album to the Academy." Special issue, *Visual Resources: An International Journal of Documentation* 17, no. 4 (2001): 373-382. London: Overseas Publishers Association.

Menpes, Mortimer and Dorothy Menpes. *World Pictures: Being a Record in Colour.* London: A. & C. Black, 1902.

———. *The Darbar.* London, UK: A. & C. Black, 1903.

McAndrews, Edward. *American Indian Photo Post Card Book.* Los Angeles, California: Big Heart Publishing Company, 2002.

Miedema, Virgil and Stephanie Spaid Miedema. *Mussoorie and Landour: Footprints of the Past.* New Delhi: Rupa Publications, 2014.

Mitter, Partha. *Art and Nationalism in India, 1850-1922: Occidental orientations.* Cambridge: Cambridge University Press, 1994.

———. *The Triumph of Modernism: India's Artists and the Avant-Garde 1922-1947,* London, Reaktion Books, 2007.

———. *Much maligned monsters: A History of European Reactions to Indian Art,* New Delhi, Oxford University Press, 2013.

———. *Indian Art,* Oxford, Oxford University Press, 2001.

Morse, Anne Nishimura, J. Thomas Rimer and Kendall H. Brown. *Art of the Japanese Postcard: The Leonard A. Lauder Collection*

at the Museum of Fine Arts, Boston. Boston, Massachusetts: MFA Publications, 2004.

Mr. Mortimer Menpes House: An Experiment in the Application of Japanese Ornament to the Decoration of a Japanese House. In *The Studio,* 1899. *The Victorian Web.* Accessed December 2, 2009. http://www.victorianweb.org/art/design/japan/menpes.html.
Murray's: A Handbook for Travellers in India, Burma, and Ceylon:[...] etc.; the Native States, Assam and Cashmere. 15th ed. London/Calcutta, John Murray/Thacker, Spink & Co., 1938.

Muthiah, S. *Madras Discovered: A Historical Guide to Looking Around, Supplemented with Tales of 'Once upon a City'.* Chennai: East West Books, 1987.

———. *The Spencer Legend.* Chennai: East West Books, 1997.

Neumayer, Erwin and Christine Schelberger, eds. *Raja Ravi Varma, Portrait of an Artist: The Diary of C. Raja Raja Varma.* By C. Raja Raja Varma. New Delhi: Oxford University Press, 2005.

Neve, Arthur. *The Tourist's Guide to Kashmir, Ladakh, Skardo, &c.* 18th ed. Lahore: Civil and Military Gazette Press, 1946.

Neville, Pran. *Nautch Girls of the Raj.* New Delhi: Penguin Books India, 2009.
Oonk, Gijsbert. *Asians in East Africa Images, Histories & Portraits.* Arkel, Netherlands: SCA, 2004.

Palaces in the Night: The urban landscape in Whistler's prints. Cambridge, UK: The Fitzwilliam Museum.

Penn, Christopher. *The discovery of the life and work of A.T.W. Penn, pioneering photographer of South India.* Worplesdon, UK: 2008/2010.

———. *The Nicholas Brothers & A.T.W. Penn: Photographers of South India 1855-1885.* London: Bernard Quaritch, 2014.

Phillips, Tom. *The Postcard Century: 2000 Cards and their Messages.* New York: Thames & Hudson, 2000.

Picture Postcard Annual. Nottingham: Reflections of a Bygone Age, 2005-2013.

Pinney, Christopher. "The Nation (Un) Pictured? Chromolithography and 'Popular' Politics in India, 1878-1995." *Critical Inquiry* 23 (Summer 1997): 834-867. Chicago: The University of Chicago, 1997.

———. *Camera Indica: The Social Life of Indian Photographs.* Chicago: University of Chicago Press, 1997.

———. *Photos of the Gods: The Printed Image and Political Struggle in India.* London: British Library, 2008.

Pinney, Christopher and Nicolas Peterson, eds. *Photography's Other Histories.* Durham and London, Duke University Press, 2003.

Pitt, Leonard. *Paris Postcards: The Golden Age.* Berkeley, California: Counterpoint, 2009.

The Postcard Album: Magazine for Old Postcard Printer and Publisher Research, no. 22-28. Published and largely written by Helmsfried Luers, Rastede, 2009-2013.

Price, Frederick. *Ootacamund: A History.* 1908. Reprint, Chennai/Bangalore/Hyderabad, 2002.

Prochaska, David. "Thinking Postcards." *Visual Resources: An International Journal of Documentation* 17, no. 4 (2001): 383-399. Oxfordshire: Taylor and Francis Journals.

Raheem, Ismeth and Percy Colin-Thome. *Images of British Ceylon: Nineteenth Century Photography of Sri Lanka.* Singapore: Times Editions; Colombo: Ceylon Tobacco Co., 2000.

Ramamurthy, Priti. "The Modern Girl in India in the Interwar Years: Interracial Intimacies, International Competition, and Historical Eclipsing." *Women's Studies Quarterly* 34, nos 1, 2 (Spring/Summer 2006): 197-226. New York: The Feminist Press.

Rothfeld, Otto and M.V. Dhurandhar. *Women of India.* Bombay: D.B. Taraporevala & Sons, 1928.

R.B. Holmes Papers 1900-1948. University of Canterbury Library, Christchurch, New Zealand, 2005.

Rice-Sayre, Laura. "Veiled Threats: Malek Alloula's *Colonial Harem,*" in *boundary2* (1989): 351-63.

Ryan, Dorothy and Miller George. *Picture Postcards in the United States, 1893-1918.* New York: C.N. Potter, 1982. Distributed by Crown Publishers.

Sampath, Vikram. *'My Name is Gauhar Jan!': The Life and Times of a Musician.* New Delhi: Rupa, 2012.

Sante, Luc. *Folk Photography: The American Real Photography Postcard, 1905-1930.* Portland, Oregon: Yeti Publishing; Verse Chorus Press, 2009.

Sharma, Brij Bhushan. "Fred Bremner's Indian years." in History of Photography Vol. 13 No. 4 (1989), pp. 293–301.

Siebenga, Rianne. "Colonial India's 'Fanatical Fakirs' and their Popular Representations." In *History and Anthropology* 23, no. 4 (2012): 445-466.

Sigel, Lisa Z. "Filth in the Wrong People's Hands: Postcards and the Expansion of Pornography in Britain and the Atlantic World, 1880-1914." In *Journal of Social History* (Summer 2000): 861-885. Pittsburgh, Pennsylvania, 2000.

Smith, J.H.D. *The Picture Postcards of Raphael Tuck & Sons.* Colchester, UK: IPM, 2000.

Smith, Jack H. *Postcard Companion: The Collector's Reference.* Radnor, Pennsylvania: Wallace-Homestead Book Co., 1989.

Solomon, W.E. Gladstone. *The Charm of Indian Art.* London: T.F. Unwin Ltd., 1926.

———. *Mural Paintings of the Bombay School.* Bombay: The Times of India Press, 1930.

Statistical abstract relating to British India from 1903-04 to 1912-13. London: His Majesty's Stationary Office, 1915.

Statistical abstract relating to British India from 1910-11 to 1919-20. London: His Majesty's Stationary Office, 1922.

Staff, Frank. *The Picture Postcard & Its Origins.* New York: F.A. Praeger, 1966.

———. *Picture Postcards and Travel: A Collectors Guide.* London: Lutterworth Press, 1979.

Steel, Flora Annie and Mortimer Menpes. *India.* 2nd ed. London: A. & C. Black, 1929.

Strip, Percival and Olivia Strip. *The Peoples of Bombay.* Bombay: Thacker & Co., 1944.

Thacker's Indian Directory. Kolkata: Thacker, Spink & Co., 1899-1930.

The Times of India. Bombay, 1899-1905.

Tropper, Eva and Timm Starl. *Format Postkarte: Illustrierte Korrespondenzen, 1900 bis 1936.* Vienna: Photoinstitut Bonartes; Fotosammlung Albertina; New Academic Press, 2014.

Wolff, Laetitia and Todd Alden. *Real Photo Postcards: Unbelievable Images from the Collection of Harvey Tulcensky.* New York: Princeton Architectural Press, 2005.

Vandal, Pervaizan Sajida. *The Raj, Lahore & Bhai Ram Singh.* Lahore: National College of the Arts, 2006.

Varma, Ravi and E.M.J. Venniyoor. *Raja Ravi Varma: The Most Celebrated Painter of India (1848-1906).* Bangalore: Parsram Mangharam, 2007.

Vernede, R.V. *British Life in India: An Anthology of Humorous and Other Writings Perpetrated by the British in India, 1750-1947 with Some Latitude for Works Completed after Independence.* Delhi: Oxford University Press, 1995.

Weill, Alain. *Art Nouveau Postcards: The Posterist's Postcards.* New York: Images Graphiques, 1977.

Weinstein, Laura. "Exposing the *Zenana*: Maharaja Sawai Ram Singh II's Photographs of Women in *Purdah*." In *History of Photography* (London) 34, no. 1 (February 2010): 2-16.

Wiles, Burt, Bruce Anthony et al. *Picture Berkeley: A Postcard History.* Layton, Utah: Gibbs Smith, 2005.

Woody, Howard and Thomas L. Johnson. *South Carolina Postcards Volume I.* Dover, New Hampshire: Arcadia Publishing, 1997.

Wright, Arnold. *Twentieth Century Impression of Ceylon: Its History, People, Commerce Industries and Resources.* 1907. Reprint, New Delhi; Madras: Asian Educational Services, 1999.

Acknowledgements

My first and greatest debt is to my wife Kamini Ramani, and to my daughters Natasha and Yasmeena, who inspired and supported me so completely over the decade it took to finish this book.

Thanks to family, friends and accomplices from a global network, from my mother-in-law Rukmani Ramani, sister-in-law Ranjini Manian, Sneha Prabha Datar, and S. Muthiah in Chennai; F.S. Aijazuddin in Lahore; (the late) Michael and Prue Stokes, Sophie Gordon, Christopher Penn, John Falconer, Rosie Llewellyn-Jones, (the late) Bob Scoales, Hugh Ashley Rayner and Ann Chidley in England; Ernest Neumayer and Christine Shelberger, Waltraud and Leon Torossian, and Brigitte Neubacher in Vienna; Ismeth Raheem in Sri Lanka; Leonard Pitt, Lew Baer and the San Francisco Bay Area Postcard Club, Rajen Dalal and Linda Burch, Shyam Lal and Rami Randhawa, and (the late) Liz Perle in San Francisco; Yasmin Khan in Washington DC; Rianne Siebenga in the Netherlands; Marion L. Griffin (nee Holmes) in New Zealand; Tasneem Mehta and Farooq Issa in Mumbai; Rahaab Allana in Delhi and the dealers and collectors everywhere who keep old postcards vital and circulating. Eric Basir of Photografix in Chicago beautifully restored most of these images to the state originally intended.

Thanks to the archives that keep the gems from dissolving, as ephemera is wont to do: The British Museum, The New York Public Library, The Austrian National Library, the Wiener Stadtmuseum, The Royal Collection at Windsor, the University of Canterbury Library, New Zealand, the Victoria and Albert Museum, The Henry J. Ransom Center, The Bancroft Library and the San Francisco Public Library.

And, of course, there would be no book without Bipin Shah, who nurtured it from the dimmest of beginnings through many iterations. Many thanks to editors Carmen Kagal and Suguna Ramanathan; for the index, Rosemary Anderson; and Amit Kharsani for design. The exemplary Gopal Limbad, Neha Manke, Rakesh Manger, Sheena Menon and Mithila Rangarajan at Mapin are responsible for the production as well as editorial and design efforts that vastly improved it. Without publishers like Mapin, *Paper Jewels* would never have seen the light of day.

Dedicated to my mother Thera Khan (1933–2016) for having shown my sisters Sorayya and Ayesha and myself how to find great beauty in the smallest of things.

It Has Been Well Said That

A Tuck Postcard is

A Present to the Child

A Handclasp to the Man

A Kiss to the Maiden

A Memory to the Old

Raphael Tuck & Sons Paper Envelope
Native Life in India Series #8993

The Alkazi Foundation for the Arts

The Alkazi Foundation for the Arts is a registered charitable trust in New Delhi (India), dedicated to the preservation of the cultural history of South Asia through extensive research on photography from the personal archive of art collector, E. Alkazi. The Alkazi Collection of Photography (ACP) includes an array of photographic material in varying formats, primarily shot between 1850 and 1950; and prior as well as subsequent scholarship from AFA focuses extensively on the interlinked zones of the 'metropole' and the 'colony' through anthropology, social history as well as art history.

With exhibitions and publications like *Paper Jewels*, we are pleased to support and collaborate with associated collections that speak of subcontinental connections as part of area studies around art's globalization and globalism—the unprecedented diffusion and proliferation of image-making practices as well as hybrid print cultures and their place in a transnational sphere. Through such publications, the terms of engagement with images emanating from an archive broadens to include and privilege lesser-known tropes and genres, old and new media, popular and traditional formats that have all evolved with the passage of time, maintaining their subtle trace to the past–a deeply dynamic source of exchange.

Hence as lens-based media from the 19th and early 20th century is reimagined in a diffferent socio-political context of the present, we are eager and delighted with projects that speak of photography's re-vivification in different forms, its illusory futures, its conceptual depth as well as its absorption into allied arts fields. Early photography and its practices of dissemination make us reconsider how information and data distribution even today lays claim to strategies that were developed a century ago and grew thereon. The authors of those images, the systems of distribution that supported them, and the patrons that commissioned them, lend us an expanded arena of references to envision their intellectual inclinations, their aesthetic tendencies, and, finally, their insights into journeys across the world.   —Rahaab Allana

Dr. Bhau Daji Lad Mumbai City Museum

Dr. Bhau Daji Lad Mumbai City Museum, the erstwhile Victoria and Albert Museum, opened to the public in 1857 and is Mumbai's oldest museum. It showcases the city's cultural heritage and history through a rare collection of fine and decorative arts that highlight early modern art practices as well as the craftsmanship of various communities of the Bombay Presidency. The collection also includes miniature clay models, dioramas, maps, lithographs, photographs, and rare books that document the life of the people of Mumbai and the history of the city from the late eighteenth to early twentieth centuries.

The museum, once in a derelict condition, underwent a comprehensive five-year restoration by INTACH, Mumbai chapter, supported by the Municipal Corporation of Greater Mumbai and the Jamnalal Bajaj Foundation. The project won UNESCO's international Award of Excellence for Cultural Conservation in 2005. The museum re-opened in 2008 with an extensive exhibitions programme and is committed to promoting art and culture through education.

The exhibitions programme explores the importance of the collection, the city's history and the issues confronting it as well as contemporary art and cultural practice. A series of curated exhibitions, titled 'Engaging Traditions', invites artists to respond to the museum's collection, history and archives. Several distinguished contemporary artists have participated in this programme.

The museum has partnered with international institutions, including the Victoria and Albert Museum, London, British Council, British Library, Dresden State Art Collections, Solomon R Guggenheim Museum, Museum of Modern Art, New York, Ermenegildo Zegna Group and Guild of the Dome Association, in an effort to facilitate international cultural exchange. The museum works with international and local foundations and curators to expand the cultural discourse.

The museum's education and outreach programme aims to build and diversify its audiences. A rich selection of programmes includes film, music, theatre and courses and lectures on the history of Indian and international art.

 ART HERITAGE

Founded in 1977 by Ebrahim and Roshen Alkazi, Art Heritage is a gallery that is committed to promoting established and young artists through its educational programming and collaborations, it seeks to sensitise its audience to a deeper comprehension of modern and contemporary art in a global context.

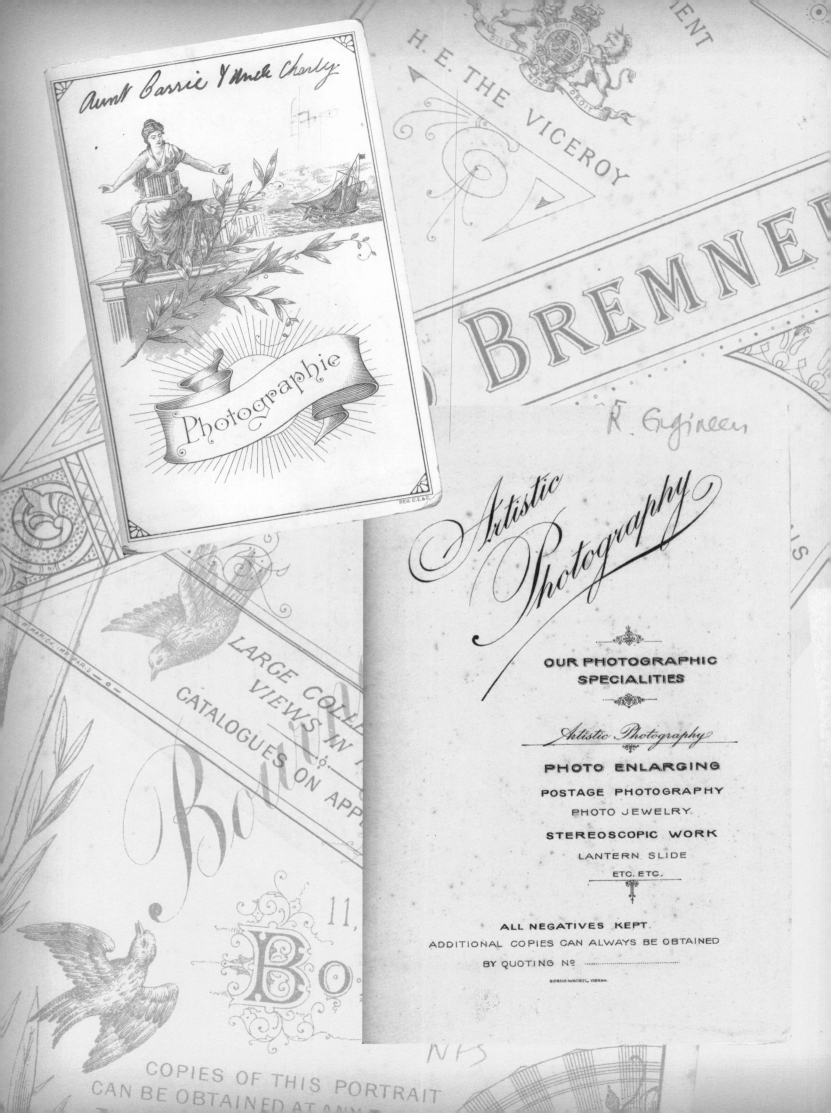